Over the Rainbow Bridge

Marlene,
maui is the best!
Enjoy Cory.
aloha,
Shirley Enebrad

Shirley A. Enebrad

BOOK PUBLISHERS NETWORK

Book Publishers Network
P.O. Box 2256
Bothell • WA • 98041
Ph • 425-483-3040
www.bookpublishersnetwork.com

10 9 8 7 6 5 4 3 2 1

Printed in the United States of America

LCCN 2009903544
ISBN10 1-935359-13-4
ISBN13 978-1-935359-13-5

Editor: Julie Scandora
Cover Designer: Laura Zugzda
Typographer: Stephanie Martindale

Contents

Acknowledgments

I would like to thank my loving family for all the support and love they have given me. Without them this book project would never have happened. My husband Steven Geller, my biggest fan, taught me to trust and believe in myself. He supported me every inch of the way and forgave me the time I have spent at my computer instead of with him and the girls. Steve, my daughters Brie and Keili and now my grandson Cory Keawe have been my soul and inspiration for this book. I wanted them to know Cory as I did…a brave, loving, feisty, endlessly compassionate boy.

Big hugs and lifetime love to all my friends who helped us live with dignity and love during the good times as well as the dark horrible ones. To Mama Lynn, Donna, Cherri, and Keller - we made it! Also huge thanks and love to Drs. Frank Balis. Barbara Clark, Bill Womack and Mike Morton for their tender care of my wonderful little boy.

Mahalo nui loa to Sheryn Hara, Julie Scandora, Stephanie Martindale and Laura Zugzda for taking such good care of my son's story and treating it with loving-kindness. You ladies are awesome!

I hope this book will touch the hearts of everyone who reads it but most of all I hope you will get what you need from Cory's life teachings. As he gave his love and wisdom so freely I give you my thoughts and prayers. Remember, according to Cory "Life is what you make it."

In memory of Cory and all the courageous children like him who bravely accepted the challenges of cancer with strength and dignity. We should all learn from their selflessness, integrity and courage.

This book is dedicated with love and gratitude to my grandfather, my parents John and Jesse, my son Cory, my dear friend Alycia and all of our loved ones who are waiting for us on the other side ~ Over the Rainbow Bridge.

Introduction

Over the Rainbow Bridge

I always felt Cory was a wise old man in a little boy's body. He was constantly coming up with the funniest little ditties and the most profound philosophies. And what insight! He taught me all about life. In fact, he taught me how to live.

My pal Joe Kogel describes life as "a string of moments." Another friend, Elisabeth Kubler-Ross, talks of the best moments as those times when you experience unconditional love. She even tells stories about Cory to illustrate her point. I am willing to share with you some of the precious moments I spent with Cory.

Please understand that Cory's opinions and experiences were strictly his own. Even though he was basically un-churched, his level of spirituality and depth of faith in God was quite phenomenal. I am writing about Cory's beliefs of what happens in life and after death not in an attempt to convert anyone but to offer comfort to those facing the inevitable. As Cory always said, "We're all going to die someday, so the important thing to remember is to live your life as best as you can and be the person God wants you to be and that way you will make the most of his gift."

I hope Cory's story will also give strength to those who are trying to understand the death of a loved one, especially parents grieving the death of a child. His experiences certainly gave me strength.

A newly bereaved friend called me a few years ago. Her father had just died a few days prior. His death had been very sudden. My friend was so lost in her grief she could barely function. She asked me, "How can I cope? How did you do it?" I was halfway through one of my most profound stories when she cut me off and denounced Cory's stories as pure fantasy. My friend's angry response made me sad for her lack of belief in God or an afterlife but did not daunt my faith in Cory's experiences. Besides, how could a little kid know all this "far out" or "woo woo" (as I call it) stuff that went on in our lives?

Here is the core of Cory's tenets. First and foremost, he believed in God. He believed that our souls return many times to the Earth plane in different "packages" (his word for bodies) because we could not possibly learn all of our lessons in one lifetime. He also told me that everyone has a mission or purpose for being here each time. The common goal of all souls is to get to the highest level of understanding so that they can then choose not to return to a physical body but to fulfill their goal of being close to perfection and live in heaven with God.

One of the most profound issues he talked about was suicide. "Taking your own life is like spitting in God's face. The greatest gift God gives us is life so we are not supposed to destroy it." He also stated that we get to choose what we will learn and the companions we will have to help us accomplish those lessons. He told me that he knew what his mission was as Cory. His purpose, he said, was to help me (his mom) understand the path I was to take in life. That path was to help other moms and dads get through the same sorrowful journey of pediatric cancer and all of its peaks and valleys. And Cory knowing his purpose made it easier for him to face a short disease-filled lifetime with great understanding and dignity. He begged me not to be too sad at his leaving, promising he would always be with me and that he would love me "forevermore."

Cory also told me that our souls do not diminish or "go away" when our bodies die. Our souls just move on to the next "level" or phase of learning. All this growth takes place in God's presence. He told me that he would be back in a healthy body someday. He

Cory, five years old

explained his decision to come as Cory. He described the agreement he made to have a short lifetime with cancer. It was eerie to hear him say that he knew the disease would kill him. He went on to say it was all a trade-off for a "bumper" life afterwards. "Bumper" means an easy, fun, free-of-pain life. He was quite young when he told me this, and I know that he did not know the word "reincarnation," but it sure blew my mind when he would talk about such things.

Let me start from the beginning.

Premonition

The Weird Kid

As the fog rolls in
Around my head,
I feel nothing
for I am dead. As the fog rolls in
Around my stone, I feel nothing.
I am alone.

Shirley Enebrad, age 10

Have you ever just known something, had an intuition that something would happen *before* it did? My family was driving along Half Moon Bay in California. The fog was low, thick, and billowy, like clouds that somehow got lost. For some reason, I looked out the car window and imagined, in my mind's eye, an old-fashioned tombstone with the rolling fog engulfing it. Then I wrote down those morbid lines about being dead and alone.

Later, when my mother found the poem, she became quite alarmed. Apparently she thought ten-year-old children shouldn't think about such morose subjects as graveyards and death.

She called me into her bedroom and sat down with me. Very carefully, she asked me what the heck had prompted me to write about death. In a matter-of-fact tone of voice, I told her that when I grew up and had a child, this child would become very ill and eventually die. I went on to describe how it would be a heavy burden, but that was okay because others would learn from us how to deal with the pain of death and dying.

Well, she'd thought the tombstone thing was weird, but now; I'd really done it. My mother bit her lip and probed on. What would my child be sick with? I answered that I didn't know that part yet. She asked me if I was certain it would be my child and not me. I said, "No Mom, it won't be me. I will survive my child's death." Mom asked how I knew all this. And I replied, "I just know." Then I went outside to play, and I forgot the entire incident for several years.

When I was twelve, my sister Rita was babysitting for a couple down the street. They had two little ones, and one had been born with Down's syndrome. The Down's child was like a little angel but it looked to me like a lot of work for the young parents especially on a 24-7 basis. I felt sorry for them. I prayed to God not to give me a burden that heavy. When I expressed my fears to my mother, she said, "God doesn't give us burdens we can't bear." I would live to regret ever hearing those prophetic words. So would Mom.

Around the same time, my father's younger sister, Deloris, telephoned out of the blue to tell us her husband, my Uncle Bob, was very ill. He was one of my favorite uncles. He was young, vibrant, and very handsome. And, at only twenty-nine years of age, the doctors had just told him that he was dying. They told him that he was the youngest case of prostate cancer they had ever seen. Even though my father's family was quite enormous, no one had ever been diagnosed with cancer before.

As a child, I had never heard the term "cancer" until then. Overhearing my parents' concern for my uncle, I could tell it was very bad news. Then something inside me clicked. I went to my mother and said, "Mom, I know what my child will die from. It will be cancer." I can still see my mother's face, visibly shaken by my declaration. She shook her head and put her arm around me. I think she just didn't know what to make of me; I had always been "the weird kid." Even my grandfather had said I was the strangest one of the bunch.

When my brothers and I were small, we lived with my mother at my grandfather's house. My dad was a merchant seaman and was not around much. My mother was very close to her father, and she felt it was important for us to know him. Besides, living with him relieved her somewhat. Single-parenting five kids must have been tough.

My grandfather was a powerful man. By "powerful" I mean that he could command an audience no matter where he was. He could be standing out in the garden talking about how to grow garlic and tomatoes, and it would sound like a politician's most polished speech. He had been a minister in Hawaii before he came to the mainland. He was extremely religious, usually strict, but also very kind. He read the Bible every night before he fell asleep and every morning before he got out of bed. It always amazed me that he read and re-read that same book over and over again.

When I was preschool age, while my brothers were all getting ready for school, I would hop into my grandpa's bed. He enjoyed reading the Bible out loud to me. My mother says I would often challenge the stories in the Bible as being too fantastic to believe. Oddly enough, my grandfather respected my skepticism. He would shake his head with a laugh and ask my mother, "Where'd you get this one?"

My grandfather was the most wonderful person in the world to me. He didn't let my questions ruffle him in the least. He would answer, as best he could, and encourage me to think about how formidable the ancient times were as described in the Bible. He never chastised me for my disbelief. My mother says my brothers never once questioned Grandpa about the Bible. I guess they just took it at face value. I look back now and appreciate the respect he afforded me even as a small child. His acceptance deeply impacted my life and my self-esteem.

My grandfather's cultural beliefs made him a very interesting man, too. Thanks to him, we grew up naturally believing in ghosts and spirits; we weren't made to feel afraid. I just thought that everybody could see them and had stories about them.

When my grandfather was a young boy, his father died. His mother eventually remarried, and her new husband was very cruel to my grandfather. He had a son, too, and he clearly favored his own child. When my grandfather was around eight or nine years old, his father appeared to him in the cane field where he was playing. His father's ghost told him to run away because his life was in danger from the stepfather. According to the ghost of his father, the stepfather wanted my grandpa out of the way so his son would inherit all of the property. At that time, in that culture, when the patriarch died, everything was left to the oldest son.

So the ghost of my great-grandfather encouraged him to get away and told him that the land was not worth his life. My grandfather somehow managed to run away to the big island of Hawaii and finished raising himself.

To survive, he shined shoes on the docks when the ships came in. Then as a young man, he became a *paniolo* or "Hawaiian cowboy." He rode a beautiful white horse on the range and craggy hills on the island. He later worked as a supervisor on horseback in the vast pineapple fields of Lanai.

His days as a *paniolo* were apparently very lonely out in the remote areas and not very fulfilling. After several years, he realized something was missing. He needed to find more meaning to his life. He felt called to do the work of the Lord, and with the help of the YMCA, he hung up his chaps and spurs to become a Methodist minister. Sounds like a fairy tale, doesn't it? It did to me, too, when I first heard it. I always thought he was telling me tall tales, but he was telling the truth. They really did have cowboys in Hawaii. In fact, the Hawaiian cowboys created the very first rodeo. And the *paniolos* have a revered legacy in Hawaii.

While he was a young, single minister, both parents of a local family died. They left five children behind. My grandfather adopted them. He paid for their care and assumed responsibility for their upbringing. He later married my grandmother, fathered my aunt and my mother, and moved to the mainland.

His example of Christian charity lived on in my family. My parents essentially adopted two of my best friends who needed housing and parental guidance when we were adolescents. That's how I finally got two *hânai* sisters. (*Hânai* is Hawaiian for foster/adopted children.)

My grandfather's talk-stories were exciting. He regaled me with them every morning after our Bible story time. I cherish the memories of snuggling with him and hanging on his every word. I am so thankful for everything that he taught me. His Bible lessons were the foundation of my belief system and how I came to view the world and my life. When things don't go as well as I would like, I just think back to my grandfather's words of encouragement and understanding. He would tell me, "Don't give up; you don't know what tomorrow will bring," or, "God's blessings are all around you, but it's up to you to look for them." Grandpa's teachings about being more accepting of the unexplainable has always helped me to keep an open mind and an open heart.

When I was twenty-four, my husband and I decided to have a child. It didn't take long for me to get pregnant and we were both very excited. Mom and I had never mentioned the weird intuition I'd had when I was ten. But, in the back of my mind gnawing at me was the faded memory of the premonition. I refused to acknowledge this memory during my pregnancy. I never did tell my husband, thinking he would really think I was a kook. When I gave birth to a happy, healthy, beautiful seven-and–a-half-pound boy, I completely dismissed all my fears as ridiculous. I should have known better. One very important lesson my grandfather taught me was, "You can't explain everything away, and sometimes you just know things." One lesson life has taught me is, "Everything happens for a reason. You may not understand it or like it at first, but there's a reason." Sometimes it takes years to figure out the purpose or find meaning or value in what happened. Believe me, I know how hard it is to get past the pain and sorrow even to find enough strength to look for a positive angle to a bad situation.

Let me explain. This was Cory's life.

From the Beginning

I was almost a complete whacko-fanatic about what I ate during my first pregnancy. No junk food, only healthy snacks, apples instead of cookies or candy. I drank way too much milk in my effort to give the baby plenty of calcium. I was very careful, and it paid off. I was extremely healthy during my pregnancy.

Labor was another matter. For those who've not had the experience, labor pains are just as awful as you've heard. Since the baby wasn't "engaging" (that's the healthcare term), since the baby was absolutely stuck (my description), my pains were worsening, and there was no end in sight. Some foolish person decided it would be a good idea to take x-rays of my pelvic area to see what was keeping him from making his entrance into the world. I was so out of it, I couldn't stop them. Because I had read a book by Dr. Helen Caldicott, I was vehemently opposed to the use of x-rays. She's the doctor who single-handedly stopped the French from conducting nuclear testing in the South Pacific because the fallout was contaminating the water supplies in Australia and just about every island in the South Pacific. Her book says, "One x-ray to a pregnant abdomen gives that child a

40% higher risk of developing leukemia." To this day I'm not even sure just how many x-rays they took.

The anesthesiologist was tied up in surgery, and by the time he got to my room; I was cussing like a sailor. Then he made his biggest mistake: He stuck his head in the door to my room and with a stupid smile on his face said, "So, the little girl is having some pains, huh?" I came unglued. I cannot even write what I said to that poor man. My mother would die of sheer embarrassment, but my father the stevedore would be very proud.

To make a long story short, Cory became distressed after a lot of pushing and shoving on his little body from the outside. I was exhausted, too. When his heartbeat tripled and then dropped to practically nothing, the doctor arrived and without hesitation said, "Let's go!" No sooner did he speak those words than I started gagging. I am a first-class gagger. Itty-bitty birth control pills made me gag. The dentist would always groan when I came through his door—yes, I was *that* bad. So the doctor raced me down the hall (not great for nausea) to the operating room. They strapped down my arms and slapped an oxygen mask on my face. Well, forget the fear of childbirth by emergency caesarian section. I was freaking out because I was afraid I'd toss my cookies in the oxygen mask! *No one will know, and I'll die from gagging,* I thought. I was struggling desperately to free my arms so I could rip the horrid mask off my face. I broke the arm strap, which was confining my right arm. I did it with such force it's a miracle I didn't break my arm in the process. I whipped my hand up to pull off the mask, and by that time the anesthesia guy caught on that I was having a problem. Breathlessly, I explained my situation and begged for water to rinse my mouth, mouthwash…anything. Without saying a word, the doctor plopped a breath mint into my mouth and whisked the mask right back onto my face. They couldn't replace the arm strap, so they had to wrap a towel around my arm and have someone lean on it!

"*This nightmare is getting worse,*" I thought to myself. "*I am a gagger who cannot handle sucking on a throat lozenge when I'm upright, and this doctor has stuck a deadly breath mint in my mouth while I am flat on my back!*" I was concentrating so hard on trying to move the mint to the front of my mouth I can barely remember when the doctor cranked up the gas. In a stupor, barely conscious, I remember hearing a faint little whimper. "Boy, what a tired sounding baby," I thought someone said. Later I realized it was my own thought. Next thing I knew, there was a masked stranger holding a bundle with a little scrunched-up face and dark, curly hair in front of me. I could barely open my eyes to see him. After what seemed like two seconds, the masked stranger rushed the bundle away. I remember thinking to myself, *"Gee, his dad will be so disappointed. He looks like my side of the family; in fact, he looks just like my brother Tim."*

The room suddenly became very noisy and hectic. I was apparently bleeding more than was normal. Trying to make out what the people in the room were saying, I suddenly got the notion that I was bleeding to death. *"Great, I got to see my baby for two seconds, and now I'm gonna die."* Then, I felt myself going back under...or I was extremely tired and went to sleep...I'm not sure which. At any rate, I went out.

I woke up hours later in a dimly lit room with no recollection of how I came to be there. I wondered where my little guy had been taken. Boy, was I ever sore. I tried to move around but felt pretty much as I imagined a waterlogged piece of driftwood feels. It was very quiet and very boring. If it hadn't been for the pain from my stomach incision, I would've thought I was dead. Now, that's what I call bored.

Eventually, someone showed up to check on me, right about the time I was drifting off to sleep. Isn't that always the way in hospitals? They want you to get rest, but they bug you all the time!

It took a couple of days for the fog in my head to lift. Then they brought me a little *haole* baby with light brown, straight hair. *Haole* is the Hawaiian word for "white" or "foreign." At first, I didn't recognize him because my one glimpse in the operating room had been brief and his hair had looked black and curly. I made an offhand remark about his skin and hair coloring being different than I'd remembered from the operating room, which sent the nurse into a tailspin. She checked our armbands and Cory's ankle band to make sure they matched. *"Finally, some excitement!"* I thought.

The first day Cory and I had to get acquainted. I was lying in bed and had him sitting on a pillow, which lay across my stomach. I was telling Cory how glad I was to finally get to meet him face to face and that I was sure we would have a lot of fun together. All of a sudden he took hold of the thumbs on both of my hands and pulled himself up into a standing position. I was speechless. Here was a brand-new baby staring me straight in the face and standing on his own powerful little legs and arching his back. He smiled at me. I blurted out, "I don't think you're supposed to be able to do this!" My thoughts went immediately to my premonition. *"Uh oh."* You may wonder why that was my first response. I have no idea. I guess it made me worry that he was just too advanced and his life was somehow in "fast-forward."

Cory was born March 18, 1976, long before rooming-in was in vogue. The nurses called me in the middle of the night to see if I wanted to play with him. They accused him of pushing himself up on his hands to survey the sleeping babies around him. Then he would reportedly start screaming and wake up the whole nursery. Of course, he would then go back to sleep. The nurses were convinced that he knew exactly what he was doing.

When I took him home, he was the best baby I could've hoped for. He slept well and ate on schedule, just like clockwork, every three hours. And he never cried. But I was a nervous wreck! There was a knot of fear at the base of my stomach that I kept trying to ignore. Now you're probably thinking I was one of those new moms that worried about everything, right? No comment.

When Cory was three months old, I was ironing in the living room. I had placed him on a blanket in the middle of the floor. He played with his toys happily for a while. I turned around and noticed that he was off the blanket heading for the fireplace. *"No way,"* I told myself. *"He couldn't have done that."* I put him back down and pushed his toys away from him to the other side of the blanket. I sat down to observe. He immediately pushed himself up on his arms and scooted across the blanket to get his toys. *"This isn't happening!"* My brain refused to accept this scenario. I picked him up again and moved him to the corner of his blanket. Before I even sat down, Cory began pulling on the blanket and was able to scoop up his toy! *"Whoa! I just watched a three-month-old baby use logic and reasoning,"* I thought. I knew then that he was indeed in fast-forward. In earnest, I began to worry about my prediction. I had never told anyone but my mother about it. Who would believe me? They would think I was nuts. My mother never mentioned it to anyone either. It was our scary secret.

Cory's strength was phenomenal. He swam at four months. He sat alone at five months. He walked and talked at six months. He became bored with nursing, so I weaned him to a little cup at six months, too.

When I think back to what he was like prior to diagnosis, I can close my eyes and picture quite vividly the spunk and humor that I miss so much. Cory had such tremendous spirit! A very active, little boy, he was agile beyond his years. In fact, he was all boy, and yet at a very young age, he displayed a very compassionate nature. And what a sense of humor he had! I love to hear his friends tell stories about Cory's practical jokes.

Fiercely independent, Cory had to be watched very carefully. As I mentioned, he learned how to swim at four months old. Cory loved the water. His swimming instructor said, "Cory must think he has gills." It was always a struggle to get him to come up for air. When he was six months old, he could swim the width of an Olympic-size pool with one breath! A couple of times Cory was supposed to jump off a wooden box and swim to the instructor who was treading water in the middle of the pool. Cory would jump in and swim in the opposite direction! Sitting on the side of the pool watching him swim around like a polliwog was exciting, even amusing for some parents, but frightening for me.

I have loving memories of him as a baby-sitting in the Tupperware drawer in our kitchen with bowls on his head. He would wrap his favorite "Blanky" around himself like a cape, put a bowl on his head, and grab a wooden spoon for a scepter. Even at a young age, Cory knew his position in our house...King of the Tupperware Drawer!

A remarkably happy baby, Cory would lie in his bed in the morning and play for hours. Eventually he would get bored and want out. Instead of crying the way most little babies do, Cory would sing out, "Good morning," until I would go in to get him. If I didn't hear him and respond, his voice would get louder and louder. Then one day when he was around eight months old, Cory discovered how to get over the crib rail. Well, that was the end of Cory's good morning song. After he perfected his method of escape, I could expect to wake up with him tapping my face or kissing me. He always had a triumphant smile on his face as he said, "Good morning." It was obvious that each day excited him even as a small child.

After scaling his bed, Cory found he really liked climbing and was quite good at it. Those doorway safety gates couldn't stop him. He just figured out how to get a toehold, and he could flip his body right over them like a miniature pole-vaulter.

We had a standard-sized refrigerator, but it was still taller than I am. One memorable day, I walked into the kitchen looking for Cory and found him sitting on top of the fridge eating cookies out of the cookie jar. I almost had a heart attack. He was nine months old! With the biggest, most mischievous smile, he said brightly, "Hi Mom!" as he kicked his little feet, which were dangling down around my eye-level.

I took a deep breath (not the first, or the last) and calmly said, "Don't move, honey. Mama wants you to come down now." I reached up for him to slide off towards me. It was so high up that I couldn't have pulled him down, so luckily he was cooperative. (I guess he'd had enough cookies.)

After I got him down, I asked how he had managed to climb up there, and he scrambled back up to the top. First, the little rascal pulled out all of the drawers to create steps. Then Cory hoisted himself very athletically up onto the counter top. Next he opened the dish cupboard and climbed the shelves like a ladder. He was so agile. The last thing he needed to do to get where he wanted, which was next to the cookie jar, was stretch a little leg over to the top of the fridge, and plop, he sat down.

I stood there utterly amazed. Cory at nine months had just devised and executed a plan that I bet most three-year-olds couldn't do.

Sitting on the kitchen floor with him in my lap, I explained how scary it was for me to have him climbing up so high and asked him not to do it again, for my sake. Cory nodded and said he understood. Then he grabbed my face between his two little hands, looked me straight in the eyes, and said, "But how will I get cookies when you're not around?" I tried not to laugh in front of him because he was being so serious. That was always tough with him.

When he accompanied me to the grocery store, he would ride in the cart. Little Mister Friendly would say hello to *everyone*. If the person didn't acknowledge him, he would get louder, always giving him or her the benefit of the doubt. He chose to believe the busy shopper hadn't heard him. It always hurt his feelings if the person he was interested in did not respond. So one day, we were standing in line, and the object of his attention continued to ignore the friendly overtures. He finally decided it was a desperate situation and he would have to go above and beyond. He kicked back in the grocery cart and started singing Eric Clapton's song, "Cocaine." I was absolutely mortified. Every little old lady in the grocery store looked at us with horror, or maybe it was disgust; I'm not sure which. The more I tried to hush him, the louder he sang. I finally gave up and just stood there with a weak smile on my face. I avoided shopping at that particular grocery store for a few months, even though it was the most convenient one to my house. I hoped in time people would forget the reason for my very embarrassed, red face.

A very verbal child, Cory, at one year, could carry on conversations with adults. He could dress himself, clean his own room, and put together a hundred-piece puzzle faster than my brother Tim. (Tim was thirty!) My brother's wounded ego prompted him to accept Cory's challenges time after time. Tim never won.

For one so young, Cory was a very competitive but also a very compassionate child. Once when my mother was ill with the flu, we stopped by to see her. One-year-old Cory stood beside her bed and leaned over to kiss his grandmother's face. With a big tear rolling down his cheek, Cory said, "I hope you get better soon, Grandma." Cory's obvious caring impressed me. It showed me he understood my mother was not feeling well even though, up to that point, he had never been sick nor had he seen her that sick.

Cory's independent nature was sometimes hard on me. For example, one day when Cory was about fifteen months old, he was in the back yard playing with our dog. His father was out in the yard, too, but must have gone around the side of the house. I looked out the window just in time to see Cory running through the neighbors' back yard on the heels of Quackszer, our dog. I could see from my vantage point that if they continued on it was only two more back yards before they would hit a busy roadway. I ran screaming out of the house for Cory's father to catch them. Fortunately, he caught up with the two escapees just before they hit the very busy street. The fence I had been requesting for years went up the very next day.

Not long after that incident, Cory scared the daylights out of me again. He thought it was a joke. Cory was playing in his playroom, and I was in another part of the house. I heard a sound like a door closing, so I went to check on him. The bugger didn't answer my calls. I ran around inside the house calling and calling. Cory was nowhere to be found! Then I ran outside and scanned up and down the street. I ran to the back of the house. I even went back upstairs to look out from upper windows. It was especially "crazy making" for me since Cory had run off after Quackszer before. I was trying to decide whether I should call someone for help when I heard Cory's distinctive giggle. It was coming from somewhere inside the house. I followed the sound until I found him hiding in the corner behind a big armchair in the playroom. Cory popped up and shouted, "Peek-a-boo!" I was so relieved to see him but so emotionally drained from freaking out that I wanted to spank him and smother him with kisses all at the same time! He got the kisses.

After I calmed down, I sat the little joker on my lap and explained how I didn't think it was as funny as he did. Cory looked into my eyes with his big brown pools of wisdom. He was just under two, but I know he understood because he never did anything like that to me again.

We had many talks about not talking to strangers. It was not too surprising to find Cory at less than two years old sitting on our front porch calling out to people as they walked past our house. He would introduce himself and declare them no longer strangers. At this same age, Cory and his swimming buddy, JB, would stroll around the women's shower room at the pool in wide-eyed wonder. They were such adorable little toddlers—with one thing on their minds: checking out the women's boobs in the showers! Cory called them "boobies," of course, always at the top of his lungs. "Look! JB, look at *those boobies!*"

Cory's boob obsession got so bad he would sit on the edge of my bed each morning and rattle off the list of names of everyone he knew who had boobies…"Auntie Cherri, Auntie Donna, Auntie Rita…" When he started to include the gorilla on the television show, *The Electric Company*, I got worried. I asked Dr. Mike if he thought Cory's obsession was a problem. He laughed so hard he almost cried. Then he told me a funny story about his daughter who had approached people during a dinner party and declared each person as having either one private part or two, depending on their gender. She pointed to the part she was referring to just so there was no mistake in their knowing what she was talking about. I decided not to sweat it.

Then one day I caught Cory sitting under his crib looking through a *Playboy* magazine, which apparently belonged to his father. (Yeah, sure, he just read the articles.) After this episode, I had a chat with both of them about keeping such materials out of the house. Cory pouted more than his dad did.

One day, I was in his playroom, folding laundry. He was playing on the floor. He looked up at me with his big beautiful brown eyes and asked quite seriously, "Do you remember when I was big?"

At first, I was taken aback but calmly responded, "No, I don't. Can you tell me about it?"

"Don't you remember when I was bigger?"

I remember thinking to myself, *"What is he talking about? He's only fifteen months old!"* But I replied, "No, honey, I'm sorry. I don't remember. Please tell me about when you were bigger."

"I was ten and you were twelve. I got a new horse and named it Star. My name was Tony and yours was Marsha. You were my big sister."

Talk about feeling zapped into the "Twilight Zone"! I asked Cory where we lived back then. At first he said he didn't know. Then he thought about it for a few seconds and said, "Out in the country...in a place called Kentucky."

I ran to get some paper and something to write with so I could take notes. As luck would have it, just as fast as he'd gotten into this fantastic story, he got bored and didn't want to talk about it anymore. *"What an extraordinary child!"* I thought. My only question was, *"Why me?"*

When Cory was around seventeen months old, he pulled a television set down on his chest. Once again, he was climbing. I was in the kitchen, cleaning, when Cory apparently decided to climb up on the television. It was on a cart, which rolled around on casters. When he pulled himself up and stepped on the shelf below the television platform, it must have moved backwards. Cory was clinging to the set with both hands, so when the cart slid away from him, his weight launched the television forward right on top of him. I heard a big crash and ran out to where he was pinned under the set. His coloring was ashen, and the impact had knocked all of the wind out of him. I literally flicked the TV off him with barely any exertion. Adrenaline is amazing in those situations.

I ran upstairs with his lifeless body and dialed the number to Dr. Mike's office while dressing myself.

At first, the nurse didn't seem too concerned. I reacted angrily and ordered her to put Dr. Mike on the phone. He picked up. When I explained what had happened, Mike told me to bring him in for a chest x-ray. He assured me my worries were valid.

The doctor's office was only about nine miles away. Part of the trip was on a highway. We were halfway down the road, and I started to notice truckers smiling and waving at us. I turned to look at Cory in the back seat and found he was grinning and waving at every vehicle that we passed. Then I began to wonder if I had overreacted. Since we were so close, I decided to take him in anyway for the chest x-ray. Mike had mentioned a concern about his thoracic membrane separating from his chest wall.

We got there and went through the exam and x-rays. Cory was fine. We left. On the way home I stopped off at my cousin's house. Sue lived between our house and the clinic. We chatted for a while, and Cory played with her children, Tanya, Kevin, and Tamara. Sue kept trying to reassure me. As far as we could tell, Cory looked fine.

It was getting close to naptime, so I decided to take him home, and on the way, he fell asleep. Once we got home, I carried him up to his bed. I kissed him on the forehead and headed downstairs. When I reached the bottom, my knees turned to rubber and buckled under my weight. I collapsed in a heap.

I crawled to the bathroom. I was able to fill the tub with hot water. Then I managed to undress myself, and I climbed into the tub. I soaked there for hours. I was so exhausted. I marveled at how my body had responded to the situation. I really hadn't tuned in to how frightening the whole ordeal had been for me.

At Cory's second-year "well baby" checkup, Dr. Mike found oddly shaped blood cells in his routine lab work. It freaked Dr. Mike out enough that he sent us to the local hospital for more sophisticated blood tests. When the doctor at the hospital withdrew the blood from his arm,

Cory looked up at me in terror. He had never experienced such pain before and didn't understand it. Immobilized by fear, his eyes filled with tears and he cried, "Mommy? Why is he hurting me?"

I felt awful. By his expression I could see how confused he was. His mommy was standing idly by letting a stranger hurt him with sharp objects. It must have been even more confusing since he had been feeling fine up to that point. No one at this small hospital could figure out exactly what the problem was with Cory's blood. They quickly threw in the towel and sent us on to Children's Hospital and Medical Center in Seattle for more testing.

At the time, all I knew about Children's Hospital was that they had a great reputation and were famous for pioneering bone marrow transplants for kids. An enormous facility, it was rather intimidating the first few times we went there. The hallways seemed endless and impersonal even though they had great murals painted on the walls where the hallways intersected. Have you ever noticed that people don't like to make eye contact in hospital corridors? They react rather like people in elevators.

Cory was a trooper. On the way there, I had explained to him that a new doctor would be taking more blood from his arm. He nodded as he looked up at me through the long, dark lashes that covered his sweet brown eyes. He told me that he would be brave. The whole procedure was over in a matter of minutes. Cory was indeed brave. His eyes pooled with tears, but he didn't complain.

Afterwards, we were told to check back with the hospital in four weeks! For some reason, still a mystery to me, they were sending the blood work to a laboratory in Ohio for testing. I wasn't too sure I could last that long without knowing what was wrong with Cory's blood. As I learned the hard way, that was just too bad.

We decided to take a trip to visit some friends in Colorado to take our minds off the blood tests. The first night there, we went to a unique Mexican restaurant set inside an old church in Denver. The restaurant had a different theme in each room. We went from room to room in complete awe. There were strolling minstrels, a puppet theater, and shoot-'em-up cowboys running around hooting and hollering. Cory's personal favorite was the Acapulco-style cliff divers. He was so impressed.

A few days later at our friends' house, Cory went outside after a huge rainstorm. There was a giant puddle of water about knee-deep in the front yard. I don't know if he was showing off or if he just wanted to imitate the cliff divers, but Cory arched his back and dove right in. The mud was thick. Cory quickly changed his mind about swimming. He arrived at the door covered from head to toe with dark, almost black mud. After I took a photograph (one of my favorites), I carried him straight to the bathtub. It took three or four tubs full of water to rinse him clean. I cleaned mud out of his nose, ears, and every other orifice. We had a quick chat about asking for permission to go swimming and not just jumping in any ol' puddle of water. It didn't take much to convince him.

We all had a wonderful time visiting friends and TJ's uncle and his family. It was such a nice distraction I didn't consciously worry about the test results. If we had stayed home, I would have been an emotional wreck.

Coming home from that trip was memorable, too. The drive to the airport took about an hour or so. Cory seemed fine. At the airport he begged me to buy him a small bag of corn chips. Of course he gobbled them right down. We boarded the plane and things still seemed fine. We were in the air for a short time when my little sleepyhead pulled away from my chest, where he'd been nestled quietly since takeoff. He looked me square in the eye and said, "Uh oh, Mommy." He nailed me good, all down the front of my shirt, even on the inside. It wasn't too horrible, though, because it was a mixture of undigested corn chips and about a third of a tube of toothpaste! For a reason known only to mischievous two-year-olds, Cory had had a strange last-minute compulsion to snack on a big glob of toothpaste. He had never done anything even remotely similar to that. Eating toothpaste was a new one on me.

Cory's toothpaste episode briefly distracted me from obsessing about the appointment. As soon as we had boarded the airplane, I had started tensing up. Even when I concentrated my efforts not to think about the test results, scary thoughts crept into my mind. The earlier tests had given indications of two blood diseases; both were untreatable and fatal.

Cory

The day after we got back, we went to Children's Hospital to meet with the hematologist. I was so worked up by then that I thought I was going to lose my mind. All I could think about was my childhood premonition about having an ill child. On the way to the meeting, I began to wonder what my life would be like without my little boy. I just couldn't imagine. He was such a joy and filled my life so completely. At this point, I was even thankful for the mess he'd made down my shirt on the airplane the night before.

We sat quietly in the waiting area. I was struggling to breathe. As we sat there I looked at my darling baby boy's face and silently prayed to God to let him be. When a nurse came to get us, my stomach turned, and I felt dizzy.

Walking the fifty feet or so into the meeting room seemed surreal. I really thought I'd faint or throw up, but I didn't. The doctor was great. He came in and got right to the point. He said, "There's nothing wrong with your kid. We have no idea what the heck was going on with his blood, but it is fine now. It was probably screwed up because he had some kind of virus or a series of viruses, and it caused the cells to be mal-shaped. You can go now and have a good life."

Without asking a single question, we jumped up and ran out of there. We got outside and started whooping and hollering. In my mind, I just kept saying, *"Oh God, thank you for not letting my premonition come true."*

When life settled down again, I realized I was pregnant. I had been so stressed out that I hadn't noticed. One day at work someone dropped a pile of computer printouts on my desk. This was way back when the ink smelled like chemicals. I took one whiff of the paper and had to make a beeline for the ladies' room. Maradee, my co-worker, followed me to see if I was okay. I was fine after breathing untainted air in the hallway. I sat in the ladies' room for a few minutes with my head between my knees. As Maradee and I walked back to our desks together, someone lit up a cigarette, and I almost passed out from the smell. Maradee said, "You better check your calendar. I think you're pregnant." After the initial shock wore off, I was very happy and excited about having another baby.

That May (1978), my niece, Kimberly, had her First Holy Communion. Cory, who was two, and I were seated next to my sister Rita, her husband, John, and their younger daughter, Jenifer. The entire congregation had their heads bowed in prayer. I felt a nudge from Cory who exclaimed loudly, "Mommy, where's God? I want to see him. You said this is God's house, and I want to know why he's not home for cousin Kimi's party. Huh? Huh, Mommy? Where is he? Where's God?" I tried to shush him by reminding him to whisper. He tried very hard to whisper, but it was so quiet in the church that it didn't matter. I told him God was there but that we just couldn't see him. He didn't care much for my answers, so he kept asking the same questions over and over again. I guess he was hoping for a better response. As he got frustrated, his voice got louder. I tried to put my hand over his mouth. He pulled away and demanded to know again, "WHERE is God? WHY isn't God home? Why can't I see HIM? He's missing Kimi's party!" By this time, everyone in the church was laughing. I was rather embarrassed; as Cory's questions made it quite obvious we didn't go to church much.

To make matters worse, he then caught a glimpse of Jenifer scratching the side of her nose, and he shouted, "Jaffy, DON'T PICK YOUR NOSE!" Jaffy (short for Jaffener, which was how Kimi had pronounced her name at birth) was mortified. I'm sure she wanted to clobber him. I'm not sure she ever forgave him for the humiliation and the false accusation.

My pregnancy was healthy, but our lives had become quite stressful toward the end. My marriage had begun to unravel. Counseling was holding things together, but even that was a stretch.

Brie (sounds like bry not bree) Noel'e (sounds like noel-A) was born January 27, 1979. We had a crowd of people at the hospital that afternoon awaiting Brie's arrival since her birth was a planned C-section. Cory was thrilled and proud to be a big brother. He wasn't the least bit jealous. He was very protective of his baby sister right from the start.

He was such a great little helper, too. He liked to hold her on his lap and tell her stories, sing her songs, or just look at her face and fingers and toes.

One day Brie was in her doorway-bouncing-swing-type of contraption. Cory apparently wanted her to have more fun so he spun her around a number of times and then let go. I found her bouncing from one side to the other off the doorjamb. Poor thing could hardly breathe. Cory was standing there clapping with delight. I asked him why he had wound her up, and he told me that she had looked bored.

Cory was such an agile child. That's a bad combination with fearless in a three-year-old. Once, we were out in the front yard, talking to a neighbor whose child had followed him down the street on his bicycle. Cory wanted to try out the bike. I wasn't too worried about it since Cory had never ridden a two-wheeler, and he certainly couldn't reach the seat on a bike that size. I took my eyes off him for one second. Next thing I knew, he was hurtling down the hill on the bike. His balance was amazing. He had never even sat on a bicycle. We started running down the hill after him. He yelled back over his shoulder, "How do you stop this thing?"

I yelled at him to steer the bike into my parents' yard. Their yard was on the corner just before a very busy intersection. He followed my instructions and spiraled around their yard to slow the bike down. He managed to lay the bike down gently in the grass just as I reached him. I was winded from dashing down the hill. He stood up with a huge smile on his face and said, "That was FUN! Can I do it again?"

When Brie was about four months old, Cory took swimming lessons at the neighborhood pool. There was a cute, little, blond girl whose name was Christina Moloney in his class. Sitting on the sidelines, I met Christina's mother, Lynn. She had a baby, Jami, who was about six months older than Brie. We discovered Cory and Christina were signed up for the same preschool class at Raggedy Ann. Raggedy Ann was *the* local preschool in our area. Lynn generously offered to give Cory rides to and from preschool so I wouldn't have to wake Brie from her naps. Lynn and I became best friends, as did Cory and Christina. Later on so did Brie and Jami.

Lynn and I attended art classes together and found we had a lot more in common than our children. Both of our marriages were straining, and neither of us was happy. There's nothing like sharing a bit of misery to forge a lifelong friendship.

The Little Ghost

The house TJ, my husband, and I bought had been built in 1922. From the first night we stayed in the house, I knew it had a resident ghost. I was alone in the house, putting shelf lining in the kitchen cupboards and talking to my mother on the telephone. I told her I could feel a presence in the house, which made me feel as if I was not alone. No sooner had the words left my mouth than the oil painting, which was hanging in the kitchen nook, crashed to the floor. I asked my mom to hold on while I checked to see what had happened. I went around the stove peninsula and picked up the picture. The nail was still securely on the wall, and upon close examination, I could see that the string was intact on the back of the painting. Seeing this gave me a slight case of the "heebie jeebies." But having grown up with my grandfather's talk-stories about ghosts quieted my fear. The ghosts in his talk-stories weren't strangers; they were usually relatives or someone he knew. But, still, I wasn't afraid.

I went back to the telephone and told my mother about the string and the nail. She casually quipped, "Yep, you're right. You're not alone." Then she asked, "Does it feel okay? It doesn't feel evil or heavy does it?" I didn't even need to think about it. Whatever or whoever was present felt fine.

I was frequently alone at night as my husband worked the late shift. I usually stayed up late to do needlepoint or read. Quite often I heard footsteps on the stairs or doors creaking somewhere in the house. It didn't freak me out. I just got used to it. I even talked aloud to him sometimes.

One time when Cory was a toddler, I asked my brother GG to baby-sit for me while I went to work. I had folded a load of laundry and left part of it on the couch in the living room. This was when Underoos, matching underpants and T-shirts, were "in." I took a call not too long after arriving at work. My brother wanted to know where Cory's Underoos were. Slightly annoyed, I said, "They are right there on the couch."

He came back to the telephone and said, "Nope, not there." I didn't know what to tell him. He searched everywhere, and they were just plain gone. We never did find them...a dozen sets of underwear vanished.

When Brie was a brand new baby, my mother was staying with us to help out. She asked me to lay fresh clothes for baby Brie for after her bath. I put out a pretty pink nightgown, an undershirt, a diaper, and a clean receiving blanket. Then Brie fell asleep. About an hour later, Brie woke up again and was ready for her bath. My mom went to grab the post-bath clothes I had laid out, and the nightgown was gone. Poof! Vanished completely. Mom and I searched and searched for it. We NEVER found it.

What was the other funny thing that kept disappearing at our house? Whiffle balls and bats. I purchased more than a dozen of those darn toys, and they always disappeared within a day or so. That's why I presumed the ghost to be male and childish.

Over the years we had other items disappear never to be seen again. I always thought I would find a stash somewhere in the farthest reaches of my attic but never did.

Sometimes late at night, in the middle of the kitchen floor, I would find toys that I had put away when the kids had gone up to bed. There would be balls rolling and sometimes a top spinning. A few times I woke up to find every light on the main floor turned on and my stereo blaring. Some of my friends were afraid to stay overnight at our house.

The kids and I got to the point where we just lived with the knowledge that we had a resident ghost.

Diagnosis

Diagnosis: Unknown

*I*t was Christmas time 1979. Brie was a baby approaching her first birthday. Cory was three, almost four. Brie, Cory, and I spent a lot of time at Southcenter, the local mall, that year. On at least two occasions Cory complained that his legs hurt. A very active and energetic little boy, Cory rarely complained about anything. Both times, I thought his little leg muscles must have been tired because I had walked him around too much. So we went home.

The week of the holiday, Cory's energy level went up and down like a roller coaster. One day he was his usual spunky self, and the next, completely lethargic. The flu was going around, and I kept believing that's what was causing Cory's lethargy and muscle pain.

Each day that Cory looked sick and wanted only to be held, I told myself, *"Tomorrow if he's not better, I will take him to the doctor."* Well, the next day he would be up and running around, so I thought, *"Oh good, he's getting better."*

On Christmas Eve, I came down with the flu myself. I remember thinking, *"Okay, that's why Cory's been this way. He's fighting off this bug. He's really okay."* When I recovered within twenty-four hours, my inner alarms started going off. If it lasted only twelve to twenty-four hours with me, I figured something was terribly wrong because Cory had been going up and down for nearly a week.

Christmas morning dawned, and Cory was too sick to play. That was confirmation enough for me. I told myself, *"If he's too sick to play with all of his new toys, he is **definitely** sick. No matter how he's feeling tomorrow, I'm taking him into the doctor."*

The next morning, I made an appointment. Cory's appearance had changed dramatically. His little hands looked like wax with no color variance in his nails. His eyes were as bright as ever, but his face was so pale it was almost green. I was truly frightened by his unusual coloring. With a sinking feeling in the pit of my stomach, I drove the nine miles to the pediatrician's office.

When Dr. Mike took one look at him, he was visibly shaken. Without saying a word, Mike left the room and came back in with a colleague. I shrank back into the woodwork and just watched them. Call it mother's intuition, but in my heart, I knew something was drastically wrong with my son.

The two doctors began discussing Cory's red blood cell count. Each one guessed his hematocrit (red cell) count to be around 18. I found out later that normal for Cory's age and weight was 40. Dr. Mike looked under Cory's eyelids for color. There was none. He turned Cory's little wax-like hands over and peered at his nails. Again, there was absolutely no color at all. The other doctor left shaking his head. Mike said, "For some reason Cory is extremely anemic, and as a result, his heart is racing like mad. I want you to go get blood drawn in our lab, and then meet me back here for the results."

We trudged over to the clinic's lab. It was in an adjoining building down several hallways. At this point, Cory was running back and forth down those hallways. We reached the laboratory, and I turned in the blood test request slips. Cory was very cooperative and didn't even wince when the lab technician drew blood. I think it was because the lab technician was so gentle and kind. She talked to him throughout the procedure, not necessarily to distract him but to reassure him. Her name was Jo-Jo. She was so friendly Cory didn't even feel the needle poke. It didn't take more than a few seconds. We meandered back to the pediatric section of the building to await the test results. Mike had instructed me to return to the back hallway near his office.

Sitting on a wooden bench outside Mike's office, I could hear him conversing with someone on the telephone. Cory was playing happily on the floor at my feet. Suddenly down the back hallway, I heard the footsteps of someone running toward us. I looked up and saw that it was Jo-Jo, the woman who had drawn Cory's blood. It was truly scary to see how fast she was running, and by the look of concern on her brightly flushed face, I knew it was bad news. Jo-Jo rapped frantically on Dr. Mike's office door. I saw him open the door as she rushed in waving the test results in the air. I barely heard her say the number, "8."

A few minutes later, Mike opened the door, and Jo-Jo left. He motioned for me to come in and asked his nurse, Barbara, to play with Cory in the hallway. Barbara and Cory were laughing as they raced down the hall, when Mike turned to me and asked, "Did you hear what she said?"

Nodding, I looked at him with a scared look on my face and answered, "Yeah, but she didn't really say his count was '8' did she?"

Mike had a wonderful way of being direct with parents. He shook his head from side to side in dismay and said, "Yes, she did. He has one-fifth of the red blood cells necessary to carry the oxygen throughout his body."

I stammered, "Didn't you guys think it was more like 18?" Mike nodded the affirmative. I said, "Well, what do we do now? Any idea what's causing it?"

Again shaking his head, Mike replied, "I've got a call in to Children's Hospital, and when they call back, I want you to listen in on our conversation with this other telephone so you can answer any questions they might have, okay?"

My next thought was to ask how this severe anemia was affecting his body. "With what you know right now, what is the worst thing that could happen to Cory?" I really was preparing myself for the bad news. I didn't think I could be lucky enough for it to be another fluke. In the depths of my soul, I knew the time of facing down my premonition had arrived.

Mike thought for just a moment before answering, "Well, his heart is pumping overtime to make up for the lack of red blood cells. I'm not sure how long it's been overworking like this, so I guess the worst thing would be his heart could get tired and stop pumping."

I didn't feel like asking any more questions. That was one scenario I didn't want to imagine dealing with. Then the telephone rang. We both picked up, and I listened as Mike explained to a Dr. Baker at Children's Hospital what the situation was.

The doctor asked me how long Cory had been noticeably pale. When you live with someone and see him everyday, it's hard to see change like that unless it's very dramatic. I told him about the flu-like symptoms and Cory's energy level seesawing. The only noticeable change I could comment on was from that same morning.

Mike and Dr. Baker made arrangements for me to take Cory directly to the hospital. Dr. Baker wanted Cory admitted so they could run a series of tests on him to determine what was causing the anemia. Plus Cory needed a blood transfusion right away.

Cory and I drove home first. I stopped at my mother's house where I had left Brie. I fed Brie and explained to my mother what the doctors had said. My mom and I thought it best for me to leave Brie with her. I telephoned Cory's father and asked him to go with us to the hospital. Initially, he did not want to accompany us because he was scheduled to work overtime. I insisted, and eventually he agreed to go with us. His attitude concerned me. I could almost feel him withdrawing emotionally from the scariness of the situation. I was not looking forward to dealing with the enormity of a medical crisis by myself.

We drove to the hospital in silence. I kept thinking how weird it was to be heading for Children's Hospital. Two years had passed since our last blood scare. I wondered if there was some connection. I thought, *"Maybe the first time was a warning."*

Once there, we filled out a bundle of paperwork, and Cory was admitted to a private room on B-3. B-3, we found out, was the section of the hospital reserved for little cancer patients.

We waited in the room for the lab to send someone to draw more blood for more tests. Cory was feeling healthy so he just took everything in stride. But I was growing more anxious with each passing minute, which turned into hours. The hospital personnel took a very long time to get the blood tests going. Even more aggravating was that no one told us how long we would have to wait.

A few hours after Cory was admitted, we were still sitting around. Cory's father decided to go to work instead of waiting with us. I didn't argue with him about his decision to leave. I was not at all surprised he didn't want to stay since he had been reluctant to accompany us to the hospital in the first place. My fears were really beginning to mount—not just about my childhood premonition but about being abandoned to handle it alone.

Hours and hours crept slowly by. I started hounding the nurses to ask the doctor to speed things up. It made no sense to me that it could take so long. I had to practically throw a tantrum to get cooperation. I had been patient long enough. I demanded an explanation.

Finally, they sent a technician to draw blood. Then more time went by, and finally around 3:00 p.m. I saw Dr. Baker running down the hallway toward Cory's room. I knew he must have gotten the results. He ran breathlessly into the room and said, "I did not believe that Cory's counts could be so low because he is so active! The lab at Kent Medical Center was right; his hematocrit is an 8 and his hemoglobin is a 2. We have to transfuse him right away! I have sent for blood from the blood bank. We've never had anyone with counts this low! He shouldn't even be able to pick his head up. This is a record low for this hospital! I've never seen anyone with a hemoglobin count of 2!" (The normal hemoglobin count for Cory's age and weight was 12.)

"Aha," I thought, *"that's why it's taken so long. This guy didn't believe the low lab results from Kent."* I was rather irritated that his personal bias against a smaller clinic had made him so blasé about my son's blood work. He also failed to tell me it could take hours to get the blood necessary for the transfusion from the blood bank.

The doctor hooked Cory up to an IV. Looking back now, I'm not sure what was in the bag. Even with an IV in his arm, Cory's energy level was still high. With the IV bag flying, he was racing up and down the halls on a tricycle while holding on to the IV pole. Dr. Baker said, "What's he like when he's not sick? Does he fly?"

The day turned into night, the novelty of being at the hospital had worn off, and Cory just wanted to go home. He was not feeling too badly, and I think he was bored. I explained to him that the doctors wanted to see him again in the morning just to be sure he was going to be okay."

Everyone was asleep on the wing. My eldest brother, Tim, showed up to check on Cory and me. He also brought baby Brie up to the hospital so I could nurse her before bedtime. My brother didn't know what to say so he just joked around. As kids, he had always been my protector. I know it must have been painful for him to see me that stressed out. Plus, he had been wounded in Vietnam and, as a result, was hospitalized for several years. I think identifying with Cory was tough on him. I was sad when they left for home. It had been a long, arduous day.

Around ten o'clock I was sitting in the dark listening to Cory breathing and reckoning with the idea that my childhood intuition was becoming reality. Suddenly the quiet was pierced with a shrill cry from Cory as he sat straight up in bed clutching his chest. I ran for the door screaming for the nurse to get a doctor.

A team of healthcare professionals came running into the room, and I was pushed out into the hallway. My mind raced to recall Mike's words from that morning: "His heart could get tired and stop pumping." I was leaning against the wall outside his room. Through the shade I could see shadows hovering around my son's bed. My strength was wavering, and I really felt as if I was going to lose it. I prayed to God that my son would be saved. Then, as if in a dream or an old TV western when the cavalry rides up at the last second, I saw someone running down the hall toward me dangling several bags of blood. My spirits leapt as I realized the blood was for Cory. I slumped to the floor and sobbed with relief.

After what seemed like a lifetime, the team of doctors and nurses left his room, and I was motioned to come back in. Cory was sound asleep and appeared to be resting comfortably. I stood next to his bed and offered a prayer of thanks to God. The doctors told me that with the blood transfusion his heart would be able to return to normal.

I could not sleep. Sitting up on the little foldout, plastic vinyl covered couch in the corner of Cory's room, I contemplated our future. It was then that I knew my marriage would not survive this crisis. All I could think of was, *"Why am I being forced to deal with this nightmare alone?"* After a while, I told myself, *"I can't expend any more energy wondering about it. Time will tell."*

The next morning Cory's cheeks were rosy pink again, and he looked completely healthy. His appetite was good, and his energy level was practically normal. He played, but the hospital playroom held his interest only for a few hours at a time; Cory wanted to go home to his new Christmas toys and his baby sister.

This hospital stay would last only four days. Being on a cancer ward was weird. The hall lights shone brightly twenty-four hours a day. The activity outside our door was sporadic. Cory's room was private, so there was little or no opportunity to talk with other parents. I felt completely isolated. No one came to visit us, either, not even Cory's dad who couldn't handle seeing Cory in the hospital bed for more than a few minutes at a time. My only guess was that family and friends were too scared to know what to say, so they just stayed away. Except for Cory, my only contact was with doctors, nurses, lab technicians, and janitors. I didn't leave his room at all.

After a battery of tests, the doctors remained stumped. They could not determine the cause of Cory's anemia. In frustration, they released Cory with a plan to have Dr. Mike check his blood once a week. They told me it could be another fluke in his body's blood-manufacturing process. One theory was that it was a transient anemia, as if I was supposed to know what that meant. I was learning quickly that being a mother took massive inner-strength.

With fear and foreboding, we went home without answers. Everyone was clueless. I felt overwhelmed seeing so many doctors who worked on this type of problem everyday completely baffled as to what was wrong with my child.

The next four weeks were a blur to me. I can't remember a single thing that happened, other than Cory's blood checks came back normal each of the first three weeks. The only explanation I have is that God got me through those long weeks.

Then the fourth blood test showed Cory's white blood cells were out of whack. His platelets were still okay, but it was very puzzling that first the red cells were deficient and now the white cells were too plentiful. Mike calmly explained the changes to me. I'm sure he thought I was listening, but I was only half there. I heard him make the call to Children's Hospital again. This time they didn't want us right away. They said we could come in the following morning. I drove home in silence, dreading the morning.

One of my best friends, Donna Schwendeman, worked for a pediatrician so I called her to ask what she thought about Cory's mysterious blood condition. Donna calmed my fears saying it was a curious turn of events, but she thought I should have complete trust in the doctors at Children's Hospital. I didn't sleep a wink.

The next morning, Cory and I dropped Brie off with my mother again. This would turn out to be a sad and familiar routine. We had to be at the Hematology-Oncology clinic by eight o'clock.

When we arrived at Children's, the outpatient side of the hospital was deserted. We wandered into the clinic, and a doctor we hadn't met before was there to greet us. He escorted us to an examination room. He introduced himself to both of us. His name was Frank Balis. And was he ever tall! A very nice man with a great soft-spoken bedside manner, he won both of us over immediately. Dr. Balis went on to explain what tests he planned to run that morning.

After hours of testing and waiting, Dr. Balis, or Frank, as we came to know him, told us we could go to lunch. He also said, "I'm not sure what is going on with Cory's blood, but at least it's not leukemia. It's possibly a transient anemia or maybe even aplastic anemia, but again, at least it's not leukemia. So, go ahead and go to lunch, and I'll see you back here around one o'clock." He even mentioned bone marrow transplants as a possible solution to aplastic anemia, as if they were no big deal.

John, my sister Rita's husband, surprised us by showing up right about the time we were leaving for lunch. He offered to drive us to McDonald's. Of course, Cory jumped up and down, squealing with delight over that idea. It was nice to have company; I wasn't very hungry, though.

We had lunch, and I filled John in on the morning's events. He was very supportive. Then just before 1:00 p.m., he dropped us off back at the hospital. I was getting a bit nervous, but when he offered to stick around for moral support, I declined. I told John and myself that because the doctor was so upbeat before lunch, I was sure there wasn't a problem. I smiled at Cory, and we strode back to the clinic with me exuding a false sense of calm.

Back in the bustling clinic, which had filled up since morning, we were escorted to yet another examination room. In it were two hard plastic blue chairs, a small examination table, a sink, and in the corner, a box of toys. Cory found the new toys to play with right away.

Shirley, Cory, Brie

I just sat there waiting. I wondered if they shuffled kids from room to room because of the toys; maybe it was to keep them from being bored since everything they did seemed to take so long.

It was quite a long time before we heard a knock at the door and in walked Dr. Balis. He had a sad look on his face as he briefly hesitated at the door. *"Boy, this isn't looking too good,"* I thought to myself. Frank walked over and sat down. He reached over and took my hand. I thought, *"Uh oh, the ol' Dr. Welby routine."* (When I was growing up, Dr. Welby was a television doctor played by Robert Young, who was supposed to be the perfect doctor but I thought was pretty schmaltzy.)

I looked down at his big hand covering mine, and I got scared... not just mildly scared either. My brain was shouting, *"This is serious!"* I looked into his eyes and saw pain, fear, and guilt. My brain screamed, *"Uh oh."*

Then Frank said, "Shirley, I'm so sorry, but I prepared you in the wrong way. What it looks like we're dealing with is leukemia."

I heard the words but my brain only absorbed the "looks like" part. I looked at Frank and replied, "I know it *looks like* it, but what *is* it?"

He repeated himself, and I then repeated my question, "But what *is* it?" I'm sure he was thinking, "Hello? Is anybody in there?" When I finally understood what he was telling me, I made him go back to the lab and check again. My brain was stuck on his words from that morning; "At least it's not leukemia."

"How could they be so wrong?" I kept asking myself. The poor guy told me that he was shocked, too, and he had in fact checked it several times before he told me. I insisted, and he agreed to check one more time, just for my sake.

When he left the room, I stared at my beautiful, bright, lively, three-year-old son playing in the corner. He looked so darn healthy. I wanted to collapse into a puddle and cry my eyes out, but I was afraid it would scare him. Instead, I internalized all my fears, fought back the tears, and tried to concentrate on what would happen next.

Frank Balis, bless his heart, came back into the room with sagging shoulders and sat down beside me again. I looked him straight in the eyes as he said, "I'm sorry, Shirley; it **is** leukemia." He was in worse shape than I was.

"Okay, what are we going to do next?" I asked. "What is the plan?" Frank's face brightened a little as he started explaining treatment options. He was smart enough to warn me that I probably wouldn't be able to retain more than 30 percent of what he was telling me. "Give it a try," I said.

Frank was a "fellow," which I discovered later meant he was doing an additional residency. I guessed he hadn't done too many of these "bad news" talks, because he was so shook up about it. On the other hand, I also believe he is a very compassionate man who has chosen the right profession.

As Frank left us alone in the room, he mentioned that a nurse would be stopping in to talk with me. A few minutes later there was a knock at the door. I dreaded opening the door. I just didn't feel like meeting anyone new and having to carry on a conversation while my whole world was crumbling. It turned out to be a pleasant surprise. Instead of another stranger to talk to, it was my friend, Donna Schwendeman. I'll never forget what she looked like: very Danish with blonde hair and huge blue, saucer-like eyes. We are close to the same height. I opened the door, and our eyes connected. I could see the care and concern in her eyes and also the question. I gave her a hug for being there and whispered in her ear that it was leukemia.

Donna told me that after we had talked the night before, she researched Cory's symptoms in her textbooks. She realized that we would need her support. She immediately started to cry, and I shushed her. I knew that if she cried, I would too. My biggest fear was that if I started, I wouldn't be able to stop, which would freak Cory out for certain.

We sat and talked about the diagnosis. I explained as much of the treatment plan as I could remember. The nurse showed up at the door, and I shooed her away. I just wanted to be with someone that we knew, someone that I knew loved Cory. Donna stayed with us for several hours until Cory was admitted to the hospital. The doctor wanted to begin high-dose chemotherapy immediately.

Once we were admitted, I telephoned my brother Mark and asked him to go find my mother and tell her about Cory's diagnosis in person. I did not want to tell her on the telephone. In fact, I knew I could not tell my mother, period. I was sure just saying the words would turn me into a blubbering fool, and then I would be of no use to Cory.

After my mom got the bad news, she called me to find out how we were doing. We talked briefly; then in a hushed voice she asked, "Do you remember what you told me when you were ten?"

I said, "Yes, Mom."

Then she asked, "This is it, isn't it?"

I tearfully replied, "Yeah, I think it is." We never mentioned it again. I knew then that the premonition was starting to come true. Cory's odyssey was just beginning.

Dr. Mike called to say how sorry he was. I felt so connected to him at that point. He had been there when both of my children had been born, so he had known Cory almost from the moment I had. But it was his courage to cry and share how upset he was about Cory's diagnosis that endeared him to me for life, not just as a doctor or a friend but as a human being.

I'll never forget Cory sitting up in the hospital bed asking me that day, "Mommy, are I sick?" He was so confused by all of the painful procedures when he truly didn't feel bad to begin with. He was so cute. Every time a lab technician or nurse poked him for a blood test, even if it was in the middle of the night, he would say, "Thank you."

There's a big red toy box with a latch on it in the outpatient Hematology-Oncology clinic. Whenever children get a bone marrow tap or a spinal tap, they get to choose an item out of the red box. Cory was so good during the medical procedures that the doctor carried him all the way to the clinic to get a few prizes. Cory chose a toy for himself and one for his sister. The doctor tried to convince him to pick two things for him since he'd had the pokes, but Cory said, "No, one's enough. I want to get a prize for my baby sister." The nurses told me that in the history of the red box, no other child had ever been so generous.

This act of generosity became Cory's M.O., his modus operandi—whenever he had to endure painful procedures, he always chose one prize for himself and one for Brie, too.

That first night in the hospital, a resident came to ask me about family medical histories. She then went on to say, without quoting statistics, that most marriages don't survive chronic illnesses. In fact, she said, "This type of illness can destroy good marriages, but bad marriages never make it." I think my face turned red. I remember wondering how she knew.

Brie's first birthday party was in Cory's hospital room. Poor little baby, she had no idea what this diagnosis would do to her future. I watched her smush her birthday cake with her chubby, little fingers and wondered how we would survive this darn disease.

Cory was hospitalized for a week that time. He tolerated the chemotherapy well. The doctors seemed to find comfort in the fact that the changes in Cory's blood cells went in stages, first red then white but never platelets. It didn't make *me* feel any better.

They gave me a book about leukemia. It had a wonderfully descriptive explanation of what leukemia cells do in a person's bloodstream. It used the image of rabbits in a room, multiplying like crazy until there is no room to move around—no room to get anything done in the room—and eventually no room for anything but the squished rabbits. Leukemia is made up of immature, useless, white cells that, like rabbits, keep multiplying and crowding out the other cells, which are needed to sustain a body's functions.

The most traumatic occurrence of Cory's two hospital stays happened one afternoon when Cory was off playing in the recreation room. The orderly cleaned Cory's room too well. When we got back to the room, I tucked Cory in his bed for a nap, and we discovered "Blanky" was gone! My normally happy-go-lucky little boy began to cry hysterically. The nurse came running in to see what was causing the commotion. When I explained the circumstances surrounding his abnormal behavior, she panicked. Apparently anything accidentally tossed into the laundry around there has a low probability of ever being seen again. The nurse took off running, and I followed her. Luckily the laundry bags were still on that floor. We found them in a room piled high with huge blue drawstring bags. We looked at each other, and she said, "There's good news and bad news..."

As Murphy's Law would have it, we found the blanket after we had dumped every last bag out on the floor. Cory was so happy to see his best friend; our work was well worth it.

The First Year

With the amount of time we would be spending at Children's Hospital, I knew it was necessary to prepare Cory for some of the unusual sights sometimes found there. He was a compassionate child. It didn't take much explanation for him to understand why I wanted him to talk with me privately. He knew that if the sight of a disfigurement bothered him he should whisper to me and not speak so loudly that the child could hear him.

It also didn't take long for my lesson to be put to the test. As we were leaving the oncology clinic one morning, a toddler with braces on both legs using a walker passed us. Cory's grip on my hand tightened, and he whispered, "Mommy, I need to talk!" We stopped in the lobby and sat down. I asked what was troubling him. His eyes filled with tears. He was still whispering, "Mommy, what's wrong with that baby's legs?"

"Honey, I guess the baby was born with legs that don't work quite right."

"But why, Mommy? Why did God do that?"

"Well, I'm not so sure it was intentional. But, look, the baby has learned how to walk, and it doesn't look like it hurts."

He started to cry bitter tears. He said, "It's not fair! That baby can't run or ride a bike. It must be so hard to play." I held him and tried to comfort his wounded heart. He pulled back and with tears streaming down his cheeks, he said, "I'm so lucky. I only have leukemia." Then, I started to cry. He was such an incredible little boy. Afterwards, we got up, and I carried him out to the car.

A few weeks later, we were at Dr. Mike's office. By choice, Cory received some of his chemotherapy shots there instead of at Children's. While we were waiting for Mike, Cory found an anatomy book. He thumbed through it until it grossed him out, but he was quite interested in the images of the heart.

At the following hospital appointment, we were placed in a large waiting room. A young woman was there with two small children. One was a baby who apparently had cancer, and the other had a tumor-like protrusion on her face. I forget what they're called, but they usually go away and aren't a big deal. Cory took one look at the child's face and jumped to his feet.

"Mommy, take me to get a drink of water. Please!"

"Here's some water right here, Cory."

"No, Mommy, I want water in the hallway." He cocked his head and bobbed it toward the door. I noticed he had a pleading look in his eyes. We went out to the hallway. As soon as we were a safe distance away from anyone's earshot, Cory said, "Mommy, why does that baby have a heart growing on her face???"

"That's not a heart, honey. It's okay. I'm not sure what it's called, but it isn't a heart. Did seeing it scare you?"

"Yes, it did. I saw a heart in Dr. Mike's book. *That* sure does look like one to me. It has veins sticking out all over it, and it's real red and yucky looking. It's supposed to be in her chest, keeping her alive, not on her face."

"Okay, listen. When we go in to see Dr. Balis, you can ask him. I'm sure it's okay. It's not a heart, and the baby will be just fine, honest."

A short time later, we were escorted to an examination room. Cory jumped up on the examination table and waited. Frank came through the door, and Cory practically attacked him.

"There's a baby in the waiting room with a heart growing on her face! Is she going to be all right???"

"Oh, sure she is Cory. That's not a heart. But I can see why you thought it was. It looks like one, doesn't it?"

"Yeah, it does. It doesn't look right on her face."

Frank so understood; he just patted Cory on the shoulder and reassured him that the child was fine. In fact, she wasn't even the patient. She was just there for her sister's treatment.

The first year after Cory's diagnosis was completely regimented. Our lives revolved around hospital and clinic visits. Within weeks of diagnosis, remission was achieved with the toxic chemotherapy medication. Remission means the leukemia cells are held down to a count of less than 5 percent in the person's bloodstream.

The side-effects were interesting. With the Prednisone came a warning from the doctors about food cravings, especially salty foods. For the first few weeks, Cory didn't seem to be reacting the way the docs had predicted, so I didn't think too much of it. Then, in the middle of the night, I awoke to find Cory standing next to my bed holding his tummy. He literally begged me to get up and fix him breakfast. He wanted crisp bacon, peanut butter toast, and hot cocoa. It was about 1:30 a.m. I tried to talk him out of the bacon, but he started crying. So I thought, *"Oh well, it'll be okay just this once."*

I hopped out of bed and threw on my robe. He followed me downstairs to the kitchen. I fixed the bacon, toast and cocoa just they way he wanted it. Cory made sure of that. When he was finished, I put him back to bed.

About an hour or so later, he was back asking for the same menu! This went on all night long. Then I understood what the doctors were talking about. It was nerve wracking because I knew Cory wasn't supposed to have salty foods because of water retention and other blood pressure-type problems, but he was impossible to dissuade or even distract. He begged, pleaded, cried, cajoled...you name it. For weeks after that, whenever we drove down the street, Cory would beg me to stop at every fast-food restaurant we saw. He cried a lot during that period.

Some of Cory's treatment visits took all day long. For tax purposes, I kept track of the trips to the various medical facilities in a date book. Looking back on the routine now, I can see how brutal it really was. When you are living with a long-term illness that takes so much time and energy, you can't afford to examine the process too closely—it would make you crazy.

As I look back, even sadder are the notations in the date book about the chemotherapy and radiation treatments he underwent and their devastating side-effects. On Cory's fourth birthday, his hair began to fall out in clumps. We visited some friends, and here's what I wrote:

> *Cory's hair is very thin on top and in front. He left masses of it all over Brian and Shirlee's couch when he got up to leave. He was so embarrassed to have made such a mess, more so than being bald.*

Complaints of ankle pain, mouth ulcers, and radiation burns were interspersed in my daily notes with momentous events such as Brie's first tooth and Cory learning to tie his shoes. But the predominant notations were the countless reminders to administer Cory's medication. I look at the notations, and I can feel the anxiety well up inside me all over again. The following are typical entries from near the beginning of his treatment:

> *February 11: Three doses of oral Prednisone at 8:00, 2:00, and 8:00. Trip to Kent Medical for shot of L'Aspariginase [a drug administered intramuscularly, usually in the thigh muscle]. Dr. Mike found Cory had an ear infection, but Amoxicillin won't affect his chemo treatment so that's a relief.*

> *February 13: Three doses of Prednisone at 8:00, 2:00, and 8:00. Trip to Dr. Mike's for L'Aspariginase. Cory is afraid of leg pokes and tries so hard to be brave. What a brave three-year-old he is!*

> *February 22: same drug instructions. Trip to Children's for meds and tests. END OF INDUCTION - REMISSION! (Long drawn out day.) Noticed Cory's foot drop...*

My glossary:

Induction is the first phase of chemotherapy. It's when the patient is bombarded with heavy-duty drugs to try to kill off the bad blood cells.

Cory's at his fourth birthday

Remission is the state of being cancer-free. With leukemia, though at that time, it meant having less than 5 percent of the patient's white cells in the blood sample leukemic or immature.

Foot drop is where the child's leg muscles are affected by the drugs, and he cannot walk heel-toe, heel-toe. The foot points down, and he ends up walking with a slapping motion. In Cory's case luckily it was temporary.

With Cory's remission, we were able to get beyond panic and fear mode into survival mode. At least the kids and I did. TJ, my children's father, as I'd feared, did not deal well with Cory's illness. He lost his job within three weeks of Cory's diagnosis. Then he refused to look for work or to help by taking Cory to his chemotherapy and radiation treatments. His behavior put more pressure on me, and I was already straining under carrying a full load.

There was one very unusual complication noted in my date book.

May 18, 1980: We were on Hood Canal at my Auntie Anita and Uncle Ed's when Mount St. Helens erupted. We could see the ash off in the distance coming toward us. We ran back to our car and headed down the hill to get Cory indoors before the ash reached us. Cory developed a croupy sounding cough. The cough lasted several weeks. He coughed so hard it hurt his chest.

Have you ever had a complete stranger confront you with a personal question? When Cory was bald for the first time, right after his fourth birthday, we had people walk up to us at the shopping mall and ask, "Why are you bald?" or something really insensitive such as, "What happened to your hair?" One stupid person said, "Why did your parents shave your head?" It was truly amazing.

As Cory's new hairs started to grow back in, they were light blonde, almost white. Then after a few days they started to turn dark. It was weird. I was convinced that that couldn't happen, so I thought it was dirt. I soaked him in the tub and then scrubbed his little head with a washcloth. Finally he said, "Mommy, you're rubbing too hard." Well, upon closer examination, I realized it was his hair color changing, and he had radiation burns on the back of his head. I had to apologize. I felt so badly about scrubbing too hard.

Cory's blood counts were so low at times he couldn't run the risk of being around other people and their germs. This meant no school, no church, no going anywhere—not even to the grocery store! Cory got so bored. This was before VCRs were available. For a very social little boy, being stuck at home with no other children his age to play with was the pits.

One night, I scanned the entertainment section of the newspaper until I found a late night showing of Disney's *The Lady and the Tramp*. It was perfect. The movie was scheduled to run long after most children had gone to bed for the night.

I bundled Cory up in warm clothes and put a surgical mask over his face, and away we went. It was a surprise for him. He was actually thrilled just to be out of the house.

The theater was virtually empty. There were maybe three or four people down near the front. I kept Cory in the last row of the center section. I wiped the arms of the seats we sat in with a disinfectant.

Of course, Cory wanted refreshments, and I had come prepared: I had sneaked in a small plastic bag filled with popcorn and a Tupperware cup with juice. He absolutely loved the movie. In fact, he thought it was a private showing just for him because he couldn't see the people down front. My "Mommy can do anything!" quotient went way up that night. *The Lady and the Tramp* movie must have been a fluke because after that, I could never find late night showings of movies appropriate for child viewing. Believe me, I tried.

Gifted School

ory's favorite thing to do was to attend school. He loved to learn. He also craved the social aspects of school. Always an incredibly bright student, school was easy for Cory.

When he was four, Cory was being seen by Dr. Archie Bleyer at the University of Washington Hospital to prepare him for brain radiation treatments. The doctor couldn't get over how smart and funny Cory was although I thought Cory was being rather sarcastic, especially for a four-year-old. At one point, Dr. Bleyer asked Cory to stand on one foot. Cory promptly walked over and stood on the doctor's foot. Then he started laughing. Cory had overhead my friend Donna tell me a story about a friend's child doing that during a check-up at her office. Cory apparently thought it amusing enough to do it too.

Then Dr. Bleyer asked Cory to tell him how many fingers he was holding up. He responded with, "Two," "Four." Then, the third time Dr. Bleyer asked him, Cory put his hand on his hip, cocked his head to one side, and blurted out, "What's the matter, Doctor? Can't *you* count?"

Dr. Bleyer asked if I knew about the gifted school at the University of Washington. I had to tell this guy, "Look, I'm still trying to cope with the leukemia diagnosis. Worrying about school is not a priority."

He pushed harder. "This kid needs special attention. He should not be in a regular school."

I finally had to say, "I cannot deal with that right now. Believe me, I know how smart he is. He is scary smart. But right now, I have a baby, an unemployed husband, and no thoughts about school this fall."

Dr. Bleyer's message was twofold. He not only felt Cory needed to be in a gifted school, but he wanted me not to lose sight of the fact that even though Cory was sick, we needed to focus on his future *apart from* his disease. I have always appreciated the interest he took in Cory's education and the valuable message he gave me.

Days later, I received a telephone call from one of the school's administrators. She offered to let Cory jump the waiting list. I thought, *"Man! They really want him to attend this school!"* I told her Cory was too burned out emotionally and physically to take entrance exams. I was assured that wouldn't be necessary—Dr. Bleyer had contacted Dr. Hal Robinson, the psychologist, who with his wife, Nancy, ran the University of Washington's Early Entrance Program and the Child Development School. Dr. Bleyer had described his observations of Cory's mental abilities, and that had eliminated any need for testing at the school.

Instead, we received a huge packet from the school in the mail. The instructions enclosed were quite specific. I was to have Cory answer several pages of questions, draw a few pictures with very few instructions, enclose a few of his own drawings, and mail it back.

Reluctantly, I sent back the completed packet. Dr. Robinson called a few days later and insisted that I allow Cory to be a part of the University Child Development School. I was so torn about whether or not to send him to this special school. They finally convinced me by explaining that he needed to be with children who were at the same level of intelligence. I thought back to the time when he was around two and I caught him in the back yard at my mother's house standing on top of the doghouse. He was throwing a ball while two neighbor boys twice his age were fetching it. I also acknowledged that he was the preschool teachers' helper because he already knew everything they were teaching the rest of the class. I agreed to send him to the school.

In the fall, Cory attended the school, which was located on campus at the University of Washington in Seattle. The first time I drove the car pool, I was convinced the school administrators had made a big mistake. One of my riders, a boy named Kevin, also four, was sitting in the back seat, reciting every major body of water in the world! And to top it off he knew every state, its capital, and each one's most important agricultural crop! I remember thinking, *"Wow, Cory's smart, but I'm not so sure he fits in this category."* I parked my car and went in to discuss my concerns with Joy. She laughed and insisted that Cory was every bit as gifted as the other children in the school. She explained that some kids are exceptional in one or two areas and weak in others, but she insisted that Cory was very bright in all areas. I shrugged my shoulders and left, but I was still worried I hadn't taught him enough geography. Heck, I didn't even know all that stuff Kevin had been reciting.

But Cory thrived in that environment. He was extremely outgoing and got along well with his classmates and teachers. The school director, Joy Menke, told me he was not only extremely bright, but he was the most socially adept child she had ever worked with. She described how the kids would go to Cory with their problems. He would put his arm around their shoulders, listen to them carefully and then dispense his advice. He was the four-year-old "Dear Abby" of the playground.

The Overdose

We had been asked to participate in a drug study at Children's Hospital. Frank, Cory's doctor, was studying the efficacy of Methotrexate. The arrangement was that we would give Cory his medication and then catch all of his urine for twenty-four hours and drop it off at the hospital lab. We had to change the day to dispense his medication from Friday to Thursday because the lab would not be open on Saturday to run the tests.

On our first attempt, TJ let him go to the bathroom at the hardware store, which negated the experiment. He didn't seem to understand or care about the importance of what Frank Balis was trying to accomplish.

When I broke the news to Frank, he reluctantly rescheduled us for the following week. Then he took me aside and expressed his concerns about TJ possibly giving Cory the wrong medication, or worse, because he didn't seem to be in touch with the reality of the situation. With an earnest look on his face, Frank warned me to be careful.

The next Thursday came, and I gave Cory his Methotrexate and reminded TJ to catch ALL the urine in the container and refrigerate it. This time TJ followed my instructions. I dropped the specimen off at the hospital's lab on my way to work. I was relieved that it had gone okay that time.

But the words of Dr. Balis continued to rattle around in my head. I was so depressed about everything. The situation with TJ was not getting any better, and I had a hard time going home from work. At work, I was so busy I could immerse myself and not think about my home life.

One night, some of my friends were stopping off after work for drinks and dinner, and I was sorely tempted to join them. But I was really tired, physically and emotionally, so, instead, I went straight home. My children were napping late so I grabbed the newspaper and curled up in my favorite chair. A few minutes later, Cory appeared in the doorway and began to whimper. Even from across the living room, I could see blotches on his cheeks. Feeling very uneasy, I jumped out of my chair and went closer for a better look at his face. He had petechiae (webs of blood veins) all over his cheeks. Panic-stricken, I asked his dad what happened to Cory's face. He replied, "It's nothing. He's been sleeping all afternoon. He probably slept on one of his toys."

I said, "It looks like a reaction to Methotrexate, but that can't be because he had that yesterday. It wouldn't take this long to cause such a reaction!"

Terrified, I was running for the telephone to call the hospital.

His dad casually replied, "No, I gave it to him this morning. It's Friday. Remember?"

"No, it wasn't in his pill box today because we changed it to yesterday for the experiment. *Remember?*"

"But it's Friday. You forgot to put the pills in his box for today. So I got some out of the bottle."

I was dialing the hospital and simultaneously suppressing the desire to commit homicide. My husband had overdosed our little boy on a very toxic drug, so potent that he could have it only once a week!

Finally I reached the oncologist on call. She asked me which hospital I was closest to. When I told her, she instructed me to, "Bring him here as soon as possible. I will meet you at the pharmacy, not the emergency room."

When I arrived at the hospital, I scooped Cory up and ran down the hallway and up a few flights of stairs. He was beginning to cough up blood. I was relieved to find the doctor waiting at the pharmacy with a syringe. She gave Cory an injection to the back of the throat. Afterwards, she put him in a room for observation. My heart was pounding hard. Then she took me by the arm and guided me back out to the hallway. Now remember, I had never met this woman before. She was obviously annoyed as she hissed at me, "How did this overdose happen?" I told her my husband had forgotten that we changed the medication day because of the drug study we were involved in. I was trembling with fear and anger. (My anger was not directed at her.)

She told me it was her duty to report the incident to Child Protective Services. I begged her to talk with Frank Balis before she did anything. Without a word she turned and walked back into the room where Cory was resting. She kept Cory under observation for several hours before allowing me to take him home. She said, if I hadn't brought him in when I had, he would have died. As it was, the mucous membranes throughout his body were raw and bleeding from the toxicity of the drug.

The doctor gave me a syringe filled with the second dose of the antidote to take home. I wanted to have it administered by Dr. Mike.

As I drove home, I heard Frank Balis' voice expressing concern about Cory's safety because his dad seemed so removed from the reality of the situation. I thought, *"Boy, is he ever perceptive!"*

Minutes later, right about the time I realized my gas tank was empty; I got pulled over by a policeman. He wanted to tell me my taillights weren't working. My purse was at home where I'd left it in my panic to get to the hospital. I did not have money, or my driver's license, or any ID. In total disorientation, I began to cry. I could hardly tell this guy what had happened; I was crying so hard. He felt so sorry for me that he followed me to the nearest gas station and asked the attendant to check my lights. Fortunately, Cory was sleeping soundly by then.

The policeman even paid for my gas. But the attendant could not fix my lights. He guessed it was an electrical problem. The police officer wrote me a note for use like a hall pass. It read something like, "This poor woman has been through enough hell for one day. She is aware her brake lights are out, and she has a perfectly good reason not to have her license with her. Please do not ticket her." I asked him for his name so I could reimburse him for the gas he'd paid for. He didn't want me to return the money, and I have no idea what his name was. He was our guardian angel in the night, and I will never forget his kindness.

When we got home, it was after midnight, so I carried Cory up to bed. I slept in the rocking chair in his room. In the middle of the night, Cory awoke, crying pitifully. He was in terrible pain. His nose and throat membranes were bleeding and his tummy hurt. I cried with him as I cradled him in my arms. When I couldn't quiet him and it became obvious the Tylenol wasn't working, I called Dr. Mike at home. I explained what had happened, including the threat of Child Protective Services, and asked if there wasn't something else I could give him for the pain. Mike picked up on the fact that I didn't want to call the oncologist. He offered to call Children's for me. I was able to give Cory a rather large dose of Tylenol. Then we arranged for me to bring the second dose of the antidote to his office in the morning so he could give Cory the shot.

In the morning, Cory and I drove to Dr. Mike's office. He injected the antidote medication and then asked his nurse to take Cory out in the hall to play. He turned to me and said with total compassion, essentially the same thing Frank, the oncologist, had said the week before. But he added, "I have watched you deal with this entire situation by yourself. Why are you putting up with this? Besides, what are you getting out of this relationship? You would be better off alone. At least you'd know your kids would be safe."

I was angry with TJ for a number of reasons, but the overdose was the last straw. I knew then that I had to make a decision about the future. I became a single parent within weeks.

The decision wasn't that hard to make because there was so much water under the bridge. Initially, I was afraid Cory's immune system would falter if he was stressed out by his parents' getting a divorce. One session with a social worker at Children's Hospital calmed my fears. She was wonderfully supportive as she reminded me how kids, even kids with illnesses, adapt to change.

Brie, Cory, holding cousin Jeffrey

Gordon Raine, one of my best friends since we were nine years old, responded to my decision to become a single parent by saying, "Are you sure you're doing the right thing? No guy is going to want you with two kids, especially when one of them is sick." I thanked him for his honesty, but I already knew with my entire being that I was doing the right thing for me, and my kids. Besides, I couldn't have cared less about a relationship at that point. I just wanted peace in my home and the knowledge that my children were okay.

At the same time I became a single parent, my friend Lynn became one, too. It was great. We co-parented and fumbled through each phase together. Our first big test as single mothers was putting together bicycles and other Christmas gifts for our children. It was a hoot! Lynn and I were drinking champagne and wielding screwdrivers as if we knew what we were doing! With each accomplishment we exclaimed, "Who needs men? We can do this stuff!"

I had purchased a toy kitchen set for Brie. There must have been a thousand screws. Lynn and I got through the stove and sink okay, but by the time we started putting together the refrigerator, we were too cocky. After screwing on about two hundred screws, we realized, much to our horror, that we had the back panel on upside down. We fell on the floor laughing hysterically. Then we poured ourselves more champagne and started over. It was a very long but fun night.

My children called her "Mama Lynn" because she was a second mother to them. I could not have made it through Cory's treatments without the support of my parents, siblings, and friends such as Lynn, Cherri, and Donna. I had pulled friends and family aside to ask that they help balance out the amount of attention Cory was receiving so Brie wouldn't feel left out. They were all very understanding about it and assured me they would do everything they could to make Brie feel secure and loved. As a family, Cory, Brie, and I had a lot of fun despite Cory's illness. And the rough spots were made a lot smoother because of all of the love and support we received from family and friends. You know that African saying about it taking a whole village to raise kids? It's true.

The hospital and clinic visits were so frequent I could work only part-time. I kept the books for a printing company in a building full of young, vibrant, outgoing people. It was a fun place to be if you had to go to work as I did.

There was an interesting guy with long hair who worked one floor down from me. He would come by the doorway to my office a couple times a day. Once in a while he would say hello, but he seemed very shy. Usually I would look up in time to catch him sneaking a peek into my office. I was so caught up in taking care of Cory and Brie; I didn't give him or any other guys much thought.

A few months went by, and my friend Debbie began teasing me about my admirer. Debbie was in charge of planning the upcoming company Christmas party. I wasn't planning to go. My experience had always been that those types of parties were mostly for couples. She hammered on me for days. When I told her why I was reluctant to go, she suggested I ask the shy guy with the long hair if he needed a date. I didn't even know his name!

The day of the party, Debbie kept hounding me. Finally, on impulse, after I'd gotten up the nerve to call him, I found out that he had already left for the day. Whew!

I went home and decided just to hang out. My friend Ronna Pavone called and wanted me to go dancing. I mentioned the company party, and she said, "Vancouver's? Wow! Let's go!"

We got there after the party had been underway for a while. Vancouver's was a restaurant/disco right on the water at Lake Union in Seattle. The food was fabulous, and there was plenty of alcohol.

I was sipping my first drink when I saw the shy guy walk in and scan the room. Within seconds he was standing in front of me, stammering, "Did, did you come here alone?" No introduction, just that. I guess he wasn't as shy as he seemed.

"Well, yes, I did. Why? Do you need a date?" I said glibly. "And if that's the case, what IS your name, anyway?"

"Mike Keller. Do you want to go downstairs and dance?"

"Sure, let's go." We went downstairs with a group of people and staked out one of the tables ringing the dance floor. Keller took my elbow and guided me out to the center. I hadn't been dancing for quite a long time and loved it. The next dance was slow. When Keller's hands got within inches of mine, there was the strangest thing I had ever seen. Sparks were literally flying between us. I decided not to have any more alcohol.

We both said, "Wow! What was that!!??" It was exhilarating and scary at the same time. I could feel this was no ordinary connection.

When we went back to our seats at the table, Keller told me he had been interested in me since the previous summer. He had been a guest at the company picnic and had seen me with my family. He knew I was married, but something about me inspired him to take the job when it was offered to him.

I thought, *"Oh great, the first guy I strike up a conversation with since my marriage ended, and he's a weirdo stalker."*

But he explained that when he had surveyed the room that evening and had not seen my husband, he'd run across to me. Noticing I was not wearing my wedding rings, he'd felt safe in asking me to dance.

We danced the night away. He was so funny, bright, and completely irreverent. We discovered we had attended the same high school and had several mutual friends, even though he was several years older than I was. When the party ended, he and his friend wanted Ronna and me to go out to breakfast. I decided to take it slow and easy, so politely declined the offer.

The next workday, he blew in to my office and handed me a beautiful red rose. He mumbled a quick, "Thank you. I had a wonderful time at the party," kissed my hand and left. He had completely reverted back to the "shy guy." I sat there looking from the rose to the empty doorway. My friend Debbie witnessed the whole exchange, and she gave me a sly smile.

This was the beginning of a very intense relationship, and not just for me because when Keller met my children a few weeks later, it was magical. I stood in the alcove watching Keller, Cory, and Brie play house with Brie's new toy kitchen set, and I felt a sense of wonder. The three of them clicked. But I wasn't ready for another relationship. I wanted and needed time to learn who I was, and that definitely meant remaining unencumbered romantically. I knew I had to be careful because my children were so taken by him.

When I started to relax about being single and going it alone, poetry began to flow out of me. They weren't all great poems, but they were insightful and sometimes mystical. I would dream the words while in my alpha-state of sleep. The alpha-state is that hazy, dreamy, foggy state just before waking. I call it the "woo woo" state. If you've ever seen that old episode of the *Twilight Zone* where the little girl rolls off her bed into the wall to another dimension, which is wispy fog and rather eerie, that's what my experience of the alpha-state is like. (Yes, I saw that episode of the *Twilight Zone*. And ever since then, I refuse to sleep next to the wall.)

I trained myself to stay in this realm so I could write my poetry down before I woke up. If I woke up all the way, the words would immediately vanish. It took awhile to figure out how to stay under and write at the same time. I kept a note pad and pencil next to my bed for these occasions. Later I couldn't always read what I had put down on the paper, but recording the words was always an adventure.

The first poems that came to me seemed to be my subconscious working through all the pain I had not dealt with in my life. The words of these poems bubbled up from my seeming unconscious but obviously still functioning mind when I was spending a lot of time with Keller. There was something so freeing about him. I'm not sure I can describe what it was, but on a subconscious level we were connected... by what, I don't know. It scared me a little, but nevertheless, I derived comfort from the words. I kept my poems in a little red leather book on my bedside.

One of the first poems I wrote, in December 1980, was about relationships.

Affinity

Two souls wandering separate—alone
One looking but not searching, the other
Searching but not finding, the perfect mate,
The soul with the aura the same hue of blue
The meandering soul, happy and content
To exist alone... yet still wandering
The tired, broken, tattered soul gave in
To life, and could never happy be...
The love of life was gone from her
And she resolved to be alone.
Then one day, the meandering soul

Took her in and gave her love.
It filled her heart with warmth.
Could this be the elusive hue of blue?
At least there was some hope.
Together they strolled away one day
Through the magic of their affinity,
To wander through time endlessly...
Not separate but as one...

Keller and I had great fun over the next few months. But I began to worry about the kids becoming so attached to him. He was a wonderful friend to them, and once I finally came to the realization that it was okay for my children to love him, then I easily let go of the fear.

Keller loved to play soccer. Cory, Brie, and I went to cheer his team on. Cory decided after the very first game that soccer was the sport for him. I signed him up for the local fun league, and with Keller's coaching and coaxing, Cory learned to love soccer, too. No one could tell Cory had leukemia. He was as rambunctious and energetic as the rest of the players. At the time, he was in a good remission. There is so much just running, especially at that age level, that he didn't have much opportunity to get hurt.

One day, Keller and I were talking about Cory's treatment and how I was coping financially. He said, "Marry me, and you won't have to worry about insurance." Keller had been wounded in Vietnam and was still entitled to military benefits. Well, I wasn't even divorced yet. Then I found out neither was he! He had been separated for at least five years but had never made any moves to make it permanent.

He called his estranged wife and told her he wanted a divorce. She said something like, "Not in my lifetime!" Since she refused, and he wasn't ready to launch a huge legal battle, I blew off the whole idea. As far as I was concerned, it was a cosmic sign. Besides; I didn't want to push him. I was actually relieved because it saved me from making a decision. Besides still working on self-discovery, I also knew the amount of energy it takes to be a single parent is bad enough, but when one of your children has a life-threatening illness, there isn't much left over to give to someone else. I didn't think it would be fair to Keller or anyone else to pursue a long-term relationship when I couldn't possibly be there for him.

We didn't break off our relationship. We essentially put it on hold. Keller had some things to sort out as well. We still saw each other and had mutual love and respect for one another, but I needed time and space. He respected my feelings. Over the years, I always knew if the kids or I needed him, Keller would be there for us, no matter what. That was such a comfort to all three of us. And many times since he has proven that I was right.

Things that Go Bump in the Night

Not long after Keller and I stopped seeing each other on a regular basis, I bought Brie a pair of red, leather Mary Jane's. Brie was so proud of her new shoes she wanted me to walk her down to my parents' house to show them off to my mother. It was pouring down rain, and I was talking on the telephone. I told her we would go when I finished my call, and the rain died down a bit. Our house was designed in such a way that she could walk in a big circle through the living room, dining room, kitchen, and hallway, and I watched her march around the house with a big smile on her face.

A minute later, I got off the telephone and grabbed her coat out of the closet. As I stooped down to put her arms in the sleeves, I noticed one shoe was missing. She was just a toddler and could not explain where it had gone. It was so bizarre because she had been moving the whole time. I don't think she could've undone the buckle and removed the shoe by herself, and Cory wasn't home. I began a thorough search of the house. I never found it. I even checked inside the fireplace ashes, but I was sure it wasn't there because I had been standing in the living room the entire time.

That night, I was so irritated about the missing shoe that I wrote a note to the resident ghost, which said, *"I am not happy about Brie's brand new shoe disappearing and want you to bring it back. Thanks, Brie's mommy."* I left the note on the dining room table and went to bed. In the morning, still no shoe. Cory looked at me over his breakfast cereal, shrugged his shoulders, and said with a sigh, "Gee, Mom, don't be mad. Maybe he doesn't know how to read."

Maybe he couldn't read, but he definitely could hear our conversations.

About this time, an old friend of mine offered me the opportunity to work for him in Boise, Idaho. I seriously considered it. He said the job would involve learning how to run a recording studio. I had worked with this guy seven years before, and we got along great. It sounded like a great challenge and a good way to start my life over.

I checked into doctors, schools, and housing in Boise. I made arrangements to go there to check out the job. As soon as I began talking about a possible move, the ghost started kicking up a fuss. A couple of times when I was home alone with my dog, Quackszer, I awoke to loud banging noises coming from either the basement or the attic.

On one particularly loud night, the dog started acting anxious. He was whimpering and whining outside my bedroom door. Irritated, I opened the door to my bedroom to listen to the noise. Quackszer, our normally ferocious watchdog that was half-wolf and half-German shepherd came flying into my room in a streak of fur and saliva. I yelled out my bedroom door, "Knock it off, damn it! I'm trying to sleep!" I slammed the door, and the noise stopped. But Quackszer slept next to my bed all that night. He seemed to have a whole new level of respect for me.

After giving it some thought, I realized the noise occurrences were increasing and seemed to coincide with my decision to check out Boise for a possible move, but the ghost didn't deter me.

Cherri, one of my best friends from our high school days of working at the Cinerama theater and one of my kids' favorite aunties, and my sister Rita offered to go with me to check out Boise. Cherri invited her new boyfriend along. We drove Rita's car. After a nightmarish weekend trip which included a ninety-dollar speeding ticket in the middle of nowhere, a broken part on Rita's car, which stranded us in a podunk town in Oregon for half a day, Cherri and her boyfriend fighting the whole time, and my so-called friend who'd offered me the job trying to rip my clothes off, Cherri, Rita, and I got so sick of each other that we came back and didn't see each other for a month. Apparently the ghost was happy I wasn't moving to Boise, because he calmed down for a while.

Macaroni Box Theory

One evening, when Cory was six years old and still in remission, the three of us were having dinner, just talking about the day's events. Out of nowhere, Cory looked across our dining room table and announced with an air of authority, "You know, Mom, energy comes from light."

I swallowed hard scrunched up my face and I looked over at him with guarded curiosity and asked "What? Where'd you learn that?"

He gave me an intense look. "It's just somethin' that I know, Mom." I did not respond. I just waited to see what else would come out of his mouth. He continued on, "When you die, your soul, spirit, energy, or essence, whatever you want to call it, lives on because energy comes from light. It never dies."

This was very profound stuff coming from a mere six-year-old! He hopped off the chair, went to the kitchen cupboard, and brought back a box of macaroni. "See, I'll show you what I mean," he said. With great purpose, Cory dumped the contents of the box out onto the table. He stood next to me, acting like the little professor. He carefully separated the macaroni from the powdered cheese packet. Then he held the box up. He pointed to the noodles and cheese—as if he were doing a television commercial announcement—and then said, "There; see. This is like when you die. Your body is just like an empty macaroni box. When you dump the noodles and cheese out, all you have left is an empty package. The good stuff is still perfect and lives on forever, but the body withers and dies. You can burn it, bury it, rip it up, or whatever, and it doesn't matter because your energy or soul lives on." The next thing that popped out of his mouth was, "So, I just want you to know that even when I die, I'll still love you." I looked up at him waiting for the next pearl of wisdom to fall. Then he said, "I will love you for infinity."

Feeling slightly queasy, I waited for more information to come from my wise, little, Tibetan monk.

Just as quickly as it came into his mind, it went away. Cory, apparently satisfied with the amount of knowledge he'd shared, went on to talk about something a little more mundane.

I wondered about his philosophical pearls of wisdom. My instincts told me he was trying to prepare me for something BIG. But I didn't want to face it.

Relapse

Double Relapse

His second year at the University Child Development School, Cory began telling everyone he was a sophomore at the University of Washington. I tried unsuccessfully to correct him. He kept insisting, "It's my second year on campus at the University of Washington, which means I am a sophomore."

Cory learned more than just academics at the University Child Development School. He learned and taught others a lot about friendship. He had his first crush there on a little girl named Jana. He learned from her how babies are made. The description was pretty accurate. It was startling. However, he was initially a little puzzled about the delivery process since he thought all babies were removed from their mommies' tummies by an incision.

He had such positive experiences there at the school. One time when we had agreed to catch his urine for testing, Cory came out of the bathroom and wanted to share with the class how warm the jar was. Randy the teacher not only allowed him to share his jar experience with the rest of the class, but they turned it into a discussion about body temperatures. When he relayed the story to me later, I knew why Cory loved the school. The teachers and staff were so supportive, and they allowed the children to stretch their minds constantly. Cory felt that the teachers were loving and kind, a genuine inspiration to him. He tired quickly of IQ tests, however.

When it was time to start looking for a school at the next level, Cory was inundated with tests. Before we knew it, the school year was almost over. Cory was scheduled for his final IQ test at the University of Washington. The day arrived for the exam, and Cory had a nasty cold. I knew he wasn't feeling well, and so did the psychologist. Who could miss it? Cory arrived with a box of tissue tucked under his arm and a gnarly attitude.

The testing room had one-way mirrors, which let me observe Cory in action. I saw that the situation began to deteriorate when the psychologist asked, "What color rhymes with head?"

Cory said, "Stink-pink—what d'ya think?"

The psychologist took a deep breath and said, "Let's try this again. What color rhymes with shoe?"

Cory cut her off and said, "Why don't you ask me something intelligent?"

The poor woman dropped the color rhyming test. She pulled out a stack of cards with black and white ink-like drawings on them. The objects looked like cartoons. Each card was filled with a hodgepodge of objects tied to a specific theme. She showed Cory a card, which featured what looked like an armless man trying to mow a lawn. Then she asked, "What's wrong with this picture?"

I saw Cory's little face change to a scowl with his eyebrows arched. I thought, *"Uh oh, here he goes."* Cory stood up and put his right hand on his hip and said sternly, "What's wrong with that picture??? It's disgusting! That's what's wrong with it. You shouldn't be showing that stuff to little kids! Let me outta here. Those drawings could give a kid nightmares. You oughta be ashamed of yourself, lady." And he headed for the door.

I jumped up and ran out of the observation room to intercept him in the hallway. The psychologist was right on Cory's heels trying to get him back into the room when I arrived. Cory refused to continue with the exam. I apologized to the woman, explaining that Cory wasn't quite himself because he was feeling poorly. She looked at me with a glare and walked off. We just turned and left.

I asked Cory on the way home what his problem was. He smiled and said, "Mom, I am just so sick of tests."

"Okay, but did you have to be so rude?"

"I'm sorry. I couldn't help it. She was asking me such dumb questions. I guess I was just not in the mood for her. I didn't mean to be so rude."

A few days later, I took Cory in to the hospital for his regular, every-other-week oncology check-up. His cold had gotten worse. That quickly became the least of our problems. Frank Balis had just left Children's Hospital and moved to Maryland to work at the National Institutes of Health. Cory was very upset about Frank's departure. Since Cory was being treated at a teaching hospital, we were lucky to have had a primary care doctor. Usually in teaching hospitals, patients see a multitude of residents, and it's rare to see someone more than a few times. I believe continuity is important to the emotional health of sick kids, so when Frank left, it was a scary time for me, too.

Frank turned all six of his primary care patients over to one doctor. We had never met her prior to this check-up.

Cory was lying face up on the examination table when Dr. Barbara Clark walked in. She had short, grayish hair and seemed sort of motherly, almost grandmotherly. She introduced herself as she started the physical examination of Cory's body. All of a sudden, Dr. Clark stopped talking, and I could see her choking back tears. She looked at me with eyes filled with unmistakable pain and then looked back down at Cory. I followed her eyes and saw that one of Cory's testes was at least triple the size of the other.

I asked Dr. Clark to step out into the hall for a moment. When we reached the hallway, she began to cry. It was so scary for me to have the doctor crying! I asked her to pull herself together for Cory's sake and for mine. She apologized and explained that Cory was in relapse. I remembered being told, *"Thirty percent of boys with leukemia who go off chemotherapy relapse in their testes."* This knowledge really scared the heck out of me. I then realized how aggressive Cory's disease was since he relapsed while he was still on treatment.

Dr. Clark composed herself and moved Cory to a different examination room. She did a bone marrow tap and a spinal tap to see if he had leukemia cells in those locations, as well. His spinal fluid was clear, but unfortunately she did find leukemia cells in his bone marrow. That really capped the day! Not one relapse but two.

When Cory was diagnosed, I was told he would definitely go into remission. Being able to keep him in remission would be the problem. According to the doctors' calculations, which took into account Cory's age, weight, and general health, he was given an 80 percent chance of surviving twenty-four months in remission. And if he made it through the first twenty-four months, he would again have an 80 percent chance of surviving an additional twenty-four months. So, if he could make it through four years, we could then start to breathe a little easier. But no one ever mentioned the word "cure" at that time. I filed that omission away in the back of my brain.

I had been so encouraged during the first twenty-seven months of Cory's remission/treatment because he had been extraordinarily healthy. He'd had just an ear infection early on in his treatment processes and then that one crummy cold a week before this double relapse was discovered. He hadn't been sick much, other than his cancer. In fact, the nurses described Cory as being, "a very healthy child who happens to have leukemia."

Barbara Clark was very upset because, out of the six patients that she had inherited from Frank, Cory was the third one to relapse in less than two weeks. I have always suspected that Frank's departure triggered something in those children that affected their immune systems. I don't know what, since I am not a doctor, but it was amazing to me that so many of his patients relapsed right after he left.

"I Want to Be Michael"

From the time Cory was first diagnosed, whenever he didn't feel well, he would cry and say, "I want to be Michael." It usually happened right after a period of heavy medication. The drugs were as bad as the disease.

His reference to this mysterious boy named Michael always puzzled me because I had no idea what he was talking about. Cory had a cousin named Michael, so I erroneously kept trying to connect this cousin to the Michael that Cory cried out for. When I tried to get Cory to explain, he would just shake his head sadly and cry pitifully but offer no explanation. I asked him if he meant his cousin Michael. He would get agitated with me and say, "No! Not my cousin! I want to be Michael!"

After the relapse, Cory cried and called out Michael's name every time he had to endure bone marrow or spinal taps. Because of the relapse, those painful procedures became much more frequent. With the relapse came a new phase of intense chemotherapy. And with the increased chemotherapy the yucky side-effects intensified. His first round of high-dose chemotherapy right after diagnosis had been easy by comparison.

Now different parts of Cory's body swelled up. His round tummy protruded quite prominently. One afternoon, while Cory was drinking juice in the kitchen, Brie, who was three, walked over to him and put her ear on his stomach. With wide-eyed innocence, she asked, "Is there a baby in there?"

"No, you big silly! There's no baby in there!" he shouted, clearly irritated, and pushed her away.

Brie replied, "It looks like there's a baby in there."

To which Cory growled, "Boys can't have babies. Don't be so ridiculous!"

"How would I know that? I'm just a little kid," Brie responded with a toss of her head. Then Cory stomped out of the room. I had to run to the bathroom to crack up laughing.

During this re-induction phase, Cory's body rejected several of the main drugs recommended for his treatment plan. He had severe stomach pain and headaches, but we could treat the symptoms only with Tylenol and antacids.

A bone marrow transplant was suggested as the way to proceed. I kept asking Dr. Clark how the double relapse had changed Cory's prognosis, but she kept avoiding my questions. After several days of this cat-and-mouse game, I was extremely frustrated. I came to the conclusion it was time to take drastic measures. I literally blocked the doorway and prevented her from leaving the room. I demanded an answer, saying, "I am the type of person who needs to know what the odds are. I need to have information so I can process the options in my mind. You are not leaving this room until you tell me what his prognosis is and what we can expect."

Backed up against the wall, Barbara looked genuinely afraid, which from my position worked to my advantage. I figured she didn't get many mothers who would do that sort of thing. We didn't know each other yet, so I'm sure she didn't know whether or not I would get physical with her. She did the wise thing and gave me an answer. "It's around 20 percent."

Of course, it wasn't what I wanted or expected to hear. So in total disbelief I gasped, "What!?"

Because of my reaction, she immediately rescinded that figure. I guess she was trying to make the bad prognosis easier on me. Then when she amended his prediction for survival and said it had plummeted to less than 10 percent, I nearly fainted. I could not believe it had changed so drastically. I thought, *How could it go from 80 percent to less than 10 percent the first time he relapsed?"* I asked Barbara, "How could this be? They told us he had an 80 percent chance to survive!" She shook her head. I could see that she was trembling. Then she said if he relapsed again, we would be given the option of whether or not to continue treatment. That certainly didn't sound like a very encouraging proposition to me.

The timing of this horrendous news was upsetting. I was bummed out that Frank wasn't there with us. Not that I didn't like Barbara, but we didn't really know her. That night, I tracked down Frank's telephone number at the National Institutes of Health. When I reached him the next day, I was surprised to find that he already knew about Cory's condition. He offered encouragement about Cory's prognosis, which must have been tough since it was so lousy. Then he sang Barbara's praises and assured me that she would be very supportive, especially if Cory's health deteriorated. I told him about having to practically tie her up to get information out of her. He laughed. He knew about *that* already, too. Barbara apparently had asked his advice on how to deal with me. She told him I was difficult and I asked too many intelligent questions. Frank explained to her that I was the kind of mom who needed the truth. I thanked him for his support and especially for his honesty.

Throughout Cory's hospital experience, there was one bright spot for him. Her name was Georgine, but we called her Georgie. She cashiered in the cafeteria. Every time Cory had a finger poke in the lab, he received a cute little felt finger puppet. While we waited for blood results, Cory insisted on running down to see Georgie. He would show her his new finger puppet, and they'd trade.

She was so light and fun. Georgie's trademark was copper red hair and kooky earrings. Often the earrings were either mismatched or funny combinations such as fried eggs on one side and a little side of bacon on the other. Whenever we went on a trip, Cory looked for funny earrings to bring back for his friend.

He liked her so much that even when it was bad news, he wanted to go share it with Georgie. She always kept her fingers crossed for him. Unfortunately, that hardly ever worked for us.

We began the procedures to determine whether or not Cory could qualify for a bone marrow transplant. The testing procedure simply consisted of Brie, my estranged husband, and me going to the lab to have several vials of blood drawn, but emotionally it was a grueling process. Again, it took what seemed like too long to get the results. The annoying thing is that they had the results on a Thursday, but we were forced to wait until the following Tuesday to hear them. And that was only after I made a pest of myself by calling every hour or so. I am thoroughly convinced the medical professionals don't understand how agonizing it is to be left in the dark.

The results weren't great. I had the closest match with four out of six components the same as Cory's, but it wasn't good enough. One of the missing components was so vitally important that without it the transplant wasn't worth the risk.

Later, I found out how horribly transplant patients suffer if the process doesn't go well. There are so many things that can go wrong. Afterwards, I was actually relieved Cory didn't have to suffer through a failed bone marrow transplant.

They were still so experimental then, too. This was long before they pioneered autologous transplants and before they ever tried transplanting non-related donor marrow. Autologous transplants are when they remove some of the patient's bone marrow and freeze it. Then, they irradiate the patient's entire body to kill off the cancer cells and re-introduce intravenously the person's own thawed out marrow.

Regular bone marrow transplants work like this: The cancer patient's whole body is irradiated to kill off the cancer cells. If there is a donor, they harvest the marrow from several long bones in their body, such as the back of the hip or the breastbone. Then the good marrow is injected into the patient's body intravenously. It's rather like planting seeds. Hopefully the marrow will "take" and grow. The patient is isolated for a hundred days in a sterile environment to prevent any exposure to germs. It's not as easy as it sounds.

Stress

During this time, I was working part-time and then eventually full-time at the printing company. My life was consumed with caring for my children. Life was hectic single parenting and trying unsuccessfully to get divorced. Add sexual harassment to all that stress, and you have a recipe for disaster. Without going into great detail, I will say the man I worked for thought he could get away with blatant, on-the-job harassment because I was a desperate single mother with an ill child. I finally quit in a blaze of anger.

I filed a discrimination charge against my former employer. I had to, because he was withholding my final paycheck and a commission that I had earned.

Want to know the weirdest thing about that particular time in my life? Everywhere I went, I was being sexually harassed. After the big, explosive confrontation with my boss, I left and went straight to the unemployment office. While there, the clerk who was explaining how to fill out the paperwork reached over and stroked my hand! I jerked my hand back and threatened to scream, and he backed off.

The next day I applied at another print shop, and the man interviewing me started admiring my hair and my legs! And the creepy guy said it out loud. I knew it wasn't the place for me, and I tried to take my leave. He began to make really weird sexist comments so I jumped up, told him off, and walked out.

In desperate need of a job, I actually went to the Los Angeles area for a job interview. I left my children in the care of my friend Cherri and my mother. While I was gone, TJ was involved in a serious car accident. His family decided it was somehow my fault. They called my house in the middle of the night and talked to Cherri. When they found out I was out of town, one of them called Child Protective Services and reported that I had *abandoned* my children.

A few weeks later, out of the blue, a caseworker showed up right in the middle of Brie's third birthday party. My parents, my sister's family, and a few friends were having cake in the dining room while I was answering a battery of ridiculous questions in the kitchen.

Then the caseworker said, "I can see there's obviously a bogus accusation against you by your estranged husband's relatives, so I'll let you get back to your party."

I thanked him for being so quick to figure out the charade and turned to walk him to the front door. Then he asked me if I would go out with him! I could not believe my ears. I practically shoved him out the door and slammed it shut.

It was beginning to feel as if I had a target on my back. I was outraged by the false report to CPS, and I was genuinely concerned about the unwanted male attention I suddenly seemed to be attracting.

Even more frightening was the fact that I had a sick little boy, and people seemed reluctant to hire me because they thought I would miss too much work.

Finally, in desperation, I telephoned Jerry Poth, the father of my friend Michael, who owned a private detective agency. Michael had been one of the people I loved most in my life. He had been my junior and senior high school boyfriend, but we had gone our separate ways before graduation. At nineteen, Michael broke his neck in a diving accident at Green River Gorge. The accident left him paralyzed, a paraplegic, with no feeling below the middle of his chest.

He was treated at St. Francis Cabrini Hospital and then transferred to the University Hospital for rehabilitation. In that year of hospitalization, I went to visit him every day.

As the swelling went down around his spinal injury, it became apparent something more was wrong with him. He began having seizures. When he came out of the seizures, Michael had no idea anything had happened. Because of that, he couldn't keep track of the frequency of the seizures, which made it hard for the doctors to know what was going on with his body.

For me, Michael's paralysis was not a deterrent. I loved him dearly. He had such a good heart. His spirits were good, and he handled his life's challenges well. On the down side, he was like an untamed horse. He had such a passion for life. A daredevil, he once drove a motorcycle in the dark with his eyes closed. Maybe intuitively he knew that he was destined to die young.

Eventually a seizure that he had while in the shower left Michael comatose. He existed in a vegetative state, withering away inch by inch, for seven and a half months before he died at age twenty.

When Michael and I were teens, we had done some surveillance for his dad. He had paid us to spy on people who claimed to have work-related injuries or were suspected of being wayward spouses. Who would ever think a couple of kids was watching? We had been quite good at it, and the intrigue had suited me. His father had always said, "If you ever need a job, just let me know."

I called Jerry because in his profession he had contacts all over the city. If anyone had connections, he did. I asked if he knew anyone who was hiring. He offered to take me to lunch. When we got there, he said he needed someone to run his office, do the books, and meet with clients. I was hesitant about accepting the offer, but I really needed the work.

The reason I held back at first was because I reminded Jerry of Michael, and I didn't want to be the source of sadness for him. I told him it wouldn't look good to have the president of the company crying in his office all the time. He promised me he wouldn't cry, and he told me that it might actually be better for his healing to have me around. I really needed a job so I agreed to take it.

Unlike other potential employers, Jerry wanted to be supportive of me, concerning Cory's medical treatment demands.

I helped him grow his company, and in return, he allowed me the flexibility to make up the time I spent at Cory's hospital visits.

It didn't happen very often, but some days I wouldn't get to work before noon.

The investigative work was fascinating. I became quite spoiled by the constant stimulation of never knowing what case would walk through the door. I knew there was no way I could ever go back to a print shop or office job again. I loved doing all of the investigative work that required a female. The idea of getting paid to play-act was a hoot. It was fun to dress up and pretend to be someone else. So many funny and very strange things happened while I worked there, but that's a whole book all by itself.

"Excuse Me, Doctor, But You're Making Me Sick!"

Cory was six years old and already sick and tired of going to Children's Hospital—finger pokes, arm pokes to draw blood, arm and back pokes for chemotherapy. One particular drug called Vincristine the nurses had to inject straight into the vein; it was so toxic it would actually burn tissue. Cory could taste it as soon as the drug hit his vein. This drug set up a modification of responses that went something like this: First, Cory would get the drug injected into his arm, and it would make him gag because the taste was so vile. Weeks later, he would just see the needle, and he would start to gag. Next time, he would get to the front door of the hospital, and he would start to throw up. Then the parking lot would trigger the reaction.

It finally got to the point where I would purposely wait to remind him of his appointment until the night before. Cory would start throwing up with the mere mention of a trip to the clinic and become uncooperative with the doctor in administering chemotherapy. He was pretty feisty and would refuse to get into and subsequently out of the car. I had to pry his little fingers off the door handles and drag him kicking, screaming, crying, and/or vomiting all the way to the hematology/oncology clinic. Once there, Cory would fight throughout the whole process. I was sweaty, nauseous, and overcome with guilt every time I had to force him to go through this.

This whole sequence of events got so bad that one-day Cory insisted he wanted to stop his chemotherapy. He said it wasn't worth it to him to feel sick all the time. All the years of my telling him it was his body and he had control over it flew back in my face.

I'm a little slow, but I finally figured out that I needed some help. Jenny Stamm, the social worker, suggested that I ask for a stress management doctor for Cory. I was totally amazed. I had never heard of a stress management doctor. I remember thinking, *"Wow! What a concept! How great! If Cory didn't hurt, he would be willing to continue his treatment."* It sounded so easy.

Apparently the stress clinic had never even considered dealing with a patient as young as Cory. They agreed to meet with us to decide if he could benefit from their treatment at his tender age. Well, he passed their scrutiny with flying colors. Cory became quite interested in the self-hypnosis and relaxation techniques that his doctor taught him. Dr. Bill Womack, a pediatric psychiatrist, became more than Cory's stress management doctor; he was someone Cory could trust. Since he wasn't involved in sticking him with needles, Cory thought he was pretty "cool."

This was back when *Knight Rider* was a very popular television program for little boys. Dr. Womack taught Cory to imagine that his body was similar to the talking car on the show. The car was filled with buttons and futuristic, high-tech gadgetry. Cory learned how to turn off the sensations in his arm so when the doctor poked it with a needle, he wouldn't feel the pain. This was a great idea and worked very well for several weeks until Cory needed to have a bone marrow tap. He kicked up the biggest fuss I had ever witnessed up to that point.

Things were getting out of hand, and Cory kept yelling at the oncologist, "Don't touch me! Call Dr. Womack! I want Dr. Womack!" I could tell how much Cory trusted Bill Womack when he completely shut down. He refused to allow them to proceed. Witnessing this episode was very upsetting for me. Cory was obviously tiring of the whole chemotherapy deal and making no bones about it. I wanted him to cooperate, but I was torn because he was fighting so hard, and they weren't listening to his concerns.

Well, we discovered when Bill arrived that he and Cory hadn't yet progressed beyond his arms. Bone marrow samples in kids Cory's age are retrieved from the back of the hipbone. So Cory needed Bill to help program his imagination so the pain to his back wouldn't be felt. Cory and Bill worked alone for about fifteen minutes. Cory thanked Bill and then casually signaled the oncologist to continue. The emergency imagination break did the trick.

This was during a period of time when Cory would intentionally aim for the oncologists' shoes when he was heaving over the side of the exam table. I watched him. He had very good aim. When I confronted Cory about doing the dirty deed on the doctor's shoes, an impish grin spread across his face into a big "bad boy" smile as he replied, "If I ever write a book about this experience, I'm going to call it, *Excuse Me Doctor, but You're Makin' Me Sick.*"

One night Cory and I went to the hospital lab after hours to get his blood drawn. This was something we did to avoid the long wait during the morning when we went there for his regular checkups. In the waiting area, we sat with a couple I knew from the parents' support group I attended at the hospital. Their little eighteen-month-old daughter had died that week. The pain of their loss was obvious. It wasn't hard to see that losing their only child had devastated them.

It was hard to know what to say. I just expressed my sorrow and asked how they were doing. The grieving mother was curt with me. The father seemed embarrassed. It was so awkward; Cory and I left and went straight to the lab.

After the lab technician drew his blood, we walked down the hall. With a troubled look on his face, Cory stopped me near the lobby and asked if we could sit down for a minute. After we were seated, Cory asked why the little girl's mother was angry with me. I told him she was just very, very sad and assured him nothing either of us had done had upset this woman. Cory placed his hands in mine, sadly shook his head, and asked, "Mommy, why does God take babies?"

I said, "Honey, sometimes God just calls them back because he loves them so much."

Cory wasn't buying it. His eyes filled with tears, and he said bitterly, "She didn't get to ride a bike or swim or anything. It's not fair. God shouldn't take babies away from their mommies. Now her mommy is mad at you because I'm still alive." I hugged him, and we got up to leave. He was silent on the ride home. I left him to his thoughts.

The next day Cory had his regular appointment for chemo and afterwards he had a stress management appointment with Bill Womack. We had to leave as soon as the appointment was over so I could get Cory to school and get myself to work so there was no time for debriefing.

Later in the day, my telephone at work rang. I picked up, and it was Bill. He wanted to know what my post-death beliefs were. At first I was confused. Then Bill explained that when Cory arrived for his stress management appointment, he was in an interesting mood. He slapped a quarter down on the desk pointed at it, and ordered Bill to "read that."

Bill did as Cory asked and read aloud, "In God we trust."

Cory implored him, "Do you believe that?"

Bill wasn't sure what to say because he didn't want to step on my toes so he replied, "Well, I don't know. You seem to have some feelings about it, though."

Cory, by now, was visibly upset. He said, "Why does God take babies and leave mommies sad?" Then he went on to explain what had happened the night before.

It apparently had been weighing on his little heart and mind quite heavily.

Bill asked what I thought he should tell Cory. I said, "Hey, you're the psychiatrist, not me. I don't know what to tell him. He's obviously still upset from last night. If it helps, I do believe in life after death and in heaven."

Bill decided he had told Cory pretty much the same things I had the night before when we had left the hospital. The explanation seemed to satisfy Cory for the time being. But Bill knew the subject would come up again, and he wanted to be prepared for it.

I will never forget the first time Cory decided he no longer wanted to go through with chemotherapy. I had to literally peel his fingers off the door handle one by one and forcibly drag him down the hall-way to the clinic. His resolve was worse than when he was vomiting from the Vincristine. It turned my guts inside out to have to fight with him and force him to hold still for the shots that made him so sick. I finally convinced him to go with me to see Jenny Stamm, the oncology social worker.

I allowed Cory to explain to Jenny his reasons for wanting to end chemotherapy. She offered to accompany us to the clinic for a heart-to-heart discussion with Dr. Clark. Cory hesitated at first; then he agreed to go with us.

Dr. Clark arrived in the examination room, shadowed by (I think I will let him remain anonymous) a young male doctor who was doing his fellowship. He had started his internship that day. The situation didn't work well for Cory. He felt very uncomfortable with a stranger there, and Dr. Clark was much more businesslike than Cory was used to or deserved.

Cory told her that he no longer wanted to be poked, prodded, and treated with toxic drugs. Dr. Clark was understandably distressed by Cory's attitude, but she made a huge tactical error. She turned to the fellow and started talking about Cory as if he wasn't in the room. That was definitely not a good strategy. Dr. Clark gave the fellow all the reasons why she thought Cory should continue with chemotherapy. Cory and I looked at each other. We waited for her to come to the realization that we were still there in the room. I shot a smirky look at Jenny who was sitting quietly in the corner. Cory finally cleared his throat and arched his back defiantly. Barbara Clark seemed to find some level of control by ignoring Cory's request. Maybe she thought she could wait him out.

Finally, Barbara begged Cory to accept the medication for just that day and then take some more time to think over his decision to quit.

Cory had been experiencing severe head and stomach pain for months. Barbara had done test after test on him with no results. They called it "phantom pain" and implied that it wasn't real. That just made Cory more convinced the drugs weren't working. That label didn't do much for his confidence in the medical people in charge of his care either.

He finally succumbed to Barbara's pressure to receive that day's dose. We left quietly but I could feel Cory's resolve solidify. He told me later he had just wanted to get out of there. (Barbara's strategy of waiting him out seemed to work.)

A few days later, we went to the movies with Brie and a couple of friends. Throughout the movie Cory kept squeezing my arm. I could tell he was in pain and offered to take him home. Cory wanted to finish the movie and not ruin the evening for everyone else. So he bravely and unselfishly stuck it out.

Afterwards we drove everyone else home. Cory and I set out for the emergency room at Children's Hospital. I started to feel panicky inside. For Cory to ask to go the emergency room meant he was experiencing terrible pain. He hated the hospital so much at that point and yet was more than ready to be taken there. It freaked me out.

Cory was whimpering in the back seat the whole ride. Halfway there, my car started acting up. It was quite late by this time, around eleven. I kept praying my car would make it. As my luck would have it, the car kept sputtering.

We got as far as the beginning of the freeway exit to the University of Washington…exactly 3.3 miles from Children's Hospital. Then, my car just made a sickening noise, gasped, and ground to a halt. Luckily, I was able to pull over to the side of the road. We got out, and I hoisted Cory up and carried him like a small child with his arms up around my neck and his legs wrapped around my waist.

I started trekking at a pretty good pace. Of course, since it was Seattle, it started to rain. I was dressed in an Aloha shirt, shorts, and sandals. Cory had on sweats, and he was only about thirty pounds lighter than I was at that point. After the second mile, I started to fade. I can remember my back stiffening up, my legs beginning to feel wobbly, and my feet starting to really hurt. Cory and I began to sing to each other. The problem with sore feet is your whole body starts aching from it. I had to ignore my body pains.

The driveway up the hill to Children's isn't all that steep but it looked like Mt. Everest by the time we reached the base. I knew I had to keep moving. Any hesitation and I wouldn't be able to climb that last incline. In between whimpers, Cory kept apologizing to me. The real bummer happened when I mistakenly walked up the wrong driveway in the dark. I thought it was the way to the ER but it turned out to be the hospital's driveway to the loading dock. I choked back a million tears not wanting Cory to feel badly about how wiped out I was feeling. I looked over my shoulder back toward the street, and it looked so gosh darn far! I knew it would be impossible to go all the way back to the street and then up another driveway. I whispered to Cory to hold on, and I scrambled up forty feet through the bushes.

I staggered in to the emergency room and stumbled to the counter. There was a huge sign laminated to the top of the counter, which read, "Do not put your children on this counter." I ignored it and promptly placed Cory right smack dab on the sign. A young man walked up and said with a sneer, "Didn't you see the sign?"

"Hell, yes, I saw the sign, but I just walked three miles in the rain with a little boy crying in pain, and I don't care what your stupid sign says. Get me the oncologist on call right now!"

Smart guy. Since he didn't want to tangle with me, he immediately showed us to an examination room. Of course, he didn't offer to carry my son. I picked Cory up and followed him, walking slowly with each step, my rubbery legs wobbling worse and worse. I moved with extreme caution and was barely able to make it the thirty or so feet to the room. It felt like miles.

We were left in that room for hours. I kept going out to the desk and asking where the heck our doctor was and what was keeping him or her. (*Note to self: Don't tick off the guy in charge of paging the doctor you need.*)

Now, I have to be fair and admit that when we first got there the emergency room was crawling with people who all looked as if they were from the same family. It was noisy and chaotic.

Once I got Cory settled down a bit, I called Lynn and asked her to come and get us. She said, "No problem." We were still waiting for a doctor to show up when Lynn arrived at the hospital an hour later.

I held Cory's hand, rubbed his tummy and his back, and tried to keep him distracted from the stabbing pain he was feeling in his stomach and the throbbing in his head. Finally, the on-call doctor showed up looking as if he'd had way too much sleep. I asked where he had been and what had taken him so long. He smiled weakly and called me by my ex-husband's last name with a. "little lady" condescension. That was his second mistake of the night! And it didn't sit well with me since by the time he showed up it was morning, and I was crazed with mental and physical exhaustion.

I leapt over the table and grabbed him by the front of his shirt. Lynn was sitting in the corner, covering her eyes with her hands. Cory was lying on the exam table wide-eyed and waiting to see what would happen next. I jerked his shirt, which of course pulled his face within six inches of mine, and said, "My name is Enebrad! Why has my son been left in here writhing in agonizing pain for hours? Now, I want you to get busy and give him Demerol or something else for his pain!"

The young doctor took a deep breath, and I let go of his shirt. He pulled back slightly and stuttered, "I-I will-will have to-have to call his doctor for permission to prescribe pain medication."

I almost went ballistic. "You mean to tell me that you are the doctor on-call and you have no authority to write a prescription for pain medication?! Then maybe you better get a grown-up in here who can!"

The poor guy left. Lynn peeked over at me as he exited the room and said, "Whoa! I thought you were gonna smack him."

"I really wanted to when he sauntered in here looking so rested and refreshed. It was as if I had disturbed his sleep." I settled down after a few minutes and waited for him to come back with something for Cory's pain. By now it was 4:00 in the morning.

The young doctor came back in and handed me a prescription. I was floored. After all the hassle to get Cory there and then being left to sit around for hours, he didn't even deliver the drugs. I had to go pick up the prescription at the hospital pharmacy on the third floor!

Lynn stayed with Cory as I found my way through the deserted halls to the pharmacy. I could barely put one foot in front of the other I was so tired and angry. It took about fifteen minutes to get the Demerol and make my way back to the emergency room.

I gave Cory the pills, and Lynn went out ahead of us to get her car. I carried Cory out to her car and strapped him into the backseat. We headed toward home. I wasn't looking forward to bringing him back to the clinic four or five hours later.

We reached home, and I put Cory to bed. He slept soundly for several hours. Lynn and I stayed up drinking tea. She kept recounting how surprised the fellow in the emergency room had been when I had grabbed him by his shirt. I felt slightly sheepish but still angry about the wait and being treated like a simpering idiot because of my gender.

In the morning I got Cory ready to go right back up to the hospital, and Lynn drove us. We stopped by my broken-down car on the way. I got out and tried to start it. Nothing happened. I decided to deal with figuring out how to get my car home after Cory's appointment in the clinic.

Cory had his blood drawn, and we headed down the hall to the clinic when coming toward us from the opposite direction was the doctor we had seen in the emergency room. He saw that I was approaching and ducked into the Hematology-Oncology Doctors' office. I could tell he was pretending he hadn't spotted us. I followed him in. He was gazing at the whiteboard when I caught up with him. I tapped him on the shoulder and asked, "Are you trying to avoid me?"

He visibly gulped and admitted, "Yes, I am."

"Well, I hope you learned a lesson last night in the ER. That is, don't ever show up hours after you have been paged with that cheery smile, looking as if you just had a full night's sleep, and then call a divorced woman by her ex-husband's last name! I know you think I owe you an apology for being mean to you, but you have that all wrong. You owe us an apology. My little boy was in terrible pain *before* I brought him up here. No one goes to the ER in the middle of the night unless he absolutely needs to. So making someone wait for hours is inexcusable."

He thanked me, and I left him to ponder all that I had said. I think he took it all in and learned from our encounter because I have heard from a number of people that he turned out to be a wonderfully supportive doctor.

Creative Solutions

When Cory was six years old, the year of his double relapse, I switched him to a small private school in downtown Seattle, not far from my office. I was very concerned that he be part of a smaller pool of kids. I figured fewer kids, fewer germs.

My children were excited about attending this little school because their cousin Julie was there, and she loved it. They had a preschool for Brie, so Cory, Brie, and Julie could all be together.

Prior to Cory's transfer to the school, I asked the director to explain to the other children attending the school (not just his class) that Cory's hair looked a little strange since what little remaining hair he had was in clumps. Of course, I was hoping they would be more understanding if they knew he was on treatment for an illness. Unfortunately, I wasn't sufficiently encompassing in my instructions.

This particular school also had an after school program where they bused in kids who attended school elsewhere. At the end of the very first day of school, Cory was playing on the rooftop playground (I said it was downtown Seattle) with several children standing in a circle. An older boy, apparently jealous of all the attention Cory was receiving as the new kid, swaggered over and planted himself before

Cory (bottom left) and his class

them. He had pushed through the other kids until he stood directly in front of Cory. The bully and Cory made eye contact. Then the bully let out a howl and began bellowing uproariously about Cory's funny-looking hair.

Without hesitation Cory reached up, grabbed a handful of his own hair (which came out with ease), and thrust it into the bully's outstretched hand and said, "Oh, so you think it's funny, huh? Well, then have some."

The bully gasped with horror as he threw the hair up in the air and ran away screaming for the teacher. According to Cory and his cousin Julie, the circle of children laughed hysterically...at the bully.

When Cory told me about it on the ride home, I asked what had possessed him to do such a thing. He smiled mischievously and said, "I don't know, Mom, but it worked!"

Well, the boy never picked on Cory again. In fact, he even apologized for his poor behavior the next day.

Private Pain

After Cory's testicular relapse, he had to have radiation to his private area. He was so brave and seemed to take it in stride. One day he showed me how dark and dry the skin was in that area. It looked burnt and crackly. But he didn't complain. He was a very brave six-year-old.

Not long afterward, I was in my office writing a report when my secretary buzzed me and said that someone at Cory's school had called to tell me to get down there right away. It was an emergency. With my heart pounding so hard in my chest that it hurt, I raced out of the parking lot. All the way down the hill, my mind conjured up horrible images of Cory falling or cutting himself somehow. Right after relapses, chemo kids' immune systems are depressed from the heavy-duty re-induction chemotherapy they go through to bombard the multiplying killer cells. The drugs kill good cells along with the bad ones, which leaves the patient lacking bacteria-fighting, healthy, white blood cells. What would be a minor injury to a healthy kid can be fatal to a child on chemotherapy.

I got to the school, double-parked, and ran inside. Cory was lying down in the director's office with a pitiful look on his face. He gave me a weak smile and looked very relieved when he saw me. I noticed the anxious face of the director, Judy, looming above him. As I walked in the door, she pulled me aside and quietly informed me that Cory had been crying, and when asked what was wrong, he complained of severe stomach pain. Judy then told me that she had never heard him complain before so she knew it had to be quite serious.

I noticed that his tummy was distended and quite hard to the touch, rather like an under-ripe melon. I asked Cory if he had eaten anything unusual. He said no, that it had been hurting for a while but that he was so busy playing he had ignored the pain.

I packed him out to the car and sped off to the hospital. Cory was lying on the back seat, moaning and clutching his swollen belly. Twenty minutes later when we got to Children's Hospital, I hurriedly parked my car, threw open the rear door, and scooped him up like an infant. With my heart pounding, I raced breathlessly toward the Hematology-Oncology clinic.

We arrived unannounced. The clinic assistant could see the look on my face and immediately ushered us into an examination room. She ran off to find Cory's regular doctor. When Dr. Clark breezed into the room, she was immediately concerned about how distended his little tummy appeared.

She then realized upon careful examination that it was his bladder. She inspected his "little unit" and discovered that a thick layer of skin had grown over the end of it and had sealed off the opening. Poor little guy hadn't urinated for probably two and a half days! Being a rather active little boy, he hadn't even noticed. The doctor asked him when he had last gone to the bathroom. Cory looked up at her as if she was a nut for asking such a ridiculous question and said, "I dunno." It was pretty obvious he was totally unaware.

The doctor clipped the skin. Cory winced and tried not to cry. He admitted that it hurt a bit. But the funniest (well, it was sad but funny under the circumstances) part happened when Cory shook his head as he turned to me and said, "After everything I've been through, this is the most humiliating experience of all!" He was so indignant. The poor little guy...

The doctor walked back in and informed us that if the skin grew back again, Cory would have to be seen by a specialist. "Great!" Cory wailed, "Now I have to have some stranger chopping on my unit! What else could go wrong?"

Well, for some reason, whenever someone gave us odds, we always managed to end up on the short end of them. Sure enough, the skin grew back, not once, but twice. Cory was not happy.

The third time it happened, the clinic scheduled Cory to be catheterized by a pediatric urologist. We were sitting in the examination room waiting. No one came in to brief us about the procedure or tell us what to expect. NOTHING. We were playing a game of Trouble (which we carried with us) when in walked the doctor and a nurse. By this time, Cory's medical chart was quite thick. We turned, expecting at least a smile and an introduction. We got neither. Commenting on the thickness of the file, the doctor started flipping through it. He asked the nurse what they were supposed to do. Nice to know these people prepare for their appointments in advance, eh?

I could feel myself growing irritated. Before I could speak up, Cory clued in to what was going on and said, "Why don't you ask ME? I know what's wrong!" Both the doctor and nurse continued to ignore him, and me, for that matter. Cory shouted angrily, "I am the patient! And I will not allow you to touch my body until you treat me with respect!"

Startled by the outburst, the doctor and nurse finally looked up as if they were seeing us for the very first time. It was bizarre. It really felt as if we were invisible to them until Cory challenged them. I then spoke up and very clearly explained to them that unless they treated Cory as they would an adult patient, they may as well pack up and leave. Rather embarrassed, the doctor lamely apologized as the nurse stood there silently nodding. To this day I cannot remember the man's name. How Freudian of me.

A few nights after the procedure, I checked to see how he was healing. Cory started to cry. I pulled him onto my lap and asked if he was in pain. He looked up at me with tears streaming down his face and said, "Mommy, I'm never going to be able to be a daddy because of the radiation treatments, am I?" There was no way I could answer him. I just held him and cried with him for all the babies he would never have in his life. Silently I prayed he would at least get to grow up and be married someday.

To Cory's tremendous relief, the skin never again grew over the opening, his radiation burns healed, and that problem remained in the painful past.

Justyn and Mary Dawn

When Brie was three years old and Cory was six, a friend, Mary Dawn, and her little boy, Justyn, moved into our house. He was the same age as Brie.

The arrangement worked out well because Mary Dawn did the laundry, cared for the kids while I was at work, and very often had dinner ready when I got home. For me, it was like having a wife.

We moved all three kids into Cory's room, and Mary Dawn moved into Brie's. Justyn and my kids weren't always home on the weekends together, which worked out great because then the kids could have some personal space. But it was a little tough for Cory to share his room with two younger kids since the little ones were always getting into his special things. The two little ones were so funny to watch. They were like a little married couple. Brie ran poor little Justyn around by his nose most of the time. The poor kid couldn't even brush his teeth without her correcting him.

Mary Dawn and I pooled our resources. That really helped both of us. We saved on utilities and amazingly we saved a lot on our grocery expenses, as it was cheaper to cook one meal for the five of us than to each do our own thing. This was true except, of course, when Cory was on Prednisone craving and devouring food as if he were a starving child in a Third World country who just discovered McDonalds was free.

Cory had a voracious craving for fried chicken for a while. The fried chicken "thing" actually lasted longer than any of his other obsessive food cravings. First, he wanted me to cook it constantly, then he wanted Kentucky Fried Chicken, and eventually he even got into the pre-cooked stuff in the frozen food section of the grocery store.

One night when he was still into the homemade chicken, I fried our last two chickens. Mary Dawn and I were pretty broke and waiting anxiously for payday.

We went out to the back yard to play catch with the kids. We played while the rest of our dinner was cooking. Then we noticed that Cory was missing. He had apparently gone back up to the house. Mary Dawn and I looked at each other and in unison said, "Oh no!" We ran up the basement stairs to the kitchen. Sure enough, Cory had eaten *all* of the chicken—and I mean all of it. There wasn't a wing left. I called my mother to see what she was fixing for dinner. I told her Cory had eaten our dinner and asked if the other kids could go down to her house. Cory kept repeating how sorry he was for eating all the chicken and then asked if he could go to Grandma's, too. My mother said, "Yes, of course you can come down for dinner."

After the kids left, Mary Dawn and I ate the side dishes. As you might imagine, after Cory stopped craving fried chicken, I never fixed it again. All these years later I still can't bring myself to do it.

At bedtime, Cory would get himself ready and then come to kiss me good night. Several times he smiled slyly at Mary Dawn and me and said, "Good night. Guess I'll go to Maui tonight." We always looked at each other and shrugged our shoulders.

One night, after Cory announced his tropical destination, Mary Dawn leaned over and whispered to me, "Do you think he's talking about astral projection?" Heck, I wasn't even sure I knew what astral projection was, but it sure sounded as if he was onto something. We asked if we could go with him.

"Find your own way there," he quipped and ran up the stairs. The next morning he said that he was tired from running around on the beach all night. After that, I never wondered why he was always so happy to go to bed at night.

Often when my kids were gone, Justyn would get up from his nap and complain, "The little boy is keeping me awake." On several occasions, Justyn accused "the little boy" of playing a drum and tickling his feet. Mary Dawn thought Justyn was just making up excuses to get out of taking a nap. I began to worry about the little ghost possibly making direct contact with Justyn.

As was his style, things kept disappearing. But then it changed. Things didn't only disappear; we had unexplained items appear from time to time, too. A yellow, child-size rain slicker was found hanging in our entry hall closet. For a while I thought it was Justyn's, and Mary Dawn thought it was Cory's. It looked like the old fashioned style from the 1950s.

Then one day, a bag filled with old dishes and tarnished silverware appeared in the corner of the living room. Again, Mary Dawn and I both thought it was each other's. I checked in the bag and thought it was Mary Dawn's camping utensils and stuff. We kept cleaning around the bag. Finally, I asked Mary Dawn if she could please store her camping stuff somewhere else. She looked at me funny and said, "I thought that junk was yours!"

I retorted, "I thought it was yours." We both ran to the bag and together we pulled out four or five chipped china dinner plates that didn't match and real silverware, also unmatched. With an astonished look on both our faces, we said in unison, "The ghost."

Then Mary Dawn jumped up and ran to the hall closet. She pulled out the rain slicker. "Whose is this?" she asked.

"I don't know; not ours. I thought it was yours."

"It's not Justyn's either."

Whoa! We thought the whole thing was pretty "woo woo." Mary Dawn was a little freaked out after that, but I just laughed.

Not long after our discoveries, on a weekend when my children and Justyn were off visiting their fathers, Mary Dawn and I made plans to meet friends at a club in Seattle in the evening. I took a nap. While Mary Dawn got ready in the bathroom I was awakened by the sound of a ball being bounced in the room above my head, in Mary Dawn's room. I was half-asleep and more than slightly irritated. I remember thinking, *"What is she doing? She knows I'm trying to sleep!"* I pulled a pillow over my head and managed to get back to sleep.

At the club that night, about eight friends and I were sitting around chatting. Mary Dawn arrived and slid in to the seat across from me. She told us all how great her dinner date was and then abruptly changed the subject. "Hey, did you hear that ball bouncing today?"

I said, "Yeah, what the heck were you doing?"

She looked quite bewildered and said, "Shirley, I'm so sure! I wasn't bouncing a ball! Besides, my room is carpeted." I started to crack up because if I hadn't been so tired and crabby I would have known Mary Dawn wouldn't be dribbling a basketball in her room. She was right; the bouncing sound came from a ball hitting a bare floor, not carpeting. And it came from our upstairs.

My brother said, "I knew your house was spooky. I'm not babysitting there alone anymore. I've always heard weird noises there—doors opening and closing, creaking footsteps on the stairs. Uh uh, I am not babysitting there alone."

Then one Sunday morning, there was a knock at the door. I looked out my window to see five little boys standing on my porch with uneasy expressions on their faces. I recognized two of them as boys from two blocks over. I assume the others were curious friends of theirs. I opened the door, and they pushed Jimmy Burch to the front of the group. Jimmy stammered, "Can, can we see, uh, your, your, uh ghost?"

"What's that?" I replied.

"Cory told us that you, uh, have uh, uh, a ghost. So we, uh, wanted to see it. Can we come in?" Well, I did not want these kids going home and telling their parents I filled their heads with nonsense. My experience has been that most people don't believe in ghosts or are so afraid of them they refuse to believe in them. I decided to let Cory handle the situation.

I closed the door and called Cory downstairs. I asked if he had been trying to scare the neighbor kids. He said, no; he was just trying to enlighten them. We had a brief discussion about how sometimes our belief system might be scary for other people and how he needed to be judicious when sharing some of the details of our life. He nodded and went outside to talk with the boys on the porch. I eavesdropped on their conversation and heard Cory tell them the ghost was on vacation!

One Saturday afternoon, Justyn came downstairs complaining about the little guy waking him from his nap again. We could tell Justyn had really been sleeping, so it didn't appear to be a ruse to get out of a nap.

Mary Dawn and I both went upstairs, and of course, couldn't see a thing. I sternly told the empty room, "Stop bugging Justyn. He needs his sleep." We went back down and told Justyn we'd had words with the little guy. Justyn said, "I don't like him. He's green and funny looking, and you can see through him." Mary Dawn was visibly alarmed. My children were gone for the week, so they never heard this account.

Exactly a week later Brie, Cory, and I were driving up the hill to Lynn's house right after naptime. Brie asked, "Mommy, what's it called when you see things when you're asleep?"

"A dream," I said.

"Well, what's it called when you see things when you're waked up?"

"*Uh oh*," I thought. "*Stay calm and answer her.*" So I said, "Reality. Why? What did you see?"

"Well, you know that little guy who wants to play with me and Justyn? He kiss-ded me awake."

"He did?"

"Yeah, and I don't want to play with him 'cuz he's icky looking. He's green, and you can kinda see through him."

I was trying not to react too much. I calmly asked her, "How tall is he?"

"Same tall as me and Justyn."

"Well, I'm not happy about him waking you up from your nap. Did it frighten you?"

"No, but I don't want him to kiss me."

"*Oh shoot*" I said to myself.

When we got home later that afternoon, I told Mary Dawn what Brie had said. We discussed it briefly and decided it was time to get rid of our ghost. Mary Dawn was worried about him scaring the kids by appearing to them. I didn't like the idea he wanted to play with them, either.

At a party my sister Penny had given, I met a woman named Liz. Somehow we'd gotten on the subject of haunted houses. She was telling stories about a house she and her husband had owned in Ballard, an older neighborhood in Seattle. It had a mean-spirited ghost. They finally moved because they couldn't rid the house of this presence she described as evil.

I called her up to get her advice as to how we should get rid of our pesky little ghost. She told me to find a Catholic priest who believes in ghosts. "A Filipino priest would probably be your best bet," she said. I thanked her and then thought to myself, "*Oh sure, piece of cake. How do you find a Filipino priest?*" I decided just to jump in my car and head for the nearest Catholic church.

In my head I composed my request all the way to the church. I knocked at the door of the rectory, and eventually a young man answered. I guess he was called a brother. I explained to him that I was in search of a Filipino priest. He didn't even look at me weird. He said, "Try the next church over." I got in my car and headed down the hill. I, again, knocked at the door of the rectory; and a Filipino priest opened the door! I was shocked at first, and then I calmly told him my story. He didn't bat an eyelash. He asked for my address and said he could come over in a few days. In the meantime, he instructed me to go to a store that sells religious items and purchase wooden crucifixes for each child's bedroom. He wanted me to bring them back to him so he could get them blessed. I thought, "*Okay, this is getting pretty woo woo, but I'll go along with it.*"

I followed his instructions, and a few days later he arrived as planned. (I do not think I ever asked his name.) The priest then whipped out a vial of holy water that had been blessed by the bishop. He went from room to room, mumbling prayers. Then he went outside, walked all the way around the yard, and blessed the exterior of the house. Then he was done. He said he would say three high masses for the repose of the little lost soul over the next few days. Three days later, the ghostly presence was gone, never to return.

Cory was really angry. He hadn't wanted the ghost to leave. "I can't believe you did it!" he shouted at me in anger. "He never hurt anyone! Brie and Justyn are just big crybabies!" he wailed. I had to sit down with him and discuss how unfortunate it was for the little ghost that he hadn't gone on to heaven. I told Cory the little ghost was probably missed in heaven by his loved ones who had since passed over. Cory pouted for a little while and then resignedly agreed that maybe what had happened was the best thing for the little ghost.

But Mary Dawn was so blown away by the whole ordeal that she packed up and moved back to Salt Lake City.

Jingle Bumps

The Christmas holiday was never Cory's favorite. I suspect he associated that time of year with the onset of his illness and the ensuing years of nausea, pain, and needle pokes.

But the celebrations around our house were always fun. It could be pretty frenetic at times, too. The year Cory was six years old my brother Tim had a great idea for a new family tradition for our children. Tim remembered how much fun he'd had going on hayrides at Christmastime when we were growing up and lived at my grandfather's house out in the country and thought it would be great fun for our children. So we gathered up family and friends. We piled up ten bales of hay in his one-ton flatbed truck he used for work, brought along thermoses filled with hot cocoa and hot cider, and sang Christmas carols. We covered a pretty big route. Afterwards, everyone came back to my house to share talk-stories, eat pizza, and tease one another about singing off-key.

Lynn, Mary Dawn, and I were in the kitchen getting snacks ready. Cory came running into the room and grabbed me around the waist. He wanted to tell me how much fun he was having. He loved parties, especially big, noisy parties with lots of family and friends. As he was hugging me, he looked up at me with a huge smile on his face and said, "Mommy, you make living fun." That warmed my heart, and even now when I close my eyes, I can still see his face and hear his voice giving me the best compliment of my life.

This was the same Christmas season we invited Justyn to go with us to the annual Seahawks' Boosters Christmas party. The club sponsored a party at the Sandpoint Naval Air Station for children with cancer and their families. It was so huge they had to use one of the hangars.

Mike Keller went with us that year. As we were walking up to the front of the hangar, Cory spotted Santa Claus emerging from a white Toyota pickup truck. He was so smart. Keller and I worried he would say something and blow the fantasy for Justyn and Brie. He just pointed at the truck and said, "Hey! Look at that! Santa came in a truck. He must be resting his reindeer." With a sigh of relief we continued on into the building. Then Cory said aloud, "That guy's name isn't Santa Claus. I know what his REAL name is!" Again Keller and I grimaced at each other and held our breath.

"So, smart guy, who is he?" Keller asked.

"He can't fool me. His name is Kris Kringle. I saw *Miracle on 34th Street*." Keller and I began to laugh. Brie and Justyn just ignored the entire incident. They were much too interested in the huge pile of wrapped gifts in the corner of the room.

When it was time for the gift giving, all three children got in line. They were very respectful and quiet. Keller and I stood on the sideline and watched as each child sat in Santa's lap. Cory and Brie politely had their pictures taken with Santa. Justyn got up there and said, "Is that a fake beard?" and jerked on the man's chin whiskers. I walked away and pretended he wasn't with me. Keller rushed up to retrieve Justyn and quickly apologized as he hurried away, announcing with each step that the child was not really his.

On the way home we had to stop at the hospital so Cory could have his blood drawn for his appointment the following morning. While we were in the waiting area, a small boy began to sob. It was obvious he knew what was going to happen to him. He cried and cried. His parents couldn't seem to calm him. Cory and Brie approached the little boy and offered their Santa gifts to cheer him up. He immediately stopped crying. When it was time to leave, his mother tried to get him to return the toys. Both of my children said, "No, we want him to have them."

It was such a sweet gesture. At one point they looked at me as if they weren't sure it was the right thing to do. I smiled at them, and Cory said, "It's okay; we have so much already."

Another family tradition at our house was (and still is) that no one can open stocking gifts or anything else until everyone is awake. That was always a problem for Cory because Brie slept so soundly and required much more time to sleep than he did.

Before Christmas morning even dawned, I awoke to a ka-thunk-ing noise. It was around 5:00 a.m., and I was curious to find out what was making that sound. I crept out of my room. My bedroom was the only one on the main floor.

As I opened my door I could hear Justyn and Cory whispering animatedly to one another. They sounded very excited. I rounded the corner and heard several more thunks. I looked up and saw two naughty little boys dragging soundly sleeping Brie by her feet. Her head was bonking and bumping on each stair! Mary Dawn apparently had been awakened by the same noise, and she appeared at the top of the staircase just as I reached the bottom..

After I tucked Brie—who slept through the entire incident—back into bed, we scolded Justyn and Cory and sent them back to their room. Mary Dawn and I decided to stay up and have tea. We didn't let the boys know, but we laughed for hours over their failed scheme to get a jump on Christmas morning at poor little Brie's expense.

San Francisco Skyjackers

D r. Clark arranged for Cory, Brie, and me to take a free trip to Disneyland and Knotts Berry Farm. It was a great getaway because we were able to stay with my Aunt Cathy and visit with relatives we hadn't seen in a while.

My father had given Cory and Brie a bag of change to spend. He had been saving his pocket change for a year. Kids always think money means coins, so they thought they were rich.

At Disneyland, Cory decided to use his spending money on a "Pirates of the Caribbean" hat, skull-and-crossbones flag, and wooden pistol. He wore that hat everywhere we went. Brie used her money to buy Mickey and Minnie Mouse dolls.

My Aunt Cathy invited our relatives over for dinner one evening. It was great fun to see everyone. Cory was in the game room learning how to shoot pool with the big boys. My Uncle Ralph was taking his turn when Cory noticed that part of my uncle's finger was missing. Cory asked what had happened to it. My uncle told him it was an old war wound.

Cory shook his head and said, "Yeah, I think I know how you feel. I have a crummy ol' disease. It's called leukemia." With that Cory took off his pirate hat to show my uncle that he was bald. "My hair keeps falling out from the chemo."

He then proceeded to run the table. It was his first time playing pool, and he almost beat all the grownups.

My Uncle Ralph was so touched by Cory's compassion that he cried when he told me the story later.

We had a great visit. Mike Torre, a friend from when we were twelve who had moved away after high school graduation, drove over from his place in Las Vegas. He took us to the La Brea Tar Pits. It was a fascinating place, and the kids and I got a kick out of the woolly mammoth skeletons and all of the different holograms.

Cory craved Lipton Chicken Noodle Soup the whole time we were in southern California. My Aunt Cathy was amazed at the amount of soup Cory consumed on a daily basis.

I indulged him, even thought it's practically nothing but salt, because when kids are on chemotherapy and have absolutely no appetite, it's very hard to turn them down when they ask for a particular food. As a mother, I always got pretty freaked out when he lost a bunch of weight. Nothing tasted or even sounded good to him, and he had no desire to eat. So when a skinny, little kid who looks like he's wasting away asks for something to eat, you really can't say no. I know I couldn't.

We finally went to the store, and my Aunt Cathy bought a whole case of the Cup O' Soups. Cory was quite happy about that.

Meanwhile, Brie was riding in the grocery cart. Curiosity got the best of her, and she pushed her finger in the mesh of the basket. It was stuck. She didn't start crying or complaining until it was swollen and turning bluish-black. Just a little more excitement I didn't need.

Earlier in the trip, Brie's body had broken out in a horrendous, angry-looking rash that she had scratched 'til it had bled. At the time, Brie's skin couldn't handle even water. Her body didn't make any oil, so I had to bathe her with special lotions. Poor little thing couldn't even go swimming. So when Cory would play in the pool, she would have to watch from the sidelines. When she came to me with the awful rash, I asked her to show me what she had put on herself. She had rubbed liquid soap all over her body, mistaking it for lotion. We had to go to an emergency room to get ointment to put on it.

So now we were in a grocery store with her finger stuck in the cart. The store manager put some vegetable oil on her hand, and we were able to get her finger out. Cory was ready to call the fire department rescue squad, and I think he was a little disappointed the incident had ended so easily.

On our way home, our plane was in need of repair at the Ontario airport. Of course, no one figured that out until we were all loaded on the plane. I was settled in with the kids and all their toys. Then they let everyone off the airplane. But I didn't want to get off, so we sat there for a while. When we did finally decide to deplane, I was surprised to see my three aunties waiting anxiously at the rail, wondering where we had been. We sat around for several hours.

Our connecting flight was in San Francisco. I knew we wouldn't get there in time to make our connection, but as time went on I began to worry we wouldn't make any connections! Cory had a chemotherapy appointment scheduled for 8:30 a.m. the next morning, and I was due back at work.

We finally made it to San Francisco. After waiting in line for what seemed like forever, we were given directions to the concourse with only minutes to make the last connection to Seattle for the night.

It was an incredibly long hike. By this time it was around 8:30 p.m., and Brie was asleep. So I was carrying a sleeping three-year-old, my purse, a carry-on bag filled with extra clothes, one filled with toys, and another bag brimming with Cory's medication.

Cory was skipping along beside me, waving his pirate flag and wearing his favorite hat.

When we got to the security checkpoint, I dropped all the bags on the conveyor belt and tried to get Cory to go through the metal detection system ahead of me. We were stopped by security. The man didn't say a word. He just motioned us back to the other side. Brie was getting heavy, and I was exhausted. It was way past my children's bedtime. I was also understandably anxious about making the last connection of the night.

Naturally, we were left standing there for the longest time. When the security guards started milling around the x-ray machine, I saw they somehow thought that two little kids and I posed a serious threat. Then I realized that they were probably freaking out about Cory's wooden gun. So I walked back over toward the x-ray system and said, "What are you guys looking at? Do you really think there's something dangerous in there? Well, why don't you just pull it out and look at it? If it looks like a gun, it's just a toy made out of wood. C'mon, I have a plane to catch!"

The security guys looked at me, and one of them said, "We can't touch anything until the police get here."

"The POLICE??? What is the matter with you people anyway?! It's a toy. It matches my son's flag and hat. This is absurd." I couldn't believe these people had telephoned the police. I slumped against the conveyor belt. I knew we'd missed the last decent flight home. The next plane didn't leave until about 2:00 in the morning. I was beginning to get angry.

I looked up to see six, giant Green-Bay-Packer-sized men in uniforms, running down the concourse toward us as if there was a riot erupting.

I said out loud, "Boy, are you guys gonna feel foolish."

The lead officer pulled our bag out of the x-ray machine and gingerly poked around in it. He pulled out the wooden pirate pistol and showed it to the others. Then I could not believe my ears when he said in a booming, macho voice, "This here gun can be bored out and altered into a lethal weapon. We're going to have to confiscate it."

"Who is going to do such a thing? Me? Him? Or her?" I said, gesturing, to myself, Cory, and then to Brie who was sleeping on the conveyor belt. One of the other officers said, "Hey, Joe, it's a toy. Let's give it back to the little boy and get out of here."

Joe said, "No, we can't do that. It's potentially a lethal weapon; we'll have to dispose of it."

Cory figured out what they were talking about, and there was no way he was going to let them dispose of his prized possession. He started to cry out, "No you're not going to keep my gun. It's mine. I paid for it all by myself!" Then he started to cry.

I was so ticked off and upset. The situation was so ludicrous it should have been laughable. When Cory began to cry, and the guy still didn't give him back his gun, I really felt like he was bordering on cruelty. This man's behavior was so stupid, and I really hate people who act stupid.

The more effort the other officers put into trying to dissuade this guy from taking away Cory's gun, the more determined he was to do it. I finally lost it and threatened to call the media. Joe turned towards me and actually threatened to arrest me!

I started laughing hysterically at that point. I had had enough. I just wanted to go home. I told this yahoo that they should really take this issue up with the Disneyland and Universal Studios people who sell toy guns to kids. I could not believe Cory was the first kid to try to get through security with a wooden pirate gun. Officer Joe demanded to see my ID. I told him to call the REAL San Francisco cops and have me arrested so I could call the news media.

We had a couple of go-rounds when finally the reasonable officer stepped in again and said, "Ma'am, I think if you would go check this gun through like a piece of luggage, your little boy can keep it." That sounded halfway reasonable, but the hike back to the check-in counter was at least a half-mile long. I asked if they would stay there and watch Brie and Cory. I figured that's the least they could do since they'd made us miss our flight. They said, "No." Then I asked if they would watch my other bags. Again the response was "No." The security guys wouldn't help me out, either. I guess I'd really made an impression on all of them.

The six giant policemen actually escorted me back to the reservation/baggage check-in counter. Not one of them offered to help carry my bags or my sleeping Brie. I didn't care. I went stomping back down the concourse to the main check-in counter. Again, there was a huge line that I had to wait in to check the darn gun. At least the clerk was nice about it. She just shook her head and muttered low, "Talk about ridiculous."

We had to box up the gun and check it through like an additional piece of luggage.

Then we trudged back to the same security check-in place. The stress and physical exhaustion began to catch up with me, and I started shaking. The kids and I had not eaten a real meal since breakfast. It was now after 10:00 p.m. We still had hours to go, and there were no snack shops or even vending machines in sight. Luckily, I had a granola bar in my purse. Cory ate that and fell asleep along with Brie.

We began boarding the plane at approximately 1:30 in the morning. By that time, I had two sleeping children and all those bags to carry on. The woman who had checked through Cory's gun showed up and offered to help me get the children on to the airplane. I could hear people grumbling about my getting special treatment. I wanted to slap them. I've noticed that airlines now allow people traveling with small children to board first. They didn't do that back then. I actually heard someone say, "Gee, if she chose to fly a red-eye flight to save money and drag those little children out this late, she doesn't deserve special treatment."

The nightmare didn't end when we landed at Sea-Tac Airport, either. I expected my brother Bobby to meet me at the gate. He did not. I wanted to cry when he wasn't there. I had to carry both kids and all our bags to the baggage claim area by myself. None of my fellow passengers were kind enough to offer to help since they all thought I was a jerk for getting on the plane ahead of them.

When we got to the baggage claim area, I discovered that Bobby had sent my other brother, GG, to pick us up. He helped haul our bags out to his two-seater Austin Healy sports car. It seems Bobby had had car trouble.

He also had our coats. I hadn't taken them with us because it was hot in Southern California, and I hadn't wanted to drag them around the whole time. That turned out to be a disaster as well, because there we were at four o'clock in the morning on a cold, foggy January day in Seattle, riding home crammed into a teeny, tiny, toilet seat-sized car. And it was raining! I was really getting crabby by that time and just wanted to get home to bed, knowing that I had only a few hours before I would have to get the kids up and drag them to Children's Hospital for Cory's next treatment.

Thinking about those twits at the airport who were fast asleep snuggled warmly in their beds while I had shivering children riding unsafely in my brother's sports car kept my blood boiling for a while—and almost heated me up.

Mind Reading

One Friday evening when my children were spending the night at my mother's house, I came home from work late. After calling around, I discovered that all my friends had already gone out. I was pretty tired anyway and had just reckoned with the idea that I was going to have a quiet night at home when my phone rang. It was my friend Lynn. She was out with some friends, and they were in dire need of a sober, "designated driver" to pick them up and take them to a dance club in Kent, a city south of Seattle. I didn't want any of them behind the wheel, so I agreed to pick them up.

When I got to the restaurant, they piled into my car, and it was a darn good thing none of them had tried to drive. We headed south to the nightclub, Meeker's Landing. Once inside, I was having a hard time hanging out with the three inebriated and belligerent women. For a while I sat at the bar and drank ice water, but staying there became a hassle. Half-drunk men kept trying to pick me up. It was an interesting experience. I realized that most people have no idea how bad they look when they've had too much to drink. It sure gave me something to think about.

Lynn came to find me, and I followed her back to the table. On the way, as we were squeezing through a narrow passageway, my eyes connected with a young Ryan O'Neal look-a-like. Lynn almost knocked me over with her elbow as we passed him. She was so obvious!

A few minutes later, the young Ryan O'Neal sat down at a table near ours. I noticed him looking over at us. I guessed he was shy because he never got up to dance.

Lynn and her friends started arguing about something one of them had said or done, and I walked to the bar to get more ice water. As I moved past his table, I heard him say very clearly, "You don't want to get caught up in that mess, do you? Why don't you sit down and talk with me for a while?"

"Sure, okay," I said, as I plopped down at this cute guy's table. *"Maybe he isn't so shy after all,"* I thought. He smiled, and we began a lengthy conversation. We danced the rest of the night. I decided I had been right. Tyler was quite shy but a lot of fun, anyway. He told me he'd just moved back to Seattle from California.

I went out with him for the next couple of days. We talked and laughed a great deal. I met him for Sunday brunch at a nearby restaurant. As we were talking, he remarked how weird it was the first night we met, how I just sat down at his table and started talking to him out of the blue.

I said, "Well, you invited me to!"

He said, "No, I didn't. I wanted to, but I was worried you'd reject me."

"Well, wait a minute. I distinctly heard you say, 'You don't want to get caught up in that mess, do you? Why don't you sit down and talk with me awhile?'"

Tyler swore he never said it. He told me he had been thinking those exact words but was too shy to make the invitation.

This odd experience was the beginning of a relationship that would last about a year and a half.

Tyler was a ski instructor. He taught Cory and Brie how to ski. An avid hiker, he taught me to enjoy hiking, too. We went hiking almost every weekend.

Cory was six the first time Tyler took him skiing. Apparently, Tyler barely had time to show Cory the basics. Cory told him, "You can go ski the big runs now; I'm just going to stay here and practice. You don't have to baby-sit me."

Tyler went back an hour later to check on Cory's progress. Much to his amusement and utter amazement, Cory was teaching a seventeen-year-old girl how to snowplow. Obviously Cory didn't want Tyler around because he skied over to him and said, "Hey, can't you see I'm busy here? I'm teaching my friend Heather how to snowplow. I can take care of myself. Go ahead and ski without me." Tyler took the hint and skied a few more runs before they left for home. He practically had to drag Cory off the slopes.

Cory was physically exhausted by the time Tyler's car pulled into the driveway. Cory took a quick bath and went straight to bed. Tyler pulled me aside in the kitchen and asked, "Are you sure he's only six?" Then with a grin he told me how Cory had given him the bum's rush on the slopes in favor of a much older woman. "Yeah, I can tell. He's your kid all right."

Spider-man!

Of all the holidays, Halloween was Cory's absolute favorite. He always loved to dress up, but every year was traumatic because he had so many ideas for costumes, and he hated to have to choose only one. So each year, when he finally made his choice, he would then choose a second for the following year's costume, too.

This particular year he decided, after much agony, to be Spider-Man. My mother and I made his costume. His facemask was really cool—a red ski mask onto which my mom crocheted webs.

Per his schedule, Cory had a clinic appointment on Halloween. I packed him, wearing his costume, into the car and headed for Children's Hospital. On the way, I stopped at my bank. Inside, as I conversed with my friend Barb, who worked on the non-teller side of the bank, Cory, a.k.a. Spider-Man, got into serious mischief. With my back to Cory, I chatted with Barb. Suddenly her eyes got BIG, and she couldn't talk. She just pointed over my left shoulder. I turned to look, and simultaneously, I heard Gary, the off-duty policeman, calling gently, "Come down, little boy." Cory, of course, ignored the man even though he was in uniform.

I ran over to where this little drama was unfolding. The interior wall he was climbing was about thirty feet high and made of huge boulders. I should've known he'd be unable to resist such a challenge. I forgot to mention how seriously Cory always took his Halloween personas. Gary, the policeman, was getting nervous. I'm sure he saw his part-time job going down the tubes if Cory fell.

I said firmly, "Spider-Man, come down from there *right now*!"

Cory sighed deeply and began to descend. "Okay, okay, I'm coming." We had a brief chat about him ignoring the policeman. Cory explained, "But I'm NOT a little boy—I'm Spider-Man. He didn't call me by the right name."

To this day whenever I stop in at that bank branch, I laugh at the memory of my son terrorizing the policeman and the bank manager.

Elisabeth

When my friend Michael was in the hospital right after his diving accident, he described to me his near-death experience. I had read a magazine article written by Elisabeth Kubler-Ross, MD, and was able to share that with Michael. It helped him to know that what he'd seen and heard wasn't necessarily hallucinatory. He derived comfort from the knowledge that many others had had almost identical experiences. With a big sigh of relief he told me he was afraid to tell anyone what had happened. He felt certain everyone would think he was nutty.

Jenny Stamm, the Children's Hospital social worker, had attended an Elisabeth Kubler-Ross workshop. She was so high on what she had experienced at this workshop that she shared it with me. I told Jenny I had long been an admirer of Kubler-Ross' work. She told me Elisabeth wanted to do a teaching film with a couple of sick children and their families at the University of Washington. Jenny asked if I'd be interested. "Are you kidding!? I'd love to meet her." So that fall when Cory was seven years old, we agreed to participate in the taping of the teaching film at the University of Washington.

Elisabeth Kubler-Ross is known as the "death-and-dying doctor." During her illustrious career she published about fifteen books on the subject of death and dying. Besides bringing the hospice movement to the United States, her most significant accomplishment was single-handedly getting American schools and universities to add death-and-dying classes to their curricula. Getting people, not just healthcare professionals but families as well, to respect the feelings and last wishes of dying patients will be her greatest legacy.

Also participating in this video project was a two-parent family with three young children. They told me that their little boy had an excellent prognosis.

While we were waiting for the taping to start, the boy's mother asked me what I did to relieve the stress of living with an ill child. I had no idea what she was talking about. She kept asking me, "Well, what do you do?" Finally, I said, "Oh, I write poetry." She looked at me with a funny look on her face and told me that she shopped. Since I barely had enough money to feed my children, I did not feel much in the way of sympathy when she described buying expensive jewelry and dining room furniture. Her husband didn't look too happy about it either. For me, it was an interesting lesson about how people cope so differently when forced to live under similar circumstances.

My children were spectacular. They were calm, composed, and interested in what was going on in. Both were drawn to Kubler-Ross. She was born and raised in Switzerland and had a very strong German-Swiss accent, but that didn't seem to bother them at all. Their interaction with her was so comfortable, as if they had known her forever.

During Elisabeth's interview, she wanted us to describe how Cory's leukemia diagnosis had affected our lives. She talked with Cory, Brie, my mother, and me. The session went beautifully, although my mother broke down in tears. I had seen her cry only a few times before that interview, and her reaction made me sad to realize how much she was hurting for us.

First of all, the kids were asked to draw pictures while we were waiting, pictures of anything. Cory drew E.T. walking toward his spaceship with a big smile on his face, saying, "Home. Home." Brie's picture got Elisabeth very excited. Her drawing was of a house. According to Elisabeth, by the colors Brie chose and the placement of the objects on the

Elisabeth Kubler-Ross and Shirley

page, her drawing indicated she has a strong sense of intuition. Elisabeth pointed out that Brie's drawing also indicated that she knew her brother was going to die. My heart shriveled up when she said that.

It was fascinating to hear her analysis of the drawings. She talked about color, content, and placement of the symbols on each page. I found out later that Elisabeth said my drawing was the healthiest she had ever seen done by the mother of a seriously ill child. Pretty impressive, eh?

My biggest concern at the moment was Brie. It was painfully obvious she was feeling like the invisible child. We would run into people at the mall, and they would immediately ask how Cory was doing. Once, after the person walked away, Brie looked up at me tearfully and said, "Why doesn't anyone ever ask about me? I'm cute." Brie's self esteem was so fragile, and she was so young that I couldn't adequately explain to her why people ignored her.

I had searched unsuccessfully in many bookstores and libraries for books that told how to deal with younger siblings of childhood cancer patients. When we met, I asked Elisabeth how to deal with Brie. She told me the reason I couldn't find any books aimed at someone Brie's age was because there were none.

Elisabeth went on to say that kids under five don't understand the concepts of death and dying, especially when the sibling was suffering from leukemia. Leukemic children don't look sick most of the time. That's why many siblings don't get it... and if they're under five years old, the concept is too sophisticated for them to grasp.

I felt a little better with Elisabeth's explanation. The only thing I had to go on was her saying that I just had to wait until Brie was old enough to "get it."

At the end of the taping, Elisabeth invited the other mother to attend her grief workshop that weekend. She looked at me and said, "You, you don't need to come." Boy, was I relieved to hear that.

I said, "Great, 'cuz if I had a week off, I'd go lie on a tropical beach somewhere and drink Mai Tais."

After the studio cleared, I pulled Elisabeth aside and asked her opinion of Cory's earlier request (during the summer) to end chemotherapy. I was feeling somewhat guilty and selfish for not being able to support his decision. I told her I just wasn't ready to let go of my little boy. She sensed that and asked how I would respond the next time he asked to stop. We both knew the request would come up again. I told her I would feel compelled to honor his request. Even though it would be painful for me, I knew I'd have to do it for his sake.

She took my hand in hers and reassured me that Cory was very tuned in to his body and his future. She cited his drawings as proof that he knew intuitively that he wouldn't survive his disease. She pointed at the drawing of E.T. and said, "This doesn't take any interpretation at all, does it?" I told her how he'd been warning me ever since his diagnosis at age three that he wouldn't grow up. Elisabeth said, "See, he's known all along. Just because he's a child doesn't mean he doesn't know what's going on in his body. Remember that and listen to what he has to say."

When the second family was added to the interview, Cory and Brie were taken off the set. Brie went with Jenny to draw more pictures. I later discovered Cory in the control booth assisting the director. He loved it. "They let me push the buttons on the control panel, Mom!" he shouted when I found him happily making new friends and learning all about video production from the crew.

Afterwards Cory and Brie jabbered on for days about Elisabeth. They were quite taken with her, and as we found out later, the feeling was mutual.

Elisabeth sent the kids an autographed copy of her children's book, *Remember the Secret*. This book became Cory's favorite. It is so beautifully illustrated. I highly recommend it for children who have a terminal illness in their family or a close friend who is sick. Coincidentally, the story is about a sick little boy with dark hair whose best friend is a little blond girl. I guess it touched him because it was so similar to his life. Cory read this book to Christina, Jami, Justyn, and Brie over and over again.

I kept thinking about what Elisabeth had said about Brie. I could only hope she would understand someday. I was still worried about her level of self-esteem and still lacked any answers about what to do.

Children on chemotherapy are at high risk if they get chicken pox. Their compromised immune systems can't fight off the effects of the disease. Cory was exposed three different times and was quarantined. Each time he was so bored. It was worse on Brie, though. She hadn't had it either, so when she was exposed, we had to send her to my parents' house to stay until the incubation period was over. Cory and I would go down and talk to her through the window. Obviously the poor kid's self-esteem problems didn't come out of thin air.

At the time my children and I were dealing with all this, the major metropolitan area of Seattle had no support groups for children with cancer and their families. I was more concerned to find one to address Brie's needs than Cory's. He understood totally; he understood better than I could.

I talked with every agency one could imagine would have a support group going. Finally, a woman at the American Cancer Society asked me, "Well, why don't you just start one?" (As if I had the time, energy, and connections to do such a thing!) That was so infuriating! I found out later how typical that attitude really was. I needed help, and the social workers from countless agencies wanted *me*—the stressed out, single mother of two with one sick child—to create my own support group and help others! You know the old adage, "If you want something done, ask a busy woman"? It's true.

The Children's Connection

A social worker by the name of Christine Daverio called one day. Jenny from Children's Hospital had referred her to me. Christine had just moved to Seattle from the Bay area, and she wanted to volunteer with a support group for children. I couldn't believe my ears! Finally, someone else cared enough to want to form a group for a very needy population. I immediately invited her over for pizza. I wanted my kids to check her out.

We hit it off from the start. My kids thought she was wonderful. Christine has a beautiful way of relating to children, which puts them at ease. She had the experience, and I had the need, so we started the group and called it "The Children's Connection."

I encouraged families who needed the support to join us. Christine recruited volunteers to interact with the kids in a therapeutic play-type group setting. We held meetings twice a month. The evening would start with a potluck dinner, which was always unpredictable—sometimes we ended up with only desserts. The kids didn't mind that at all.

Our shared meal was such a healing time. The feeling of aloneness a parent experiences while dealing with a child's illness is horrendous.

To be surrounded by loving supportive people boosted our spirits like nothing else could.

After dinner we would split up into two groups, one for children and one for parents. It was so nice to be able to share with other parents. Lynn, Christina, and Jami came with us. They were so close to Cory it seemed appropriate for them to be there so they could benefit from the support, too. The kids played or did crafts. The real magic happened when they connected with one of the adult volunteers whose job it was to help the children express themselves. Inevitably the child would open up and share his or her feelings in a safe, loving environment.

There was only one male facilitator—Steve Geller, the human jungle gym. The children loved to climb all over him. Many of the children came from single parent families headed by a woman. As was evident in my case, not many marriages survive a child's long-term illness. These children craved male attention.

Steve had been searching for the meaning of life after his grand-mother passed away. He hoped that volunteering to spend time with sick children might lead him to some answers.

Cory was drawn to him like a moth to a flame. Steve and Cory and, then soon after that, Brie became fast friends. Cory sensed that Steve had a gentle nature much like his own. Plus, Cory found out that they both liked to create art and skiing. Kindred spirits!

One Step Closer: Third Relapse

When our friend Stuart Westmorland painted the outside of our house, he and Cory became good buddies. One night, Stuart and Cory went to see an Arnold Schwarznegger action movie. When I heard Stu's car pull up in the driveway, I opened the door, expecting to see an exuberant little boy reliving the action movie he had just seen. Instead, I found Stuart on the porch with Cory sound asleep in his arms. Stuart looked very concerned. He told me Cory seemed knocked out by the pain in his head. Before Cory fell asleep, he had asked Stuart to tell me that his headache had gotten much worse. My brain immediately calculated that he had been talking about having a headache for several days. As usual for him, Cory would get involved with playing and fail to mention the severity, frequency, or length of time he felt the pain. But the pain had progressed now to the point of needing immediate attention. Alarms went off in my head. I calmly thanked Stuart for taking Cory to the movies as he carried my sleeping child upstairs to his room and helped me tuck Cory into bed.

Stuart seemed a bit nervous. I asked if Cory had said anything else about the pain. Stuart said no, but he could tell during the movie that

Cory wasn't feeling well. He had offered to take him home, but Cory insisted on staying until the end of the movie. I think Stuart was feeling that he should have brought Cory home sooner. I reassured him that it was okay. Knowing Cory, I felt he wouldn't have wanted either of them to miss the ending.

I decided to let Cory sleep since he was out like a light anyway, but I checked his breathing hourly. In the middle of the night, he woke me with an anguished cry. I ran up the stairs and found him at the top of the stairs holding his head. I wrapped a soundly sleeping little sister, Brie, in a blanket and carried her out to the car. I then ran back for Cory and carried him out. I had called Lynn and told her I needed to drop Brie off at her house so I could take Cory to the emergency room. We had done this enough times to have our routine down.

When Cory and I arrived at the emergency room, we were placed in an examination room. After a bit of a wait, a nurse came in to draw his blood. She was having a hard time finding a vein. Cory asked her politely to send for a lab technician.

After being poked for so long, veins have a tendency to roll away from the needle or collapse. This makes it very difficult to get the needle in the right place. Cory knew from experience that his veins were hard to locate. The nurse ignored him. She kept trying to hit a vein and was getting obviously frustrated. Cory became more anxious with each miss.

After two misses the healthcare person is supposed to get someone else to do the procedure. Cory again asked her to get a lab technician. He knew the lab people drew blood all day long and, therefore, would be better at dealing with the rolling veins.

The nurse seemed resentful that this little kid lacked confidence in her abilities. So she ignored his requests and tried a third time. Luckily, she hit a vein and got a vial of his precious blood. Feeling pretty smug, she wheeled around too quickly and dropped the vial. As it shattered on the floor, Cory let out a good old-fashioned battle cry, "Aauugggh!"

The nurse stood there aghast. After all of the trauma, the blood was splattered everywhere over the floor. She gave him a pleading look as if she wanted him to allow her another opportunity to dig around in his arms. Cory arched his back in defiance; pointed at the door and said with no mercy, "Get out." The nurse was cleaning up the blood and glass particles, and she looked up to speak. With a snarl Cory cut her off by saying, "Get out of here and send in a lab technician, someone that knows what she's doing!"

The nurse stood up and turned towards me. I could see in her eyes that she was truly sorry for the mishap. However, I couldn't believe she had the audacity to ask for another chance. I glared at her and said, "He's the patient, and you've had more than your share of chances."

Apologizing all the way out the door, she left with sagging shoulders. A few minutes later, a doctor that we knew strode into the room and asked Cory to show him his veins. Cory said, "No way, Doctor; I want someone from the lab to come in here to take my blood."

The doctor begged Cory to let him try, but Cory refused even to consider it. Finally the doctor gave up and agreed to send in a lab technician. The doctor seemed slightly irritated that Cory would not cooperate with him. But Cory didn't care. We were the ones who had to wait. Cory said, "I'll wait all night before I let those two touch me."

And wait we did. It took over an hour before a lab person could get to the emergency room. Cory felt it was definitely worth the wait. He knew that doctors never draw blood! He also knew that the experience probably would have been worse than the nurse's screw-up had been.

Even though we had been in the hospital for several hours and his pain had not abated, Cory was able to calmly describe the symptoms to the doctor. The doctor nodded and smiled. After the examination the doctor said, "It could be sinusitis, there's nothing to indicate a CNS [central nervous system] relapse."

Cory threw his hands up in disgust, gestured to the base of his skull and huffed, "Doctor, my pain is at the back of my head not in the front where my sinuses are!" (A very astute child who had seen way too many television commercials about sinus medication.)

I could see how uncomfortable the doctor was feeling. The medical professionals never want to admit it when a child relapses. Cory knew and I knew the pain and blurred vision were indications the leukemia cells had most probably returned. The doctor put us off, telling us to come back to the clinic in the morning for a complete check up. We played along with him, but what could we do? Cory gladly accepted the pain medication, and we went home.

When we arrived back at the hospital the next morning, a mere three to four hours after being sent home, Cory and I already knew the results. We stopped off in the cafeteria to see Georgie. Cory told her what had happened in the emergency room the night before. He told Georgie that he knew it definitely wasn't sinusitis. Not long after that we were in a procedure room getting the bad news—it was a central nervous system relapse. This meant that the sneaky leukemia cells had found their way into his spinal fluid. This is the fluid that surrounds the spinal cord and the brain. It is a very difficult area to medicate because there are so many places for the cells to hide, such as the little wells or ventricles of the brain. Also, this particular area of the human body is vital and needs to be protected so it's very well insulated.

We were still trying to come to grips with the bad news when the doctor from the previous night's misadventure in the emergency room popped in. He was very apologetic. I felt sorry for him. I think somewhere, deep inside, Cory did too, but because he was frightened, hurting, and angry, he didn't cut the doctor any slack. Looking sheepishly down at the floor, the doctor said he felt really silly for the sinusitis diagnosis the night before. Cory was lying face down on the procedure table listening. I was wondering how he would react. The nurse groveling the night before hadn't really stopped him from being brutally honest with her. Cory half-rolled over to glare at the doctor and sarcastically spat out, "There's the door, Mickey Mouse. Don't let it hit you in the butt on your way out." ZING...ouch! Cory always knew how to hit his mark.

We left the hospital that day feeling pretty sad. Cory's blurred vision scared him. The head pain scared both of us. But the relapse diagnosis made both of those concerns almost irrelevant. For some reason the doctor put off doing a bone marrow tap until Monday, and this was Friday.

Have you ever heard the saying, *"Live one day at a time"*? Health-care professionals too easily drop this little ditty on folks dealing with life-threatening illnesses. Try following this advice when you feel overwhelmed with problems. It is very hard to put everything else on hold while you try to survive one day at a time. It's all just a bunch of useless words at a time like that.

Really, the difficult part of that philosophy is dealing with the ignorance others have about your situation. It sounds so easy, but try telling your kid who is writhing in pain that maybe tomorrow the medication, which hasn't worked so far, will kick in and stop the cancer cells from multiplying like prolific little bunnies in your blood. It *ain't* that easy, especially if your common sense says, "This sounds like a lot of baloney."

Cory was brave as usual and tried very hard to keep me afloat. On the way home, we talked about the meaning of life and death, about God and his plans for us. Cory wanted to discuss the quality of life, of his life. We knew his appointment on Monday meant a return to high-dose chemotherapy and all the crummy side-effects associated with it. Cory was very clear about how important his quality of life was to him, and he did not want a pain-filled, undignified existence. He had seen a lot of suffering at Children's Hospital in four years, and he had suffered more than his fair share, too.

"I want to live, Mommy. I'm going to fight this!" he shouted to me. I was elated to hear him say that he wanted to fight since he had previously talked about stopping treatment. He began to feel angry right about the time we drove up to our house. A wonderfully healing technique advocated by Elisabeth is to externalize anger by doing something physical without harming anyone or anything. I suggested to Cory that he beat up the couch with a dishtowel. Brie ran off to get him one. He attacked the couch with a vengeance so unlike him it startled Brie. After about fifteen minutes of watching him unleash a torrent of anger and hopelessness, Brie asked if she could go to my parents' house to play. She, at least, could take a break from the bad news.

A few minutes after Brie left, Cory crumpled and fell limp on the arm of the couch, sobbing. Then just as suddenly, he gathered up his strength and with a roar ran up to his room and howled for a good half-hour. Elisabeth would have been very proud of him; for a seven-year-old, he was mastering the technique she had spent several decades trying to teach adults. When he was through "releasing his mads," he came downstairs and said, "Okay, what are we doing this weekend? I want to have a normal weekend and not think about Monday."

The Rainbow Bridge

Next Stop: Summerland

onday finally came. I had promised Cory a trip to the music store if he would agree not to fight Dr. Clark when she did the bone marrow and spinal taps. He desperately wanted the audiotape, *Thriller*, by Michael Jackson.

Cory breezed through the procedures with one goal in mind—heading for the record store at Southcenter Mall. Cory's bone marrow was clear. Dr. Clark explained what his new induction chemotherapy would be like. He would receive four weeks of oral Prednisone, intrathecal Methotrexate (that's where the drug is injected into the spinal fluid), intravenous Methotrexate, intravenous Vincristine, and a possible Ommaya reservoir. Cory became a little more interested in what she was saying when she mentioned drilling holes in his skull for the Ommaya. (It's a rubber device that looks like a jellyfish. The doctor surgically pulls back the scalp and threads tiny but long tubes through the holes. Then the Ommaya lies on the skull. The scalp gets stitched up. Then, physicians can inject the medication into the Ommaya through the scalp. The meds travel down the little hoses into the brain's ventricles.)

"No way," he said at the mere mention of the Ommaya. Dr. Clark told him he had four weeks to decide, and the only alternative would be more cranial radiation, which doctors had found never works as well.

By this time, Cory just wanted out of there. He hopped down off the table and said, "Let's go!"

We were on the freeway heading south when Cory looked at me with his chin jutting out and his back arched stiffly. Without hesitation he said quite emphatically, "I want to live. I will fight to stay alive, and that's that."

My belief at the time was that Cory could use his mind to fight off the evil cancer cells. I tried to encourage him by restating how much power his mind had in dealing with the illness.

Maybe I bored him to sleep. Who knows? But when we were just minutes from the mall, he seemed to fall asleep. I looked over at his angelic face and fought back my tears. Then I whispered softly, "I know you can do it, buddy; you can fight, and you can win." Unfortunately, I'm not so sure I really believed what I was saying.

I pulled into the parking lot at the mall. Then I gently shook his shoulder. He opened his eyes and said, "I don't mind dying, Mommy. I don't mind dying now. I'm not afraid to die and I don't want you to be afraid for me." I was shocked that he had changed his tune so quickly. I was wondering what had happened in those three minutes since he'd fallen asleep.

"Mommy, I went to the bridge, and I saw all my friends there waiting for me on the other side. They want me to come across, but I told them I wasn't quite through here yet. So you see, I won't be alone, and I'm not afraid. Your grandpa is there, and he said that he would take good care of me. He loves me even though I hadn't even been born yet when he was here on earth. He loves you and Grandma and my uncles very much, and he's there waiting for me. And Quackszer was there wagging his tail and waiting for me, too!"

Speechless and paralyzed with fear, I could not move. My heart was pounding out of my chest, my ears were ringing, and I felt nauseous. I tried to remain calm. I smiled weakly at my little boy who was so excited about his latest adventure. He went on to describe the bridge and all the people he'd seen on the other side waving to him. "They want me to come across." He continued on to say that he could not leave earth until he was satisfied that Brie and I would be okay. Also, he was concerned about my parents and my brothers and sisters and their families being in a "good space" before he could take his leave. I was overwhelmed by his enthusiasm. Over the years, I had read books and articles about such "other worldly" experiences as people who were near death seeing bridges, valleys, mountains, or rivers to cross over to get to heaven, but I knew he hadn't. At that moment, I knew Cory was *not* having a "near-death experience." He had just relapsed, but he was definitely not near death. I could not understand why he was having this bizarre thing happen to him. I know some people would refer to it as a vision or a dream, but in my heart, I know that it was so much more than that.

As quickly as he began telling his story, he stopped. The only thing he wanted to do was go to the music store and pick up his Michael Jackson tape. I was happy for the distraction. I had had enough "woo woo" experiences for one day. I prayed to God for strength and understanding.

On the way home from the shopping mall, Cory started wondering aloud how each of our family members would deal with his death. This caused him to worry about everyone. He wanted to know how I thought his leaving would affect people. I had always felt that I was a good listener when he needed to talk about his fears, but what he was saying was so difficult to hear as a mother. I finally told him that I was just a mom who needed a break. He smiled at me and graciously said, "No problem; we can talk more about it later."

That night he wasn't feeling well so he climbed into my bed. In the morning we were lying in bed snuggling. He tried to moan quietly. I asked what I could do for him and his pain, and he said, "Just pray, Mommy."

I cried with him, and said, "I do all the time, son, but what else can I do?"

He nestled closer and said, "Just love me...and when the time is right, love me enough to let me go."

We hugged one another in silence for a while. I was stunned. I knew where our conversation was heading...and I wasn't sure I could handle the trip. Then Cory said, "Mommy, you have to promise me that when it comes time and I say stop, you will make them stop. I know the doctors and everybody will try to talk me out of it again and say I can't make my own decision. You'll have to make them listen." His resolve was so evident that I had to take him at his word. I made the promise, and we fell back to sleep.

Cory was achy all day. He just lay on the couch or in my lap and whimpered with pain off and on. He dozed when he could. Brie played outside most of the time so Cory could rest. Later, the three of us went to my sister's house for dinner. Brie played with her cousins, but all Cory wanted to do was have me hold him on my lap. He was so unusually quiet all night.

The next day my sister-in-law Beverly wanted to show her support by going with us to the hospital for Cory's chemotherapy. It was unusual for us to have company along, which made it a good distraction for Cory. He was very brave during his spinal tap and intrathecal medication (that's where they inject the drug into the spinal fluid and the needle enters between vertebrae—ouch!). He got pretty ill from the IV medication and did a lot of vomiting. Afterwards, I asked Cory to show his Aunt Beverly the playroom for a minute so I could talk to his nurse, Colleen.

Colleen had just come back from vacation that morning to discover Cory had relapsed again. The first thing she wanted to know from me was if we intended to discontinue Cory's medical treatment. I explained to her it was really up to the patient, not the patient's mother, but I hoped he would want to continue because I wasn't ready to deal with the alternative at that point. She nodded sadly.

Then I told her about his fantastic journeys to the other side, over the Rainbow Bridge. She was awed. I think she thought I was a little weird, too, but she was much too polite to tell me that to my face.

Our conversation wound back around to Cory's desire to quit his chemotherapy. Even though it hurt me to verbalize it, I vowed to support his decision. I asked her how she thought the doctors would respond—would they resist or support him? Colleen promised to feel them out and get back to me.

Cory took another trip to the special place that night. He told me that the bridge was a magnificent rainbow made up of colors not seen on earth. He saw Quackszer chasing butterflies and kitty cats. He described many old friends and some new ones. "They were all healthy and happy, Mommy!"

*Summerland, God's castle, and the Rainbow Bridge drawn by Cory

He told me his biggest excitement was speaking to God. He chattered on happily, describing his first encounter with God. "God wore a long flowing nightgown type of thing. He has long, dark hair, a beard and mustache, and very dark eyes. And he was so wonderful!"

I asked what they talked about. Cory shared this much, "God says everyone comes to heaven eventually. Everyone has a job to do there; it's not all fun and games. There are schools to continue your education. You must cherish life and give love freely."

Then with a tiny bit of hesitation, Cory said, "God told me to go back to earth, and I will be called when he is ready for me and not to forget what he'd told me."

Over the ensuing weeks Cory took many trips over the Rainbow Bridge and decided to call the magnificent place Summerland. He said, "It's where the sun always shines, and they never see rain." It was certainly evident he was born and raised in the rainy Northwest. "It's like a parallel world. It looks very similar to Earth. There's water, land, trees, mountains, meadows, only much more beautiful. The colors are more intense and like nothing you've ever seen. Everything there is bright and made of light. The cottages, smaller castles, and God's castle are all made from faceted crystal. The crystal reflects the beauty and colors of the rainbow like prisms on chandeliers. Rainbows are really the bridges to heaven. If you could see a side view of a rainbow, you would recognize that it's really just a bridge. The clothing worn by the beings (who look like regular folks) is long flowing robes made of iridescent material that also reflects the light. Gardens are bountiful and glorious with beautiful flowers not of this earth. The music is tinkly and sweet. It brings joy to your ears. Everyone is happy, healthy, joyous, and peaceful. People communicate by thought, not by speaking. Loved ones are instantly recognized, even if they don't look as they did before they died."

When Cory talked about walking in God's garden, hand in hand with God, he described heaven as having different levels of understanding and existence. I imagined the side view or elevation of a tall building with numerous floors reaching higher and higher. The beings progressed to the different levels according to their experiences and their needs.

Cory asked God if his Uncle John was there because he hadn't seen him. God gave him this explanation about his Uncle's absence: "John will eventually be allowed to join the others in 'Summerland' but not until he has sorted out and made sense of his mistake, the mistake of committing suicide." God was not punishing him, but John needed to learn from his mistake so that he would not have to repeat the lesson. What was the lesson? According to Cory, "God gives us the greatest gift of all, the gift of life. If you take your own life, it isn't right; it's like spitting in God's face. Uncle John destroyed a perfectly good body, so he has to think about it." Sounded to me as if the Catholics' idea of purgatory may be valid.

With his trips to Summerland came a feeling of peace and acceptance for Cory. He knew just how beautiful existence was on the other side of the Rainbow Bridge. He got to the point where he could go there at will. He was always so excited and eager to share with me who and what he had seen. It was fascinating, listening to his wondrous tales of seeing people, even some he hadn't known, many who had long since gone to the other side. A very dear, old friend of my parents had died from a brain tumor. Cory told me how this friend ran up to greet him with a hug when he arrived in Summerland. He instantly recognized her, too.

He spent some time with my grandfather. And when he described the second meeting, I cried. My loving grandfather reassured Cory that he would be there to care for him, and he told Cory not to be afraid. He held Cory and told him how much he loved him and that he'd been watching over him since his birth. He also described how he'd been keeping an eye on my mother my brothers and me since he'd gone to heaven.

Cory saw many kids that he knew from the hospital. He kept asking me to give messages to their parents and to tell them how happy and healthy their little ones were, but I couldn't bring myself to tell them. Instead, I reported the sightings to the social worker from the hospital and let her decide whether to pass the information along. He talked of a little friend, who died after an amputation, as being whole again. The little girl, whose mother had seemed angry with me, could ride a bike, he said. He kept repeating how everyone he saw there appeared so happy and extremely healthy! These were things that would definitely impress a little boy who had spent most of his life dealing with painful procedures and crummy side-effects.

Cory loved it whenever I wrote a poem about him. He was flattered, I guess, or maybe just pleased that we had such a strong connection that the poetry just came to me. I'm not sure which.

From the discussions Cory and I had about his out-of-body trips, another alpha-state poem came to me.

Summerland

Where the sun always shines
And they never see rain,
It's all beauty, light, and love.
No one can remember pain.
Where friends and loved ones
Await the glorious day,
When the spirit leaves its earth
Body to find its way
To the crystal castle in the sky
Over the Rainbow Bridge to dwell
On high
In God's presence forevermore.
He'll be waiting patiently for you and me...
To join him in the presence of God's love
In that beautiful kingdom up above.

Message from Michael

I had never discussed my friend Michael Poth with Cory. Incredibly, eleven years after Michael's death, Cory came to me with messages from my friend that he'd met while in Summerland.

This all happened while I was working for Michael's father. Cory may have somehow heard me talk about the fact that my friend had died after he sustained an injury to his neck. But little kids don't know there's a connection between broken necks and paralyzed legs. So when Cory came to me saying that my friend, Michael, had approached him, introduced himself as my dear friend, and asked him to relay a message to me, I was flabbergasted.

Michael wanted me to know that he could walk, run, and dance and that he was totally happy there on the other side. I cried with happiness. Michael also told Cory that he knew his father felt deep sadness. And as it is with any death, there is always the guilt of not having done enough for the person or regrets about not having said the right things. Michael understood that his father had taken his coma and death very hard. He wanted Jerry to know that he was fine and well.

Cory was very confident when he came to me with Michael's messages. I, on the other hand, was a bit reluctant to rush to Jerry with such information. I thought he would think I was totally bonkers. You never know how people will respond to such strange accounts. But he loved it! The message was a huge relief for him.

For years after Michael's death, I dreamt of seeing him. My most vivid and recurring dream was of me at college, running past the library on my way to class. I would catch a glimpse of Michael out of the corner of my eye. He was always casually chatting with a bevy of cute coeds. I always ran back to find him holding court. I would blurt out, "Michael, what are you doing here? They told me you died!" He would respond, "I did! But now I'm fine. Look! I can walk, dance, and run!" Then he would run circles around me, laughing and teasing me. This recurring dream of Michael looking like his old self made me happy. Then I'd wake up.

At first, I wondered if I was just dreaming this over and over because I didn't go to his funeral. Later, I believed he was coming to tell me he was okay.

Many people that I have met over the years tell similar stories about loved ones appearing to them, too. Whether it happens during a vivid dream or a time when they are half awake, they all describe it as feeling completely different than a regular dream. That's how my dreams of Michael were.

I have actually been asked if I thought these kinds of visions or dreams were implanted in my head by the devil. As you might imagine, I didn't take that approach too well. Besides, even if there were such a thing as a devil, why would he want me to have such warm comforting feelings? Think about it.

Krisser

"**K**risser has hair! I almost didn't recognize him!" Cory shouted after he saw his little friend from the hospital in Summerland. Krisser had died months before Cory started having his out-of-body experiences. They had been on the same chemotherapy schedule, and even though Kris was quite a bit younger than Cory, they had hit if off. Kris always came to the clinic with his loving grandparents.

Cory went out of his body and saw his friend several times. Each time he was so happy and excited to tell me about it. Our little friend had been bald the entire time we knew him. That is why Cory was so enthusiastic to find that Kris had a full head of thick, luxurious, beautiful hair.

One morning, Cory came to me and said that he had seen his friend Krisser and his grandpa. "Krisser's grandpa is in Summerland! Krisser was showing him around!" I was curious, but I didn't know what to say so I just left it at that.

We went to the hospital the next morning, and as Cory's doctor was administering his bone marrow tap, she said to me, "Kris' grandpa died."

I replied, "Oh?"

Dr. Clark said, "Yes, he died yesterday morning."

I swallowed hard and said, "I know."

She looked at me and asked, "Oh, did his wife call you?"

I said, "No, Cory went out of his body to Summerland again and told me he saw Krisser showing his grandpa around." Her jaw dropped. Cory had no way of knowing; we didn't even know he'd been ill.

"Sssh, God's Here"

My friend Mike Keller and his friend Fifer had come by to bring Brie her birthday present. Poor Keller had searched far and wide for the special doll that Brie had requested. As luck would have it, he couldn't find THE doll, so while he was explaining the situation and trying to convince her the one he did get was better, I had a chat with Cory. He wasn't feeling well. He complained about the chemotherapy making his tummy and chest hurt. I took him up to bed and rubbed his tummy and back in an effort to get him to sleep. He was crying from the pain.

He rolled over onto his back and the expression of pain on his faced turned to fear. I was sitting on the edge of his bed. Cory looked up toward the ceiling at the light fixture. I asked what was troubling him. Cory answered in a raspy whisper, "Sssh, God's here."

My heart throbbed. I was gripped by fear so intense that it hurt. I asked, "Right NOW?" Cory nodded slowly. "What does he want???" I queried.

Cory whispered again, "He came to tell me to stay in my body and to stop coming to Summerland."

I was relieved because it sounded as if he wasn't going to take him anytime soon. I asked, "Why are you so afraid?"

Cory turned to me with an exasperated look on his face, rolled his eyes, and asked me, "Have you ever had God mad at you?"

I looked up over my shoulder following Cory's eyes. I couldn't see him, but Cory told me God was wagging his finger at him. Then God left. Cory told me God had said that "they" would come for him soon but not right away. The other major point God came to make? It was not up to Cory to decide when he would go. *"Wow, chastised by God."* I thought. *"No wonder the kid's scared."* He was absolutely right; I hadn't ever had God mad at me…that I knew of.

As we talked, it became clear to me how frightened Cory really was. He was mostly worried he wouldn't be allowed to stay on earth for his eighth birthday. I suggested that he explain to God that he didn't want to miss this particular birthday. Cory gave me another roll of the eyes and with total irritation said, "Gee, Mom, you just don't go around telling HIM what you want."

"Why not?" I asked. He politely ignored me and almost immediately fell fast asleep. I quietly tiptoed out of his bedroom feeling completely overwhelmed by the whole experience. "What next???" I said to no one in particular. I went downstairs and tried to digest what had happened. Keller asked why I was being so quiet. I just told him Cory wasn't feeling too great, and I was worried.

The very next night, Cory asked me to write more poetry about him and to promise I would never forget him. He was so worried that he would be forgotten. Then he broached the subject of what he wanted to be buried with. "Please put in the Care Bear Brie gave me and a picture of you, and I want my picture on my headstone." Then he fell asleep.

Cory's physical well being went up and down so much around this time. The night after God came to tell him to stay in his body; he went night skiing with my brother Mark and his family. Cory felt good and had a grand time. Then the next day he was down for the count again. He had a very rough evening. The roller coaster ride, which was the best description at the time for Cory's up-and-down physical health, was starting all over again. I felt so badly for him.

He began to make drawings for various people. It became an obsession with him. The drawings were his goodbye presents for the people he cared about. Then his entrepreneurial spirit took over, and he decided that maybe he should be selling these pictures instead of giving them away. He hit up a couple of my brothers, who applauded his spirit so much that they didn't mind paying for the artwork. Cory actually wanted to put a table out on the street corner to sell his drawings. I told him direct sales would probably be easier since the weather wasn't great and our street was so busy.

Over the next few nights Cory began to designate which belongings he would leave to his friends and his sister. He asked me to take notes as he dictated a shirt here and a train set there. He also made a separate list of things he wanted me to save. I questioned him about the save box. At first he was vague and secretive. I kept pushing him. He finally gave in and told me they would be for *him*. He was planning to come back in a new, healthy body as my next baby. He wanted me to name him "Michael."

"The Michael mystery is finally solved?" I asked.

"Yes, Mama, it will be me."

Then, he told me that he knew before he was born as Cory that he would become sick and die. He said he came to be my child. He said it would be hard but that I would survive his death. Then in exchange for a sickly life as Cory, he would get to be a happy, healthy, little boy named Michael. So, he wanted his hydroplane pictures, his watercolor art pens, and his Frank Frazzeta books kept in a safe place for his return.

I wanted to know more about his plan, but he cut me off saying that he needed to rest. He would tell me more at a later time. I placed his list on the dresser and walked out quietly.

The next night, Cory asked me to get my pad and pencil so he could dictate more instructions. I honored his request, but believe me; the smile on my face was totally fake. He began our discussion by telling me what music he wanted played at the funeral. I choked back the tears and said nothing. He went on.

He wanted pictures of his father, Brie, my parents, and me placed in his casket. It was so hard to hear those things even though he was so matter of fact about everything. When he noticed that I was crying, he wiped my tears and said, "Mama, wipe those tears from your face.

I will be back in God's loving embrace. Please don't weep for me. I promise you, I'll always be beside you at the speed of thought. Whenever you think of me, I'll be there."

Kindred Spirits

Jenny, the social worker at our hospital, introduced us to a little boy named Aaron and his mother, Brenda. They had just moved to Seattle from Atlanta. Aaron had just finished his treatment for T-cell lymphoma. His mom and stepfather decided to move to Seattle to start a new life, rejoicing that Aaron had survived his cancer.

Four days after they got here, Aaron relapsed. They didn't know anyone, so Jenny wanted Cory and me to meet them so we could offer our support. I was reluctant at first because we were dealing with the emotions of Cory's recent relapse ourselves. I wasn't sure I had the energy to offer anyone else support. Cory convinced me it was the right thing to do. When we met Aaron and his mom, it was magical. This was the sweetest little boy I had ever met. He had such a wonderful little spirit. Aaron and Brenda's relationship was inspiring.

When Aaron was able to leave the hospital, we invited him and his mother to come over to our house to play. The kids played, sang, and danced all afternoon. They had so much fun dancing to Peter Alsop's wonderful song entitled, "I Am a Pizza." Holding their sides from laughing so hard, they finally collapsed from exhaustion. Aaron was between Cory and Brie's ages and got along well with both of them. The sound of giggles and outright laughter filled my house. It was hard to imagine that both little boys were desperately fighting for their lives.

Brie developed a huge crush on Aaron. It was so obvious but cute. I think Aaron was quite flattered. At the same time, Cory and Aaron understood each other on a completely spiritually based, unspoken level.

We didn't tell too many people about Cory's stories of his out-of-body experiences. I didn't want people to think he was weird. I did report them to all of his doctors, his nurse, Colleen, and Jenny. Everyone was fascinated by Cory's accounts. I was impressed by how much respect Cory's doctors gave him. No one raised an eyebrow. No one tried to attribute the experiences to hallucinations, stress, or the chemotherapy.

Teacher Not Student

Alternative School #1, aka AS#1, in Seattle was Cory's next stop for education. I chose the school because it was small and public (free) and I was impressed with the atmosphere. Cory loved it. His principal, Beverly Barnard, told me that Cory had the aura of a saint, that his very presence could calm chaos. The students and staff at this small school were very nurturing.

Cory's refusal of the Ommaya reservoir after his third relapse meant more brain radiation. In May, post-relapse, Cory kept making up excuses to stay home from school. This was not like him. He loved school more than anything else. Finally, one day I decided he was ready to go back to school. I asked what his current ailment was, and he told me that he had a killer hangnail. (I'm a little slow, but that one was obvious!) I pushed him a little harder, and Cory tearfully told me that he was having problems with his short-term memory, and it was embarrassing for him to be mid-sentence and lose his train of thought completely. He was devastated. This was a child who adored school and all that it offered. He went on to say, "Spacing out is so embarrassing, Mom. I just don't want to be there."

It didn't take long for me to find out just how frightening the situation was. When I dropped him off at school a few days later, my last instruction to him was that I would pick him up after his art therapy appointment at the Fred Hutchinson Cancer Research Center. Later that afternoon Cory called from home to tell me that my brother Bobby had picked him up from school. I asked why. He told me that he had called my brother for a ride home. Well, Cory was supposed to have been dropped off at his art therapy appointment by Karen, one of his teachers. He had completely forgotten the appointment and our conversation that morning! After that, I had to pin notes inside his pockets and pray he wouldn't forget his name, or worse...

A miracle occurred that evening. The telephone rang, and it was Elisabeth Kubler-Ross, calling from Switzerland to check on her little friend. They had an uncanny telepathic connection. Often when Cory was depressed or in physical pain, she would call him out of the blue. I told her his latest challenge was memory loss and how much that was affecting his love for school. She said, "That's not such a big problem. Put him on." Cory talked with her for quite a while and seemed so much brighter afterwards. When I questioned his renewed sense of energy and power, Cory told me that Elisabeth had given him some important advice. With a smile, he related part of their telephone conversation. "Elisabeth told me I didn't come here to be a student; I'm a teacher. She uses my drawings to comfort sick and dying people. She said adults who haven't felt a real emotion in years cry when they see my drawings 'cuz then they know there really is a heaven. So it doesn't really matter if my memory doesn't work that well right now. I can just concentrate on what I am good at and enjoy myself." He went back to school the next day, a very happy boy.

A week later was I ever surprised when I arrived at Fred Hutchinson to pick him up from what I thought was his art therapy appointment. I opened the door to the main conference room and found my son breakdancing, actually doing a head spin on the table. He never complained about hangnails or made excuses to get out of school again.

The school year ended. By summer the chemotherapy started causing more adverse reactions. On July 2, Cory again expressed feelings of hopelessness about his disease. The doctors ordered more and more tests to find out why he was in so much pain. The upper and lower GIs and a multitude of other tests did not reveal a single clue. I will always believe it was the drugs. It didn't take a bunch of scientists to figure it out. It was plain and simple: They were poisoning his body.

It got so bad on one particular day that, on our way to the clinic, I had to pry his little fingers off the door handle again at the main entrance to the hospital. He had made up his mind. He wanted to quit treatment. I convinced him to go with me to talk with Jenny, the social worker, about his decision to stop. Cory stated his case. She listened and then, to show her support, accompanied us to the clinic.

When I told Dr. Clark how Cory was feeling about ending his treatment, she immediately tried to talk him out of it. She still felt he had a strong chance to survive. She also didn't feel an eight-year-old child should be allowed to make such a drastic decision. Cory accepted the drugs that day but warned Dr. Clark he was still not convinced.

On the way home Cory told me that his frustration caused by his short-term memory loss was growing. He could not remember most of what he had experienced in Summerland because of the brain radiation. That revelation was very traumatic for Cory.

That weekend, Cory discussed his desire to quit chemotherapy with his father. When he came home after the visit he resignedly told me, "I will continue for a little while longer to satisfy Dad and Dr. Clark."

Goodbyes

In August, Cory and Aaron went to Camp Goodtimes together. Camp Goodtimes is a weeklong camp for children with cancer and their siblings. Doctors and nurses along with highly trained volunteers staff the camp so it is safe for the patients to be away from their medical centers. It is a wonderful opportunity for the children to express themselves and feel a sense of freedom from their disease for a whole fun-filled week. Many children have never been camping or away at a camp because of their illness. As for the parents, they get a break and can rest assured that their child is safely having fun. And as a bonus it's free, a significant benefit for the many families that cannot afford an added recreational expense on top of medical payments.

Aaron and Cory were so excited to share the experience together. The first part of the adventure was a chartered boat ride from a marina in north Seattle to Vashon Island.

Poor little Aaron hadn't been feeling too great but insisted on going. The morning they left, we met Aaron and his parents at the marina. While waiting for the boat, which would take them to camp, I noticed Aaron was pale and somewhat subdued. The two little buddies smiled at each other and talked about how excited they were to be heading to camp.

Their smiles faded, and two sad little faces peeked back at us as we waved goodbye to them that morning. They were both clutching stuffed animal friends as the boat pulled away from the dock. I cried at the sight of Cory's forlorn little face, but I knew he would have a great time. It wasn't like him to be afraid, but I realized he had never been away without family before. He was clinging to Danger, his favorite teddy bear, for dear life.

He came home with so many stories to tell. He made new friends, and they slept in a tent one night. Cory told me that Aaron didn't feel too great most of the time. At first, Cory felt guilty because he was having so much fun and his friend couldn't. He told me he stopped in at the infirmary to check on Aaron often. Cory told him that he was sad that he wasn't feeling well enough to have much fun. Aaron replied with a sweet smile, "Cory, I'm glad you can have enough fun for both of us!"

Not long after Aaron returned from camp, he was hospitalized. Brenda took him home on a Tuesday. When they released him, the doctors told Brenda he could die anytime. In their "infinite wisdom," they told Brenda he could possibly have five more months. We all hoped he would make it to Christmas. I took the kids to visit him on Thursday. My journal reads:

Aaron asked to be helped out of bed so he could play with Cory and Brie on the floor. They played "He-Man" and a few other games. Brenda said it was the first time he'd been able to play in a week. This would be the last time Aaron played. The angels took him back to heaven that Sunday, September 2, around 3:00 p.m. It was a bright, sunny day. Aaron made a peaceful transition with his angel there to show him the way.

Cory and Brie reacted very well. They both said they were happy for Aaron yet sad for themselves and Brenda. They expressed openly how they would miss their little friend but knew that he would no longer suffer or be in pain.

I'm very proud of my little friends. God truly blessed me with two of the most loving, caring, and beautiful-beyond-words little souls. For as long as they are meant to be with me on this planet will I cherish their love and especially their wisdom. Aaron's death has been expected since he came home from Atlanta, but it still wounds deeply. He was a wonderful little boy, and we will always remember the beauty of his soul. His love was his gift to all whose lives were touched by his presence. I am thankful that I, as well as my children, was able to be a part of his short life here in Seattle. We loved him and his mommy immediately upon meeting them. I believe he and Cory are connected somehow, and I believe more strongly in life now as a result of having Aaron in our lives.

The day of Aaron's leaving, Cory said, "He's no longer in pain, Mama, and I will be with him soon." Cory was almost too open with me sometimes. I really didn't want to hear "that." I suspect Cory felt as if he had to prepare me by dropping those little bombs on me every once in awhile.

Weeks later, Cory was asked by Brenda to go and check on her little buddy in Summerland. Cory went with great glee. Since he was going with a purpose, Cory figured he couldn't get into trouble for disobeying God's order to stay in his body.

The morning of his reconnaissance mission, a very animated Cory practically flew down to my room. With great vigor he jumped on my bed to wake me. He was electrified as he told me that his Uncle John was now in Summerland. He urged me to get on the telephone to tell my sister Rita and her daughters about him seeing John with Aaron and lots of other children.

He summarized the scene saying, "Uncle John is there. I saw him reading stories to a group of kids under a beautiful tree. And Aaron was with him! They looked so happy, Mama! And now Uncle John is in the light. Call Auntie Rita and tell her quick!" Cory was so happy and relieved for John as well as his family. He had been worried about Kimi and Jenifer because their father's death had been such a shock.

Cory was so happy to see his pal Aaron looking so healthy, too. He said, "He was surrounded by a bunch of smiling, laughing kids!" They told Cory, "C'mon buddy! Come play with us." He told them he'd be back a little while later. It was hard for me to hear that part, I guess, because I was afraid "later" would be too soon.

After that particular trip to Summerland, Cory refrained from going again. My guess is that he thought it would be best to honor God's request that he stay in his body.

At this point in time, Tyler's presence in my life was, for the most part, good for me. For someone who had never been a parent, he was very supportive. On several occasions he was there waiting for us when we got back from a chemotherapy treatment with Cory exiting the car vomiting. He would rub Cory's back and then carry him into the house. His compassion was a real gift to Cory.

But our relationship probably was not so great for him. I think it became increasingly more difficult for him to cope with Cory's illness and its inevitable course of destruction. Just hearing about Aaron's death hit him very hard, showing him what he would soon have to deal with in our family. With each passing day, the reality of what Cory was facing became inescapable. Tyler had never experienced the death of anyone he cared about and wasn't prepared to handle the inevitable.

Labor Day weekend, I took care of Quasi, Brenda and Mark's dog, while they flew Aaron's body to Florida. That prompted several long conversations between Tyler and me. He admitted it was hard for him even to think about being able to cope if Cory got worse. Therefore, he did not trust that he could be there for me when he knew I would need him the most. His second admission involved Keller. Keller was being very supportive, and Tyler felt ashamed that he couldn't be like that. He also admitted being a bit jealous of Keller's close relationship with me and my kids. He said it was like having to deal with another ex-husband.

So, after dating for a year and a half, when the going got tough, Tyler got going. I was really ticked off at first. But I had to acknowledge that my lack of commitment to the relationship didn't make him feel very secure, so why should he stick around? Cory and Brie were openly bummed for a while. Cory understood the issues without being told, but Brie was too young to figure things out. I felt bad that Cory's intelligence caused him distress that normal kids would never feel.

Cory, Shirley, and Aaron before boarding the boat to Camp Goodtimes

A few months later Brie saw a television show that warned about the dangers of smokeless tobacco. She insisted on calling Tyler on the telephone to tell him about it because she knew he occasionally chewed. She cried and begged him to stop, obviously a child with a great deal of awareness about cancer but not about addictive behavior. Tyler was very kind to her on the telephone and promised her he would stop. She got off the telephone feeling quite accomplished.

Lessons Taught, Lessons Learned

Cory's last encounter that I am aware of, with a school bully happened at AS#1. Cory missed the first few days of school because the bus schedules were all messed up. The kids at his school thought that he had died during the summer when he didn't show up the first week of classes, but they were very happy to see him when he did arrive. Cory got a lot of attention, even from much older students. There was a new boy at school who became quite jealous of Cory because of all the attention he was receiving. I'm not sure if he even knew Cory was ill. He taunted Cory and then one day for no apparent reason punched him in the stomach.

Cory told me the story when he got home. I was furious. If Cory's blood counts had been down, he could've bled to death! Cory told me not to get too excited. He had already dealt with the situation. I asked if he had brought the boy up on "Forum."

AS#1 had a system where a student who felt wronged could file a grievance against the person who wronged him or her. A panel of peers would review the grievance and render a consequence. The "Forum" was one of the things I admired most about the school. I felt that giving kids a sense of justice was healthy, plus the added benefit of the students learning that violence was not an appropriate way to resolve differences.

Cory replied, "No, Mom, I told my friend Sam (a thirteen-year-old) what the boy did, and he grabbed the jerk by the throat and threatened to punch his lights out if he ever bothered me again." So much for non-violent solutions, though I had to applaud his ability to solve his own problems.

When he wasn't feeling too well, he would trudge down to Beverly Barnard's office and nap on her couch. Beverly only had to drive him home a few times. She would offer, but usually he was quite determined to stay. In some ways it seems that just being near the kids at school was enough for him.

The year following his third relapse, the chemotherapy drugs, which are designed to destroy cancer cells, really ravaged his body. I got numerous telephone calls from him while I was at work. He always sounded so pathetic. He would often be experiencing horrible headaches and wrenching stomach pain from the drugs. Even if he were vomiting, he would still insist on staying at school.

Sometimes it was so bad that I would insist on taking him home rather than letting him stay at school. Many times halfway home from the hospital, I would be forced to pull over to the side of the freeway so he could hang his head out the door. If he could hold it, he usually didn't make it past our driveway.

One night his legs swelled up from the drugs that he'd had injected into his thigh muscles. By the time I got home from work, he was in agony. His legs were so swollen and sore he couldn't even stand up. I took one look at him, and I could see that his usually baggy sweat pants were tight on his legs.

I carried him out to the car. My friend Cherri was there and decided to go with us. The emergency room doctors said that there was nothing they could do. Cherri had never witnessed Cory in that much pain. She started yelling at the doctors. "Do something! He's in so much pain." Cherri kept repeating how inconceivable it was that they couldn't do something to help him. We finally left. I drove because Cherri was almost in as bad of a shape as Cory. It was clear to me that Cory saw his quality of life fading away.

We were invited to talk to a group of students at a nearby alternative school about Cory's cancer. The kids ranged in age from thirteen to eighteen. They were very curious. One boy, who was about seventeen, asked Cory, "What does it feel like to know that you are dying?" (He hadn't been diagnosed as terminal at this point, so I was concerned that the question would upset him. What a goose I was…)

Without missing a beat, Cory replied, "Everyone's going to die someday, so the real question is, how do *you* feel about *living*? That's what's important. When I die, I'll know I lived my life as best as I could. I have experienced more than most grown-ups. You have to treat people the way you want to be treated. Be kind and caring and don't judge others." The whole room was flabbergasted. My heart burst with love and pride for my courageous and wise little boy who sounded like a sage old soul. The teenager was speechless. Cory went on to say that until you can face the fear of your own death you can never fully live. Wow. The kids were in awe, and the adults were in tears.

Over time we were asked to speak to many groups of kids. It was a wonderfully affirming and yet comforting experience for Cory to share his feelings, insights, and wisdom. Elisabeth was so right: He truly was a teacher. Knowing he was helping others really gave him a sense of purpose and fulfillment. I believe that this was all part of a larger plan, and it certainly helped our whole family see that God's path is chosen for us and sometimes we don't get to vote.

Shattered Dreams

When you had a baby and thought about the child growing up, did you have hopes and dreams he would grow up to be president someday or make some monumental change for humanity? I did. Then one day it was all taken away by words I could hardly understand much less pronounce, spoken by a doctor I had just met. It took a while for the weight of what I'd heard to sink in. And when it did, it seemed so unfair and unreal.

The worst words I've ever heard went something like, "We'll start him on..." Then my head went into a vacuum, I was left with the sensation of waiting and wanting the train to run me over. The VERY WORST words a parent can ever hear? The ones that shattered my dreams forever were, "You were right; he has relapsed. We're not sure how long he has, maybe two to three months." I can still hear those words as clearly as I can see Cory's sweet face when I sat down with him. His eyes were questioning yet knowing. I can still see the pain in his eyes when I had to tell him that he would die.

The beginning of the end was Christmas Day. The morning went well. I walked in on Cory sitting with Justyn and Brie in a chair. He had his arms draped around both of the smaller children's shoulders.

I eavesdropped for a few minutes from the dining room doorway. He was preparing them for future Christmases as big kids. "Now, you know as you get older, you will receive fewer presents. It is kind of a disappointment; believe me, I know. But the presents are more expensive. Take this year for example; I got several Atari games, some clothes (big whoop), and some other little stuff. So you see: It balances out... numbers versus quality." Assuming it would have embarrassed Cory to know I was listening, I ran into the bathroom to crack up. This was a perfect example of who he was—big brother extraordinaire preparing Brie and Justyn for the harsh realities of the world.

That night, as I was tucking him into bed, Cory told me it was time to stop his chemotherapy. He had been away from the hospital for several weeks. During that time, he had spent three whole weeks throwing up and feeling terrible. This was the first day he felt halfway decent, almost normal. The idea of going back to the hospital the very next morning and getting chemotherapy that would make him feel yucky all over again repulsed him. He said, "I'm tired of being sick. I've gone five years on treatment for everybody else, now I want to quit for me."

As I sat and listened, he reminded me of the promise I had made him the year before. I indicated to him that I did remember the morning after his first trip to Summerland when he had said, "*When it comes time to stop, Mom, you have to make them stop.*" I reached down and scooped him up. I held him tight and rocked both of us back and forth. We cried, I'm sure, for quite different reasons—Cory for relief from pain and the obligation to put up with it for everyone else, and I because I knew my little boy wouldn't get to grow up. I also knew Cory would be brave, but I had serious doubts about my ability to handle the coming months. Supporting his decision to discontinue treatment was the hardest thing I had ever faced up to that point.

I spent a sleepless night tossing and turning. The magnitude of what we were facing weighed heavily on my soul. I wanted to escape from all the horrible thoughts running through my mind, but I couldn't get away. Sleep just would not come. I would've preferred a nightmare at that point, but I received no relief. The idea of a future without my little boy was a jumbled mass of destroyed snapshots with holes where Cory should have been.

Coleman and Cory

In the morning, I telephoned the clinic at Seattle Children's and cancelled his chemotherapy appointment. The clinic director put me on hold. The next thing I heard was a click, and Dr. Clark was on the phone. She asked why he wouldn't be in for treatment. I informed her of Cory's decision to end his treatment. She was not very happy about it, but what could she do? I remember hanging up with vague threats of court orders ringing in my ears.

When I sat down to tell Cory about the doctor's response, he smiled weakly and said, "She just doesn't get it, does she? I know I'm going to die, and I just want some good time before I go. I knew "they" were going to act this way... I just knew it."

On New Year's Day, I flew to Hawaii alone to meet my Aunt Cathy. My friends and family had convinced me to go ahead with my vacation plans. I was reluctant to go until Cory sat me down and told me that the coming months were going to be rough. He thought I should go take a break so I would be better able to deal with all the hassles and hurdles. Cory knew the battle with the hospital was just beginning to heat up and I would probably have problems with my ex-husband over Cory's decision to quit.

Before I left for Hawaii, Cory's doctor called, insisting we meet with the medical team to discuss Cory's decision to end treatment. The doctor restated that she was completely against Cory's decision to stop treatment. We set a date for the meeting, and I left town with a heavy heart.

For me, Hawaii has always been a place of rejuvenation where I feel completely at home and can make a magical connection to my grandfather. I really needed it that trip. Cathy and I had a lot of time to talk and relax. It was hard to be away from my children. It was so hard not to feel selfish about continuing on with my plans when Cory's decision to end his treatments would most likely mean relapse. My aunt convinced me that I shouldn't feel badly, that I needed time for myself. She and Cory were right. I needed to build up my strength so I could cope with the inevitable.

I tried to enjoy the beauty of the islands and especially the bright sunshine. It took real effort to pretend my life wasn't about to spin out of my control.

Cathy and I had fun times visiting several of the islands. First, we diddled around Oahu and then went to the big island. I didn't much care for that one. The locals still take sacrifices up to Kilauea for Pele the goddess of the volcano. They don't toss in virgins anymore, but to me the energy on that island felt dark and really creeped me out. My grandfather's stories of the nightwalkers (ghosts) didn't help much either.

I was much happier when we went to Kauai. I wanted to see Joyce, one of my best friends from childhood, who lived there. She had lost a baby to SIDS, and not long after that, her husband committed suicide. Her move to Hawaii was prompted by her losses. Joyce and I went out alone one evening to talk. We laughed about old times and cried about Cory's decision. After what she had been through, Joyce understood how I was feeling.

Kauai was such a peaceful place. It helped me heal somewhat just to lie out on the deserted beach near Joyce's little house. I closed my eyes, soaked up the sun, and listened to the waves lapping gently on the sand. I hated to say goodbye to Joyce when my Aunt Cathy and I left to fly back to Oahu.

We stayed on Oahu with my cousin Ralph and his wife. We did the usual tourist stuff on Waikiki. When the day finally came that I had to leave Hawaii, I was more than ready to see my babies. On the long flight home, I wrote a letter to Elisabeth. In the letter I described my emotions surrounding the upcoming confrontation with the oncologists at Children's. I think writing the letter was helping me prepare myself mentally for the hospital meeting which was scheduled to happen right after I got back.

The meeting was to be held in Dr. Bill Womack's office at the hospital. To be present were: Jenny Stamm, MSW and staunch patient advocate; Colleen Woolsey, RN, Cory's primary care nurse; Dr. Barbara Clark, his oncologist; Bill Womack, his stress management doctor; Cory and me.

Cory and I approached the door to the hospital laughing about something funny said in the car. When we reached Bill's door, we knew it was time to get serious. I was pretty much prepared just to let Cory have his say. I trusted he would very capably state his position.

We walked in and sat down to wait for the discussion to begin. Everyone was chitchatting, but Cory remained silent, lost in his thoughts. The last person to arrive was Dr. Clark.

She was the only one we knew for sure disagreed with Cory's position. Bill started the meeting by clarifying Cory's decision to end his chemotherapy. We waited. Dr. Clark went first. She truly cared for Cory, and she stressed how important she thought it was for him to continue treatment. Barbara Clark was and still is a very compassionate, caring physician. She stated her case eloquently. Cory listened quietly.

Then it was Colleen Woolsey's turn to speak. She said in her opinion it was important to support Cory's decision, acknowledging that he was the patient.

Jenny said virtually the same thing. I could tell Dr. Clark was beginning to feel outnumbered. She turned to me and tearfully pleaded, "How can you allow him to make a decision like this? He's only a child!"

I felt badly for her because she obviously cared so much. But Cory's words echoed clearly in my mind... "When the time comes to stop, you have to make them stop, Mom." I knew in my heart that I had to keep that promise, no matter how much it hurt me to let him go. Dr. Clark was seated right next to us. She was openly crying. It took me a minute to collect my thoughts. I finally cleared my throat and said emphatically, "It's Cory's body, and I have to support his choice. From the beginning of his illness, I have always taught him that he is in charge of his body..."

Before I could finish, Cory spoke for the first time "I'm not quitting because I *want* to die. No one wants to die. I'm saying I am going to die anyway, and I just want some good time. The chemotherapy makes me sick. I'm *tired* of *feeling* sick."

Barbara Clark, bless her heart, saw an opening and went for it. "Cory, just one more year, please try it a little longer." Then in desperation, "How about six months?"

"Dr. Clark, can you guarantee that I will be cancer-free if I stay on chemotherapy for the next six months or a year? Can you promise me the chemotherapy will keep me alive?"

Of course she couldn't guarantee him a single thing. She had to shake her head no and acknowledge that there were no guarantees.

Cory bravely stood his ground and said, "Well, I know I am going to die, and I just want to feel good for a little while."

With that last exchange, Bill Womack spoke up. He graciously summed up everyone's position in the matter. He acknowledged Barbara Clark's caring concern. Most important, he validated Cory's rights as the patient and asked, "How can we force him to undergo treatment he knows won't do any good?" The meeting adjourned.

Cory's classmates wanted to give him a party when they found out he had decided to discontinue his chemotherapy. Beverly described the experience as a positive one, "an experience where children learned about life and giving." Cory told some of his friends and teachers that he thought he could fight the cancer better if his body wasn't being bombarded with toxic drugs. In reality, the disease had already re-invaded his central nervous system.

Bad News

In February Elisabeth Kubler-Ross was scheduled to do a workshop and several appearances in Seattle. KOMO-TV's *Northwest Afternoon*, a local talk show, wanted to do a show with Elisabeth about ill children. She suggested they contact her good friend Cory to share the stage with her.

The producer/reporter, Elaine Purchase, called me to ask if we would be willing to participate in a videotaped story to be used for the introduction to the program. She went on to explain that we would then be on the set with Elisabeth for the live portion of the talk show.

I discussed it with my children, and they thought it sounded like fun. So I called Elaine back, and we set up an appointment.

A camera crew came to our house one evening. They hung out with us for a while, and then we chatted on-camera. A few days later, the same crew attended one of our Children's Connection support groups. While Elaine hung out with us, I mentioned off-camera my suspicions that Cory was suffering with severe headaches because he had relapsed. I told her that I intended to take him to the clinic the following day to be checked out.

It had only been a few short weeks since Cory had opted off che-motherapy, but he was showing definite signs of relapse. Headaches, muscle pain, and blurred vision had hit him all at once. I called the hospital, reporting his symptoms. Six different doctors gave me six different responses. Some were even cruel about it. One said, "Well, what do you expect? You let him quit treatment. He's probably so uptight about going off treatment that his muscles are tensing up and causing the pain that you're describing."

In tears, I telephoned Bill Womack to ask if he thought Cory's pain was psychological. He told me absolutely not. He assured me nothing Cory or I had done was causing charley-horse cramps to form in his thigh muscles.

I wrote in my diary:

February 7, 1985. Tomorrow I'm taking Cory to Children's for an LP [spinal tap] and a bone marrow tap. His symptoms have been getting worse. I already know in my heart that he's relapsed.

Cory's doctor is very uneasy. She keeps telling me it may be the flu. Right. She's had to apologize once again for her behavior on the telephone yesterday. When I called to ask about bringing Cory in to be checked, she got snotty and asked, "Why bother to bring him in if you aren't going to let us treat him?" I was so upset by that remark. I can't believe I had to explain to a pediatric oncologist that if he had in fact relapsed, he would be in need of pain control! Getting support from doctors even at a time like this is rough. I know she cares for Cory. She is very compassionate, but it seems ridiculous how difficult it is for all the doctors up there to accept his decision to stop treatment. She of all people needs to respect him as a person and as a patient! She obviously has a hard time facing death. I know she doesn't want to lose him. But what about his feelings?

February 8, 1985. I had to go to court this morning. Still try-ing to get child support. My ex-husband stood up in court this morning and told the judge that I dress my children in rags! I was outraged by his false accusations. But even if that was the case, why doesn't he buy them clothes? The family court system

*does not work properly. I really did not need this added stress
this day; I have to take Cory in for a check-up.*

My brother Bobby decided out of the blue to go with us to the hospital. It seemed odd. In all the years we had made those horrible trips to Children's, no one in my family, except my sister-in-law Beverly, had ever gone with us. Coincidentally Lynn had gone with us the year before when Cory had experienced his third relapse.

My intuition told me Cory had already relapsed, so I drew comfort in having my brother with us. But Bobby opted to stay in the waiting room during the medical procedures; everyone in my family has a phobia about needles.

Cory and I were crammed into an exam room. At least it felt claustrophobic. Have you ever been in an emotional state where you felt as if the walls were closing in, like being in that room in *Raiders of the Lost Ark*? That's exactly what went through my mind.

As soon as the needle was withdrawn, I could see the cloudy liquid that had been sucked up into the syringe. Normal spinal fluid is as clear as water. Dr. Clark and I looked at each other knowingly. My heart burst into flames inside my chest, and I had a hard time catching my next breath. Neither of us said a word—we couldn't. Even though I intuitively knew before we got there that he'd relapsed, it didn't help.

Barbara's eyes were filled with tears as she passed me with the tray holding the syringe. There really wasn't any need to send it to the lab for testing. Everyone in the room could see the fluid, chock full of leukemia cells. Those vile, out-of-control cells would soon be responsible for taking my son away from me—and we all knew it. We were all very still and remained silent.

Finally Dr. Clark suggested that we go ahead with a bone marrow tap. There would be a totally different time frame to deal with if he had relapsed in the bone marrow, as well. (If his bone marrow was involved, he would die much sooner.) Cory hated those procedures, but I begged him to let her do them; I needed the information for my own sanity.

I waited alone in the examination room for the results. Bobby had taken Cory to the cafeteria. Actually it was the other way around: Cory took Bobby down to the fifth floor cafeteria.

I had been in that particular examination room so many times over the previous five years. I can remember looking around me that day; it was so familiar yet so foreign. The room was still. The air was gone, even the air in my lungs. It hurt to breathe. I sat there blinking back the tears. I knew what Barbara would say when she came back from the lab.

The nightmare we had been living for more than five years was about to get worse. I could feel the panic set in.

Barbara Clark composed herself before she stepped into the room. Sadness followed her in like a gaseous cloud and filled the examination room. With a grim expression on her face, she told me Cory was dying. I heard her say something like, "He has two months, maybe three. But his bone marrow is clear." She then asked if I wanted to start chemotherapy again. I instantly replied, "No, he won't want that."

I agreed with Barbara's suggestion to put Cory on a drug called Decadraun to alleviate some of the horrible symptoms associated with brain involvement. With the brain swelling that was expected due to the relapse, the steroid would help control some of the adverse affects such as deafness and blindness.

Slowly, I made my way to the cafeteria in a bit of a trance. At one point, I realized I was actually feeling my way down the hall by reaching out and touching the walls. When I reached the doorway, I spotted Cory and Bobby across the expansive room. I took a deep breath and made my way through the maze of tables. I knew I had to be straightforward with him, but I was struggling with not wanting to fall apart in front of him. I had faced this problem throughout his illness, always not wanting to scare him, thinking if he saw me wavering it would cause him even more distress. Who knows what might have happened? I never tested it.

When I reached their table, my brother was looking at me questioningly. I sat down. Cory moved around the table and climbed into my arms. I held him close to me. I just wanted to smell his hair and feel the warmth of his body. After a few minutes, I choked out the hardest words I have ever had to say in my life, "Honey, you've relapsed in your central nervous system again, and the doctor says you have between two and three more months to live."

Bobby and Cory both gasped. Then, all three of us began to cry. I can't tell you how long we sat there in the middle of the cafeteria crying because time stopped. Cory finally broke the silence when he looked up into my eyes and said, "I don't want to die, Mama."

Cradling him close to me, I nodded saying, "I know, baby, and I don't want you to go either." It was a strange thing to do in the midst of a sea of strangers. I look back now and wonder why I didn't wait until we were out of there. I have no idea; I guess my internal brakes weren't functioning properly.

I don't know how we did it, but we walked over to Georgie's cash register, waited in line to see her, and gave her the grim news. She hugged us, and we all cried. Then we gathered ourselves up and walked stonily out of the building. I can't remember who drove. I do know that we didn't talk about Cory's grim prognosis on the way home. We didn't talk about anything "heavy."

When we got to our house, Cory followed me into my room. He wanted to talk about the rest of his life. I cannot describe to someone who hasn't experienced it what it feels like to have such a conversation with your child. Words are inadequate. It was like a bad movie or a nightmare that wouldn't end…not happily anyway. Just imagine knowing your child is leaving and you can never see him or her again.

Together we mapped out how we would deal with the precious little time he had left. The most important points Cory wanted me to understand were: Number One—he wanted no hospitals, no shots, no IVs, no chemotherapy to prolong his life; and Number Two—he wanted to go to school and be as normal as possible for as long as he could.

I offered to take him anywhere in the world. He said, "No, Mama, I just want to go to school and be with my friends." I asked if he wanted to go to Hawaii or Europe. "Nope, just school. That's all I want."

Since all Cory wanted was to go to school, I collected my thoughts and mustered up the energy to telephone Beverly to tell her the bad news about Cory's relapse. I told her the doctor had given him two to three months before he would die. Then I told her Cory wanted to continue going to school. She didn't miss a beat. This wonderful woman knew how difficult it would be with Cory in her school. She accepted the challenge with courage as she applauded Cory's decision.

The next thing Cory wanted to take care of was his funeral arrangements. He wanted to do it right away while he was still feeling relatively healthy. Talk about organized! Not sure where he got that gene.

He asked me to take him to the cemetery. He wanted to choose his own burial site. There were two cemeteries to choose from and as small towns go...they were on the same hill. We drove to the one on top of the hill first. It had a neon sign. Cory said he just couldn't imagine being buried in a place that had a neon sign. "Even if Jimi Hendrix is buried here, I just can't hang with no neon." He decided right then that there was no point in stopping. We drove back down the hill to check out the other location. Mt. Olivet is much older. It's the pioneer cemetery so absolutely no neon. That's where my sister-in-law Beverly had buried her father, Wilden. Cory had known Wilden and, like his cousins, called him "Grandpa." We found his grave on the crest of a small hill. From that spot we could see Lake Washington and beyond. We could almost make out our neighborhood on the other side of the lake. Cory looked at me and said, "I want to be buried right here, next to Grandpa Wilden."

"Okay," I said. I was feeling apprehensive about this whole process but let him have his say. As usual Cory was so matter-of-fact about everything that it made it easier for me to listen to him.

"C'mon, Mom, now let's go to the casket place."

"Oh gee, Cory, do we have to?"

"Let's go get it over with, Mom; I want to make my own arrangements. We have to do it now while I still feel good."

We drove to downtown Renton. Again, there were two mortuaries a block apart. Cory chose the one he wanted based on the architecture of the building. We went in. The elderly gentleman who owned the place greeted us. Cory said, "I would like to see your caskets please. I need to pick out my own 'cuz I'm dying." I couldn't tell if Cory's request was unusual or not. The mortician didn't flinch. He quietly led us to a room filled with caskets. It was creepy. Cory checked out each one. I begged him not to climb into any of them. I knew that would have put me over the edge. When he found the one he wanted, the nice gentleman wrote down the model number. It was sky blue metallic. He thought that was pretty cool. I could only smile weakly and nod.

Then Cory asked to see the chapel. I just followed him around and let him do most of the talking. He was a very careful consumer. They didn't really talk about expenses. I don't think I could have handled *that*. I quietly told the owner I would deal with the money part later. After Cory was satisfied that his arrangements were in order, we went home. Cory had more to take care of there. He was so focused on finishing up his business. Adults could really learn something from Cory's clear outlook. I was totally in awe of my son…again.

People often ask for my advice about how to tell their son or daughter that he or she is dying. Of course, every family has its own way of coping. Ours was to be honest and open with each other no matter what was happening. Dying children know—they just know. They take their cues from the adults around them. If the child doesn't think the adults can deal with the information, the child will just wait until the time is right. That time may never come. I have witnessed that scenario over and over. So, I guess the best advice I can offer is to be as honest as your comfort level will allow. It is also important to respect the child's comprehension level when explaining the prognosis.

Many cultures have different beliefs about whether or not you should talk about death. Some believe if you talk about it that will make it happen. The truth is it is already happening. No one lives forever, and we need to be able to let the children ask questions or speak what's on their hearts. Really just think about what is best for the patients. They deserve the same respect as adult patients according to Cory.

More TV

The next day, we went with Jenny Stamm to pick up Elisabeth at the airport. Cory and Brie were so excited about seeing her again. I desperately wanted to talk with her about Cory's news. I needed to hear something reassuring from her. She was the only death-and-dying expert I knew at the time. When I look back on this time, I am not sure what I wanted or needed to hear from her, but the feeling of helplessness washes over me whenever I think of those days just after we were told Cory's life was nearing its end. Even now it's hard to breathe as I write about it.

From the airport we drove Elisabeth to a Bellevue hospital to visit a man who was dying. Elisabeth had been asked to stop by and comfort him. Jenny, the kids, and I waited in the car. My thoughts were swirling. I couldn't help but feel sadness for the man's family. Sitting there in the car stroking Cory's hair, I couldn't help but feel the heartache and spiritually heavy sadness for my own family.

Then we drove her to the hotel. She asked the children to help her unpack. Elisabeth pulled out the laminated picture of Summerland that Cory had drawn for her. She sat Cory down on the edge of the bed and said, "This picture you drew for me has traveled with me around the world many times over. During the past year and a half, it has probably gone two hundred thousand miles. It helps people who haven't cried for twenty or thirty years to release their tears. People are so happy to know there is a heaven. It is such a healing picture. You should be very proud, Cory." He just beamed.

Cory told her that he was dying. She hugged him as he said, "I guess my lessons here are done."

We visited with Elisabeth for several hours. Then it was time to take her to the KOMO-TV studios for a live, public affairs talk show called, *Town Meeting*. I had never seen it before, so I had no idea what we were about to experience.

Jenny parked the car at two minutes to 6:00 p.m. We sauntered up to the back door, and it flew open. A frantic looking woman grabbed Elisabeth by the arm and rushed her into the building. Jenny, the kids, and I were ushered off in a different direction. We entered the studio, and there were people literally hanging from the rafters. There were no seats available, and the staff was running around trying to get us situated. The program went on the air LIVE at 6:00! We left Cory and Brie in the front row with Brenda (Aaron's mommy). Then, Jenny and I crammed into a row up higher on the bleachers. I looked down and realized that Elisabeth was the only guest. There in the middle of the set sat an empty chair. No wonder those poor people looked frazzled. We had barely gotten her there on time!

In true Elisabeth fashion, it didn't faze her a bit. Someone made a comment to her as she was being seated, and she smiled and said, "I have never been late for a TV show." The show was interesting. The audience asked her question after question, and everyone seemed to hang on her every word.

About halfway through the broadcast, during a commercial break, Elisabeth motioned for Cory and Brie to come sit with her on the set. Cory wasn't feeling well, but he pushed Brie towards Elisabeth. I was sitting up higher and couldn't say anything one way or another. I just prayed she wouldn't pick her nose or belch or something awful like that. Brie was great. She just played with a watch someone had thoughtfully given to her to occupy her attention.

The next night, Elisabeth gave a speech at a theater in downtown Seattle. It was magnificent.

Then the day after that, which was Tuesday, we had our television debut on *Northwest Afternoon*. It was just three days after Cory's terminal diagnosis. Cory wasn't feeling too great, but he loved being there with his friend Elisabeth. Cory snuggled up next to me and was very quiet throughout the interview.

After the program Elaine Purchase met us backstage. She wanted to know how Cory's tests had turned out on Friday. I told her that he was dying and that the doctor had given him an estimated two to three months longer to live. I know she didn't know what to say, but I was touched that she cared enough to come down to the studio to ask about his condition.

Forevermore

The other weird thing that happened right after Cory's terminal diagnosis was that we sort of wrote a song together. It came from the cosmos, really. That's how I explain it because I have never been musically inclined. In fact, I was kicked out of the eighth grade choir for goofing off when I was supposed to have been singing. And early on, my *Kumuhula* decided that the ukulele was not going to be my instrument. I actually flunked ukulele!

Just before we left the KOMO-TV station, Elisabeth and Cory hugged and kissed goodbye. They both knew it was the last time they would see one another.

Cory, who had been feeling poorly the whole day, was beaming. We got into the car, and he told me he knew why Elisabeth was so special to him and he to her. He said when they touched one another during their hug; he had a flashback memory of a lifetime with her as his loving grandmother. He said my mother was the mom, and he and I were siblings. We lived in what he described as a tall, skinny house where the whole block looked the same. His schoolbooks were bound with leather straps, and he described wearing knicker-style pants, a muffler around his neck, and a "dorky" hat. He said his mother worked and our grandmother (Elisabeth) would see us off to school each day. She would hug and kiss him goodbye just as she had done when we left the studio. His memory was so warm and loving it made him feel better, even though he'd been feeling terrible all day. He couldn't wait to tell my mother about his flashback. My mother and Elisabeth had also made a significant connection during the time we made the teaching videotape at the University of Washington.

Later that evening, we were heading towards home along Lake Washington Boulevard, back from Bill Womack's house where Cory had had his stress management appointment. A song began to play in my head. I started to sing it to Cory who was reclining in the front passenger seat. It was very peaceful. The words and the melody got stronger and louder in my head. Cory was half-asleep, but he listened intently. He told me he liked it. When we got home I had other things to think of, but when I tried to sleep that night the words and music kept haunting me. Unable to sleep, I finally got up and found my mini-tape recorder. I sat up in my bed and sang into the recorder what I had been hearing.

Where are you going, my little one, little one?
Where are you going, my little one, my son?
I'm going with God to the land of the light,
The light we all shine in our hearts.

Why are you going, my little one, little one?
Why are you going, my little one, my son?
I'm going with God to the land of the sun.
My lessons on earth are all done.

Why are you leaving me, baby, leaving me so soon?
Why are you leaving me so soon, my son?
I'm going with God, Mommy. Please don't cry.
It won't be long, and I'll be with you someday.

I'll never forget you, my little one, little one.
I'll never forget you, my little one, my son.
I'll always remember how you made me smile.
We'll be together again in a while.

Why are you going, my little one, little one?
Why are you going without me, my son?
I'm going with God, Mommy. Please don't cry.
I'll love you forever and my sister Brie.

This isn't the whole song, but you should be able to see where I was at, emotionally. It wasn't obvious to me at the time, but I came to realize later that it was all about acceptance. We were actually reassuring each other about the inevitable.

Back to School

Beverly told me that Cory's presence at the school after being told that he was terminal was an obvious learning experience for everyone. The students learned about life, courage, and death. The teachers were forced to look at their own mortality, which is never easy. The Seattle School District had never been faced with a terminally ill child who wanted to be in school. It was wonderful to have someone as understanding and supportive as Beverly, who embraced Cory's desire to continue attending for as long as he could.

Cory's classmates saw him dwindle in size and then swell beyond recognition. They watched as his slim body became so heavy and weak he was forced to use a wheelchair to get around. Right before their eyes, Cory went blind in one eye and then the other. Most of the children were so supportive and actually helped him get around. They truly learned not to fear being around a dying person. And they also learned that children die, too. These are powerful lessons. But maybe the most important lesson Cory taught them was to appreciate life and all it has to offer.

Holey Holy

One day as I was cleaning Cory's room, I spotted a plastic bag stashed between the pedestal of his waterbed and the wall. I had to stretch to reach it. In the bag, I discovered a pair of Cory's old sweats pants. I was very surprised to find them there under the bed because I had thrown them away months before. They were grass stained, way too short for him, and had the knees ripped out. I walked down the stairs with the pants in search of Cory.

All of a sudden I realized why he had them hidden in his room. The little rascal was taking them to his father's house when he went for visits. At first I laughed myself silly. Then I realized why my ex-husband had accused me in court of dressing my children in rags. I stopped laughing and called Cory in to my room to chat.

When I showed him the pants, he started to crack up. When he noticed I wasn't laughing with him, he stopped, and then he sat down on the bed beside me. I asked him what was up with the old sweats that I distinctly remembered tossing in the trash bin.

"You know, Mom, those are my most favorite pants!"

"Uh huh, Cory, try again."

"Ever since the doctor said I was dying, Dad keeps trying to take me to church. And I don't want to go."

"Can't you tell him how you feel?"

"I can't get him to understand that I don't need to go to church. I've walked in God's garden. I don't *need* four brick walls with a sign out front to talk to God. I can talk to God anytime, and I do!"

"And did you explain all this to your dad?"

"Yeah, but he doesn't listen to me."

"So what's with the pants?"

"Well, he kept nagging me to bring over church clothes, so I brought over the holiest pants I could find." With that we both burst into laughter and fell backwards onto my bed. His sense of humor was still intact.

Last Wishes

Cory's nurse wanted to arrange a Wishing Well trip for the three of us. Wishing Well is a Rotary Club program that fulfills wishes for dying children. I tried to convince Cory that he might really like to see the Eiffel Tower or the beautiful beaches of Maui but NO, he wanted to meet David Hasselhoff, the Knight Rider (later, the star of *Baywatch and America's Got Talent*.) He told her Los Angeles was where he wanted to go so he could meet his TV hero.

Within three days, we were on a flight to Los Angeles. Cory and Brie were so excited about meeting David Hasselhoff they could hardly contain themselves. They also wanted to see the talking car. I was having a hard time relaxing because Cory's health took a noticeable nosedive just on the two-hour flight down. He was lethargic. He complained of head and muscle pain, and that was only the beginning.

My friend Patty Rheuban and her kids picked us up at the airport and drove us to the hotel. On the way to the hotel, we were traveling down the freeway, and Cory started having breathing difficulties. I did not know what to do; he'd never reacted that way before. This was not something we had been prepared medically to deal with.

We stopped the car and discussed whether or not we should start searching for a children's hospital. Then Cory's breathing improved, and he insisted he was fine. We took the whole gang out to dinner. Patty's children were fascinated with how much a little boy on steroids could eat.

By the time we checked into the hotel, he was complaining of severe head pain. I became a nervous wreck. I didn't have anything but Tylenol with me, and it didn't seem to be helping at all. I kept debating whether or not I should call Dr. Clark for advice. It was late, so we just hit the hay.

The limousine arrived to pick us up in the morning. Lori McCormack, one of David's managers, accompanied us. I kept an eye on Cory, looking for signs of discomfort. The drive took more than an hour. David was filming his series on location at a hotel in the hills above Malibu. Brie thought the limousine ride was far superior to the airplane ride.

When we got to the hotel, David greeted us warmly. What a nice man he turned out to be. He was such a gracious host. He shot a few scenes with Cory sitting in the place of honor, David's chair. Brie sat in the director's chair. Then David took the kids outside to show them the car. There were actually three of the cars used on the show parked outside. Brie could not understand why the cars didn't talk like the one on TV. Cory had it figured out already, so it wasn't such a disappointment to him.

The kids were showered with gifts. Seriously, the trunk of the limousine was filled. I kept wondering how I was going to get all the stuff home.

We were supposed to stay for lunch so Cory could dine with David and go for a spin in the car, but Cory started feeling worse. He hung on for quite a while, but finally the pain was too much. He sadly reported, "Mommy, I got a bad headache and need to go back to the hotel. Please tell David I'm sorry, but I can't stay any longer."

Lori relayed the information to David during one of the breaks. He stopped down the production to say goodbye. I photographed him giving Cory a big, loving hug. With tears in his eyes he told Cory how much his visit meant to him. Cory could hardly believe his ears. That was exactly what he'd intended to tell David. Cory apologized for

David Hasselhoff hugging Cory

having to leave early. David and the entire crew were so touched; they were all wiping away tears as we drove off.

Once back at the hotel, Cory took a long, but restless nap. Several of my cousins who lived in the Los Angeles area came to see us. We had a nice time visiting, but I was fretting the entire time.

Cory was growing weaker right before my eyes. I wasn't sure if the trip had taken this heavy toll on him or if it was just the timing. Whatever the cause, the disease was beginning to wreak havoc on his body, and it was painfully obvious. Even more frightening was how ill-prepared I was to deal with the changes.

We were scheduled to have a private Universal Studios tour the next day, but Cory wasn't sure he wanted to go. He was leaning toward one last trip to Disneyland instead. And I was feeling that it was time to head back home to the comfort and familiarity of Children's Hospital and Medical Center.

The next morning as I was heading for the bathroom, I tripped over something on the floor. I flicked on the light and was shocked to see three or four room service food trays scattered around the room. I opened the door to the hallway to put them outside our door and found two more! Cory's drug-induced feelings of starvation and intense cravings had compelled him to order tuna sandwiches and blueberry pie all night long while the rest of us were asleep.

The next day with my Aunty Carol's help and generosity, we made it to Disneyland. I had to rent a wheelchair because Cory was so weak. The amusement park was so packed. Each ride took at least an hour. We only made it on about four or five of them. Trying to push Cory around in a wheelchair was exhausting. He wanted to see *everything* since it would be his last visit to the Magic Kingdom. We did the best we could to cover all that he wanted to experience.

The trip home was a nightmare. The reservation clerk was a big jerk. I had had to change my flight arrangements from the Burbank to the John Wayne Airport when Cory had decided on Disneyland instead of Universal Studios. I had taken care of it over the telephone and was assured there would be no problem. But when we arrived at the ticket counter at John Wayne Airport, the clerk told me he didn't have three seats together. When I told him that I had a sick child and a younger child, he told me I should've thought about asking for "special" treatment in advance. I was dumbfounded. The tickets clearly indicated I was traveling with two children.

I began to unravel emotionally. I was trying to be reasonable with a man who was blatantly rude and uncaring. He kept joking around with his coworkers while I was trying to explain to him there was no way we could sit apart. Neither of my children could sit alone, as Cory was too ill and Brie was too young. He said he was not willing to ask other passengers to shift their seats so we could have three seats together. I insisted that he at least try. I figured it would only take moving one person. I was sure some understanding person would be more than willing to trade seats. I yelled, "It's only a two-hour flight!"

The jerk finally instructed me to take up my problems with the personnel at the gate.

The folks at the gate were much more helpful. Just as I had expected, some nice person was more than happy to be rearranged a little to allow my children and me to sit together.

During our two-hour flight to Portland, the flight attendants on board never once asked if they could help me with anything. Cory was so out of it that he could barely hold his head up. I was trying desperately to keep Brie entertained and Cory comfortable. When our plane stopped in Oregon, I left the kids on board and ran off to find a telephone. I called my mother to ask her to have the airline arrange to meet us at the gate with a wheelchair. It never occurred to me that the flight attendants could have made the arrangements.

This airline was batting a thousand that day. The woman on the telephone told my mother to get to the airport early and make arrangements for a wheelchair there. When my poor mother got to the airport terminal, she approached the desk clerk and politely asked for a wheelchair. The woman behind the counter said rudely and crudely, "Why didn't you make these arrangements in advance?! You should've called in your request. We can't be doing this at the last minute. What's wrong with him anyway, a broken leg or something?"

My brother Tim had had enough. "He's dying. Is that a good enough reason for you? Now get us a wheelchair!" Fortunately for these awful people, we were all so stressed out we never got any of their names so never wrote the company about some of its insensitive employees. Instead, I vowed never to fly that airline again.

When we landed, I carried Cory off the plane. Luckily my mother and brother were right there with a driver and one of those little golf carts so we could all ride. I was physically and mentally exhausted. Brie thought the golf cart was just as much fun as Disneyland. She chattered on about the limousine ride and meeting the Knight Rider. Cory was subdued. We waited for my father to pick us up outside baggage claim. After we were all situated in the car, my father asked the kids what was their favorite part of the trip. They both shouted out, "Room service!" Then they chattered on and on about meeting David Hasselhoff, the Knight Rider, and all of the fun they had watching him tape his show.

Swelling, Soccer, and Sweets

Cory had been playing soccer since he was five years old. When he could not run as much, his coaches made him the goalie. Cory had asked that the other players not be told of his disease. He said he didn't want special treatment. I think he really didn't want pity or for his teammates to think he was physically inferior because of the disease. With Cory as goalie, they were headed for the championship playoffs, which were scheduled for the weekend right after our Wishing Well trip. Before we left, a local newspaper reporter did a feature story about Cory and mentioned that he had just been diagnosed as terminally ill, so despite his intentions, his cancer was no longer a secret.

Cory didn't make it to the soccer playoffs that weekend. His health continued to deteriorate after we got home. Keller picked us up to take us to watch the game, but Cory decided that he did not want to go. His soccer pals were expecting him to play. They had made a team spirit poster in his honor, I guess, because the coaches or the parents had seen the newspaper article. Cory's heart was aching because he couldn't play. He acknowledged that the right thing to do would be to go support his team, but he just couldn't bring himself to watch it from the sidelines stuck in a wheelchair. Funny thing, he opted for a trip to IHOP to eat pancakes instead.

Within a few short weeks of our trip to Los Angeles, Cory ended up in a wheelchair full-time and also hooked up to an oxygen tank. Things changed drastically...and way too fast.

Decadraun caused one of Cory's worst cravings. That's the drug he was taking to reduce the brain swelling. It caused him to crave Twinkies and Ding-Dongs as much as he had previously wanted fried chicken or chicken noodle soup. It seemed worse, though, because everything he wanted was sugary sweet and loaded with calories.

I took him to see Dr. Mike one afternoon. Mike almost fainted when he saw Cory. He had gained about fourteen pounds in one month. Mike gasped and said, "What are you feeding this kid?!"

I said, "Well, all he wants to eat are Twinkies and Ding Dongs. So, I go to the bakery outlet store and buy the junk by the trunk load."

"You can't let him eat all that junk! Gaining so much weight in such a short time could damage his heart! It could kill him!"

"Mike, does that *really* matter at this point?" I asked calmly. "And besides, *you* tell him 'no.' That junk is all he wants, and he's dying anyway!"

"But, but, oh, never mind..." he sputtered.

Cory was so swollen from the disease, the steroids, and the junk food. I walked in on him in the bathroom crying at the sight of his image in the mirror. He turned to me and sadly slumped down onto the edge of the bathtub. I asked what was bothering him.

"That's not my face in the mirror, Mommy. That's not me." Tears streamed down his face.

"Honey, the real you is still inside your body. I know it must be hard to see yourself so swollen, but you know who you are. Try not to look in the mirror if it upsets you."

"I used to be so skinny, and now look at me."

"I know, honey, but it doesn't matter what's on the outside does it? You know what a wonderful person you are on the inside."

"Thanks, Mom."

I hugged him, and he smiled.

Cory in Soccer Uniform

Being Normal

Cory's idea of being as normal as possible for as long as he could got harder with each passing day, especially when it came to getting him to school. Even in the wheelchair, he insisted that I put him on the bus anyway. The bus driver never mentioned that the school district had mini-vans with hydraulic lifts to accommodate wheelchairs, but I'm not so sure Cory would've agreed to that anyway.

He liked riding the bus with his friends. My biggest problem was getting him and the wheelchair up the steps and onto the bus. The driver never tried to help. It could be that she couldn't get up from her seat for some reason, but she never even offered an explanation. She would just sit there and watch me struggle to get him on the darn bus. A few times I felt as if she was irritated because I was taking so long to get him on. Towards the end, I got a little smarter and met the bus at the end of the route so that the older boys could help me lift the wheelchair onto the bus.

When Cory could no longer help himself climb up on to the bus, my brother Bobby would drive him to school for me. He didn't usually last very long, maybe an hour or two. Then, one of us would go pick him up. Days would go by, and Cory would be too wiped out to go to school. On those days, he would stay with my mom and dad.

Brie came home from school one day distressed. She reported that one of their schoolmates, a thirteen-year-old boy, had declared suicide intentions. Cory was extremely alarmed. He insisted on going to school to talk with this boy. That evening, Cory and I called Beverly. Yes, Beverly had heard the news about this boy. Apparently it was all out in the open. Even though Cory's little body was swollen and he was having a difficult time breathing, he asked Beverly to arrange a meeting with the three of them. Cory said he thought the other kids weren't very nice to this boy sometimes because he was so sensitive... and that's what Cory liked most about him. He wanted the chance to tell this boy how he felt.

The next day, Beverly and Cory met with the boy in her office. Cory told him, "All I want is to have a healthy body to stay here in. And I would want to stay. You can't give up what you have for nothing. You can get help. If you are having problems, talk to Beverly or to my mom or to my friend Dr. Womack. Killing yourself would be like spitting in God's face. God's gift to us is life, and you can't destroy it." He went on to talk of his experiences on the other side of the Rainbow Bridge, which he said taught him about people who took their own lives. They had to go to a dark place to contemplate their actions before they could enter the place of light. It wasn't a punishment but a hard lesson he did not recommend.

Beverly says that at that point she watched a potentially suicidal thirteen-year-old see that things were not so terrible. In fact, he came out of his depression with a glowing awareness.

The story of Cory's wisdom spread. Several other teens that were thinking of suicide sought him out. Beverly invited a few students that she had heard weren't doing well emotionally to talk with Cory, too. He met with each and every one of them. One young girl revealed her secret to Cory—physical and sexual abuse at the hands of yet another foster parent. She cried and expressed her fear and shattered trust. Cory urged her to trust at least one more grown-up. He suggested she talk with Beverly. He believed Beverly could help her. He begged her not to take her life. She took his advice and was immediately moved to a safe foster home. All of the students Cory counseled survived their crises, and last I heard, they are all continuing to do well.

Another one of the memorable things about Cory's last days at school was how he treated his sister. Brie wanted to follow him around constantly. I think she was afraid he would die and she wouldn't be able to say goodbye. Cory, on the other hand, felt that she was cramping his style. This was a child who wanted more than anything to feel "normal." Having his kid sister shadow every move he made did nothing but enhance his need for privacy.

Beverly called me at work to express her concerns about Cory's treatment of Brie. We both deduced that he was trying to "cut the umbilical cord" between Brie and him. But it sounded as if he was being absolutely brutal in his approach. I assured Beverly that I would talk with him.

That evening, I sat with Cory and gently asked how things were going at school. He had no complaints. I said, "What about Brie? Is she doing okay?"

Cory's response was neutral at first. Then he unloaded, "She's following me everywhere! I can't have a conversation without her hanging around. She has to learn how to take care of herself. I won't be there, and she has to be able to go it alone."

I asked him if he couldn't be a wee bit nicer about pushing her away. I said, "Honey, you don't want her to remember you being mean, do you?" Cory began to cry. He admitted his anger and frustration about dying. He even copped to the idea that maybe, just maybe, he was taking a bit of this anger out on Brie.

We sat holding each other for a few minutes. Again, I asked him to consider how she would feel after he was gone, if her last memories would be of him being mean to her. Cory acknowledged Brie's position in the whole process of his dying. But he also needed to have his struggle with acceptance of his impending death to be heard. I listened and cried for his pain.

He said, "You are all losing me. I am one person. As the one who is dying, I am losing all of you. I have to let go of hundreds of people. I think I am entitled to be upset and angry."

I said, "Yes, you are entitled. But it is not okay to take that anger out on your sister. She loves you. She will miss you forever. And you love her. Don't make her suffer your anger, too." Cory went to Brie and apologized.

Brie at six years old was very understanding. She hugged her brother and accepted his apologies with grace. However, she did continue to follow him around at school. It didn't last long, though. Soon after, Cory could no longer attend school. His efforts to get ready in the morning became too painful. Cory's prediction came true sooner than he had thought: Brie rode the bus alone.

One Last Look

Cory was blind in one eye and bloated beyond recognition, but he insisted on going to school one last time to accommodate the television camera crew from KOMO-TV.

Elaine Purchase, who had done the earlier story about our family, had asked to do a follow-up story. She recognized what a special child Cory was and how his dying with such dignity could enlighten others.

After the first television experience and several newspaper articles, we received a number of telephone calls from reporters who wanted to interview Cory. He turned them all down because he wasn't feeling well after our trip to Los Angeles. One evening he was feeling particularly grumpy and harried by the attention he was receiving. He turned to me and said; "Now I know how David [Hasselhoff] feels! Everybody wants a piece of me!"

The main reason he agreed to the follow-up story with Elaine was because she wanted to videotape him at school. He loved AS#1 so much, and he wanted people to see what a terrific school it was. He had spent so many hours on the couch in Beverly's office and had listening to her fight with the school district for funding. He told me, "I want those people to see AS#1 is not the bastard of the Seattle School

District." Colorful language, I know. I allowed him to swear to express his anger once he could not physically beat up the couch. I told him that he just couldn't use the really bad words. He had a string of words that became his mantra: S-GD-SOB. Sometimes in the middle of the night I could hear him swearing over and over again because he was either in pain or so frustrated by his physical limitations.

Elaine interviewed several people, including children, about Cory's presence in the school. Some told how they were no longer afraid of dying because Cory had taught them it was a natural part of life. Others expressed some fear that he might die at school. Beverly relayed the story about eight-year-old Cory successfully counseling suicidal teens. Cory was indeed a teacher not just a student.

Beverly assessed what she witnessed as a "Death-and-dying Curriculum of the greatest magnitude." Then she wrote, "There is not a person in this school who will ever be afraid of being near a dying person. Rather, we will look for the wisdom to learn more about life. I am left with a deep feeling of love, a strength for survival, and a most unique understanding of children and their approach to life."

Cory's last project at the school was beading a pair of earrings for me. On that last day while Elaine was there, that's what he concentrated on. I had no idea he was making me a Mother's Day gift. It was painful to watch him struggling to see with his one good eye. He would actually pry it open to see once in awhile. His teacher, Karen, helped him. I had to turn away a few times to keep the tears from flowing. I was sure he'd be embarrassed if I cried at his school.

After overhearing the kids' interviews with them telling Elaine how his dying was affecting them, Cory said to Karen, "I am so lucky, and I have so much to be thankful for." He looked up at her puzzled face and continued, "I got to be eight, and I got to see Elisabeth again."

After Elaine and the cameraman left, Cory went out for his last recess. I watched him from a distance as he traded a girl on the playground his wheelchair for a turn on her skates. Unfortunately, his balance was off, and he was so weak it would have been impossible for him to support his weight. Normally I would have been worried, but I knew he wouldn't be able to do it. But I so admired his spunk. He finally gave up trying to stand on the skates, but he wasn't upset about it. I think Cory knew there was no loss of dignity because he had made the best effort possible under the circumstances.

He told Elaine he wanted to go skiing on the weekend. Cory also had asked our friend Brian if he could come down and work at his popcorn shop in the Pike Place Market in Seattle. Our friends owned this great flavored popcorn store. Cory negotiated with Brian. He drove a pretty hard bargain, too. He wanted ten bucks per hour! Brian finally talked him down to $7.50 plus all the popcorn he could eat.

We went down there the following Saturday. Cory was so serious. He filled the popcorn orders and made change. It was a hoot...until Cory's headaches came on like a ton of bricks. Getting up and down out of his wheelchair to serve people made him a little dizzy. But it was the headaches that short-circuited his moneymaking venture. He was happy to go home, anyway, because his legs were beginning to bother him, as well.

Elaine was able to get some great footage of Cory hanging in there, though. His determination to work while hopping in and out of his wheelchair with the use of one eye showed the amazing strength of his spirit.

Birthday Bash

For Cory's ninth birthday, I searched for a way to accommodate all of the people who I knew wanted to help him celebrate. We agreed an open house would be the best. I had naively theorized that the open house would have people stopping by in shifts, but what happened? No one wanted to leave once they got there. We had two hundred visitors, and most stayed. We had a great time anyway. Poor Cory was so swollen and attached to his oxygen tank that it was hard for him to move around. He had cousins, classmates, soccer mates, and his oldest and dearest friends gathered around, and he made the best of it. He truly had a wonderful time.

Cory was an all-American boy. A few months before his birthday, he had asked me for a male Cabbage Patch doll. He wanted a new friend. I think he thought carrying Danger the bear around was a little too babyish for him. Have you ever heard that wonderful tune on Marlo Thomas' album, *Free to Be You and Me*? It's called "William Wants a Doll." This song describes a five-year-old boy's desire for a doll to love and hold and how his father and others ridicule him. Cory could definitely relate to William. I thought it was sweet that Cory wanted a doll to hug.

For his birthday, Cory got a whole wardrobe for Adam Alexander, his new Cabbage Patch friend. He really appreciated receiving the clothes because it was too painful to play with much else. He would sit up in bed and talk to Adam for hours.

The day after the party, on March 18, Cory's actual birthday, he got a telephone call from Lori McCormack, David Hasselhoff's manager. David was trying to call Cory from Australia to wish him "happy birthday" and to find out who had won the soccer championship. I was so impressed that he had remembered Cory's birthday and made the effort to call him. David's thoughtfulness really made Cory feel good at an especially tough time. Cory was more than a wee bit sad to tell him that he didn't get to play in the soccer championship with the rest of his team. He did keep to himself that he hadn't even gone to the game.

Later, Lori told me that David had been deeply impacted by Cory's courage and strength.

Five years after, quite by accident, I discovered that David had made a very nice donation to Seattle Children's Hospital in Cory's name. Apparently David didn't want a big deal made out of it, and I wasn't notified. One of my friends saw the memorial plaque displayed in the hospital. I immediately called Lori because I was embarrassed that I hadn't sent a thank-you note. She told me not to be concerned. I sent the note anyway.

Cory at his ninth birthday

Easter

Easter was a big deal to Cory and Brie. For Cory it was second only to Halloween. But I had been so distraught the night before Easter arrived that I had forgotten to purchase eggs and dye. It was a miracle I'd remembered to purchase stuff for their baskets. In a panic, I telephoned my brother Bobby to ask if he would come over and stay with my sleeping children so I could zip down to the grocery store.

All the way there, I was thanking God for twenty-four-hour grocery stores. Of course, there was no egg dye left on the shelf so I bought food coloring instead. Luckily, they did have eggs. I went straight home to boil the eggs. The food coloring was a good idea in theory, but it came out so faint on the eggs it was almost not worth the hassle. I chastised myself through the entire, miserable process. *"How could I have blown it? I just can't let Cory down!"*

Cory's bed was in the living room so he could be near the action. Our living room was steps away from the kitchen. I tried to be as quiet as possible. By 3:00 a.m., I was stumbling around in the dark trying to hide the eggs and candy for Cory and Brie to find in the morning. Our tradition called for the kids to find an empty basket outside their bedroom doors that they would fill as they followed a trail of goodies left by the Easter Bunny. (I know, I know—not much religion built into this tradition. But we would have gone to church if Cory hadn't been so sick and immune-suppressed all those years).

I didn't want to make Cory's trail too difficult because he was blind and hardly able to move around, but I didn't want to insult him, either. As I tiptoed behind the reclining chair situated across the room from Cory's bed, I stubbed my bare toe on a table leg. I grabbed my foot and hopped around in agony with my free hand covering my mouth. Unfortunately, I had yelped out a cuss word on impact. Cory stirred in his sleep. I momentarily froze. When I thought the coast was clear, I crept out of the room. I dropped onto my bed in a heap and fell asleep.

In the morning, I was awakened by squeals of delight coming from Brie, the Candy Queen. I threw my robe on and went in to check on Cory. He was sitting up in his bed, counting candy eggs. I asked how he was doing. He snapped back, "The Easter Bunny left me a lot of candy and eggs, but my trail was too short and too easy! It wasn't challenging enough, not even for a blind kid!" Then he recovered for a second and got very serious and said, "Guess what else happened, Mama?" "I *heard* the Easter Bunny!"

"You did?!"

"Yeah, it was just after three o'clock in the morning, 'cuz I heard the grandfather clock. And I heard him as he was leaving his trail of eggs and goodies for Brie and me! I *DID*! I *heard* him! He said a bad word; he said 'Oh shhh...,' but I'm not sure why."

"Ooooh?" I patted him on the head, leaned down and kissed him, and left the room to check on Brie. She was sitting on the bottom stair eating chocolate eggs for breakfast. I asked her if she had heard the Bunny, too. She replied, "No, but Cory said he heard the Bunny say a bad word." Boy, did I ever feel guilty. With one bad word and a swollen toe I had tarnished the Easter Bunny's reputation.

Several hours later, I heard Cory on the telephone. From what he was saying, I guessed he was talking to my mother. He was explaining how he had crawled around the living and dining rooms in search of the Bunny's goodies. I almost fell over when I heard Cory saying, "Yeah Grandma, you'll never believe it. I SAW the Easter Bunny! Yeah, I did. It was last night around 3:00 a.m.!" He was such a believer...

Cory loved the Easter candy, but he didn't really like to eat it. Just having it was enough for him. He was pretty weak and wasn't able to get around much. He was also dealing with the loss of his vision. So he sat up in his bed sorting and re-sorting the candy. He also counted each type of candy over and over again. Our friend, Vikki Pavone, who was also my brother Bobby's girlfriend, walked in and, without saying a word, nipped a couple of chocolate eggs from one of Cory's piles. She was sitting in the recliner in the opposite corner of the room enjoying the candy when he recounted his chocolate eggs." Aaannnteee Vikeee! Did you steal some of my eggs?" he yelled across the room. A red-faced Vikki almost choked on the egg she was eating. She apologized several times before he finally forgave her.

I tried to convince him to share the candy since he didn't like to eat it anyway. But it must have symbolized past Easters when he was healthy and able to enjoy himself because he refused to share the precious candy, protecting it as if it was gold.

R~E~S~P~E~C~T

At the time Cory was dying, hospice for children did not exist. But Visiting Nurse Services, which provided hospice care for adults, agreed to take Cory on as its first child patient.

When Cory first began getting regular visits from hospice nurses, he took it in his stride. There were two of them, and they rotated their visits. Cory complied with their requests to roll up his sleeves or put the thermometer under his tongue.

The first month they came twice. As the cancer cells multiplied and the symptoms of his dreaded disease progressed, they decided between themselves when to come on a weekly basis.

The interesting thing about having hospice help for me was that they never seemed to work for us. I don't mean that in the negative sense, but there really wasn't much communication with me at all. They just appeared one day and then fixed their own routine. I was usually at work, and Cory was usually at my mother's house during that time. So I was never included in their decisions about when and how often they planned to see Cory.

One day, Elaine Falangus, one of Cory's nurses, knocked at the door to my mother's house. My mom let her in. Cory was sitting quietly in the living room sorting his prized possessions. He carried them around in a backpack. This was a favorite past time for a little boy who could no longer be active. He looked up suspiciously as Elaine entered the room. She casually said, "Hi, Cory."

Cory's rummaging around in the backpack came to a sudden halt. Then he looked up and asked rather rudely, "What are *you* doing here?"

Elaine replied, "I came by to see how you're doing."

To which Cory said, "No, what are you doing here again this week?"

Elaine responded cheerfully, "Well, Deb and I thought it might be a good idea to start coming two times a week now."

Unruffled, Cory stared at her point blank with great consternation and queried, "Did you make an appointment? I don't recall you making an appointment."

Startled, Elaine answered, "Well, no, but..."

Cory raised his hand to silence her and then interrupted, asking, "Do you just drop in on your adult patients without making an appointment?"

Poor Elaine, obviously becoming quite uncomfortable, replied, "Well, no but..."

Cory displayed dogged determination by again interrupting to ask; "Don't I deserve the same respect as your other patients?"

Well, as you can imagine, Elaine knew that he was absolutely right in his indignation, but his reaction took her by surprise. She began to apologize profusely and suggested that maybe she should just check his blood pressure very quickly and get the heck out of there.

Cory raised his hand to quiet her again, grinned slyly at my mother, and said, "Okay, sit right there and hang on a sec." Then, he proceeded to reach into his precious bag of goodies. Elaine sat down in the chair where he had gestured. As she sat there watching him and looking rather sheepish, Cory pulled out an emery board and started filing his nails! According to my mother, this went on for about five minutes. After the first few minutes, Elaine sat quietly and waited in silence for Cory again to acknowledge her presence. He did not even glance in her direction as he concentrated on his task. He had to make sure every nail was filed just perfectly. Elaine glanced around the room. Then she stared blankly at the TV and finally down at her watch. She told me later that she was feeling rather silly, so she decided to speak up.

With some hesitation, Elaine whispered, "Cory, can we take care of this now? I got your point."

Cory arched his back in triumph, turned to gaze directly into her eyes with his one good eye and said, "Okay, I'm ready now."

Elaine sprang out of her chair to seize the moment. She wasn't too sure he wouldn't change his mind. She did the fastest checkup she could, apologizing the entire time. After she left, she stopped at a pay telephone to call me at my office. She relayed the entire incident. I wasn't sure at first if she was complaining or not. It sounded to me as if Cory had been pretty brutal. I felt sorry for her, but at the same time I could understand exactly where my son was coming from. After more than five years of being treated without respect, he was up to his ears with adults acting as if his opinion didn't count because of his age. As far as Cory was concerned, a patient is a patient, and it shouldn't matter how old or young you are.

At the conclusion of her story, Elaine promised me that she would never treat another child patient without heeding Cory's admonishment about deserving equal respect. By then, we were both laughing about what a little character he was. But at the same time, Elaine acknowledged how much she had learned from Cory and how courageous he was to take a stand.

Elaine was married but did not have children yet. I suspect she was not used to kids like Cory. And her hospice agency had never served children prior to Cory. Elaine said she was definitely unprepared for a patient his size with such a strong will. As Elisabeth Kubler-Ross, Cory's dear friend, always reminded him, he was not a student; he did not come here to learn; he came to teach. Elaine shared the lessons she had learned from Cory with her co-workers. Great ripple effect...

Flying Free

My poetry inspirations continued to come to me in my alpha-state of sleep—the hazy, dreamy, just-before-waking-up state. Cory derived a great deal of comfort from my poetry that dealt with him. I think for some sad reason, he was worried that after he died people would forget about him.

This is one of my favorite poems that came to me from different incidents with Cory. On several occasions, he'd told me not to weep when he died because he would be in a better place and all the love he brought to me would still be with me. He had also described how he would dance on the stars after he died. One time, Cory, Brie, and I were walking home from my parents' house and he pointed out which stars he thought his friends Krisser and Ian were dancing on. And during a walk downtown with me, he once remarked on a gracefully floating leaf. As he watched it drift down, the beauty of its elegance mesmerized him. And, of course, he shared Elisabeth's philosophy about butterflies. Many of his drawings featured brightly colored butterflies. He told me they represented the release of the soul from the body at the time of death like a butterfly leaving its cocoon. His wisdom and incredible insights live on in my poem.

THE FREEDOM OF FLIGHT

Don't weep for me when I have gone away.
Death is not like the end of the play.
It's like the freedom of the butterfly's first flight.
I won't really be gone...only from sight.
All the love that I brought here with me from birth
Will always be with you, while you are on Earth...
I will be back in God's loving embrace.
So please wipe those tears of sadness off your face.
Be happy I'm free from pain and despair,
Free like the birds that soar through the air.
I will always be with you, in everything you see.
Wherever you look will remind you of me...
A flower in bloom, a new bud on a tree
And even a dandelion growing in the lawn.
But please don't think of me as gone...
A kids' game of soccer, a familiar song you will hear,
Comic books, cartoons, and "Danger" my favorite bear.
Don't think of death as the end of me.
It's just the beginning of my flight to be free...
Don't mourn my passing because I will be
As one with God, all knowingness and light.
I will dance on the stars that shine in the night
Or glide like a leaf caught in a gentle breeze
Or soar on the wind with a bird's grace and ease.
Maybe hitch a ride on the tail of a kite
All with the magic and freedom
of a butterfly's first flight.

The Beauty of His Spirit

"*All I ever want is for you to remember me loving you.*"

The love of a child is so pure. My sweet little boy was lying in my arms one evening, actually half lying-half sitting up when he said these words to me. I will cherish them forever.

It all started on a Tuesday in April. I was at the Harbor Club for lunch with my boss and several clients. The maitre d' arrived at our table with a telephone. Trembling with fear, I reached for the handset. I can remember the feeling of not wanting to take the receiver knowing, if someone was calling me at the Harbor Club, that it couldn't be good news. I took a deep breath before I said hello. At the other end, the very serious quavering voice of my younger brother, Bobby, said with incredible urgency, "Sis, you better come home quick. It's bad. The doctor said she'll meet you here."

I quickly leaned over, grabbed my purse, and whispered to my boss that I had to get home as Cory had apparently taken a swift downturn in his condition. I remember the ride down in the elevator but have no recollection of getting to my car, being in my car, or driving home. My heart was pounding in my ears. I was so afraid of what I would find when I reached home.

After slamming the car into park, I rushed into the house. Cory was lying down in the living room. He looked like he was beyond the Rainbow Bridge. I swept across the room to his bedside. My poor brother looked terror-stricken. I asked what had been going on. "Cory was vomiting quite severely and now nothing. He's not moving, Sis. I'm scared."

I rushed to Cory's bedside as Bobby was talking. I could see that he was still breathing. Bobby was right, though; he was not moving at all. I asked him to call Lynn and ask her to come down to our house.

Lynn arrived to help me. I was also expecting our friend Shirlee Kimball that afternoon. I telephoned Shirlee and asked her to drop by Brie's school on the way over to bring her home early...just in case it was time for Cory to go.

I telephoned Beverly to let her know that Cory had taken a serious turn for the worse and that Shirlee would be there to pick up Brie.

No one had ever been sent to get Brie prior to that day. When Shirlee arrived, she went directly to Beverly's office, and Beverly escorted her to Brie's classroom. When Beverly and Shirlee appeared in the doorway, Brie froze in her footsteps. Her face reflected the fear that gripped her little heart. Of course, she expected the worst news possible. Shirlee tried to calm her fears by telling her Cory was still alive and by adding that the doctor was on her way to our house. Brie told me later that she thought he had already gone and that's why someone had come for her.

When Brie arrived at home, she saw that he was still breathing but unconscious. I didn't realize until then that for years she had been waiting for the other shoe to drop...always anticipating the bad news. I felt sorry for her knowing that she had been worrying all that time. She was, and is, a very private person. She would swallow the pain and hold it inside.

I hugged Brie and held her on my lap. She waited around for a little while. Then she asked if she could go outside. I think it must have been scary for her. Later, I saw her peeking into the living room at her brother's motionless body. The fear of actually seeing him die was obvious on her little face. I finally told her she could go over to my parents' house to play with Brooke and Zach, Shirlee's children.

Without a moment's hesitation, she skipped happily down the block to the swing set.

Shirlee's husband, Brian, came over to pick up Brooke and Zach since Shirlee had offered to stay over with Lynn and me to help us care for Cory.

Dr. Clark arrived that evening. After examining Cory, she breathed a sigh of relief. He didn't have a brain bleed. Apparently, his physical inactivity kept his body from flushing out the methadone, and the drug had built up in his blood, causing his condition. She wasn't sure how he would progress, but it didn't appear he would die immediately. She told us this first night would be crucial.

That first night, Shirlee, Lynn, and I fell in to a routine rather quickly. Cory was tossing his cookies all night long.

One of the two would run for clean washcloths and a towel, the other would get clean bedding, and I would hold Cory's head to the side so he wouldn't choke. By morning, we were weary but hopeful because he had made it through the night.

Lynn and Shirlee went back to their families the next evening. Cory was still comatose, but he was no longer vomiting.

Day after day, as the minutes and hours ticked by, I kept a vigil by his bedside. He was breathing but did not stir. I held his hand and stroked his face and hair while I silently prayed he would awaken. Time was meaningless, and I cared not that I had no money coming in while I was off work. I knew I would have to deal with all that earthly stuff later. I thought I had lost him without the ability to really say goodbye and tell him how much I loved him. It's very interesting the thoughts that pass through your brain when you sit for hours staring helplessly at your child. Well, some things are interesting and some are just plain weird. His drug-induced coma lasted for six and a half very long and frightening days.

On the seventh day, it felt as if something magical had happened when I heard his tiny voice in the wee hours of the morning whispering, "Thirsty...Mama...thirsty." I had fallen asleep in the chair across the living room from his bed. I was reclined and sort of in a half-sleep state since it was not all that easy or comfortable to sleep in the chair. I jumped off the chair and practically flew to his side. My heart was bursting with joy to hear him speak. In a heartbeat, I acknowledged his request and ran to the kitchen to get him refreshment. Cory was only able to take two sips of juice, but it didn't matter; he had come back from limbo land, and I was thrilled.

Sitting beside him on the floor, I clutched his little hand. He asked me in his weak little voice, "What day is it, Mama? Did I miss Mother's Day?"

I laughed and said, "No, honey, but don't you worry about that. I'm just so happy you're awake." Mother's Day was not important to me, but it definitely was to him. Little did I know just how important it was to Cory until later when I had time to think about it. I was just so relieved that he had come out of his coma.

I asked how he was feeling and where he had been. He said he was feeling airy, not quite grounded. Of his experience he described mostly just sleeping and listening to the activity around him. He said he could hear and sense those around him. He laughed when I told him about Uncle Mark, Uncle Tim, Shirlee, Lynn, and me drinking Amaretto out of coffee mugs with our ice cubes tinkling while his doctor had been there the first night of his coma.

We were being silly together again. That's all that seemed to matter. I was afraid to think beyond that moment. Knowing you have absolutely no control over your life or worse, over your son's life, is beyond gut wrenching. I can only describe it as feeling like treading water with legs so tired that the pain radiates up your body and permeates your entire being.

While Cory was becoming less and less interested in his surroundings—actually seeming to be asleep most of the time—the days stretched out. They felt long, scary, and hollow. At the time, I felt the pain and sadness of his impending death with every second as it slipped away, knowing that soon he would no longer be with me. Not only would he not be with me, but also he wouldn't be there to share his life with his sister, my parents, and his uncles, aunts, cousins, or friends. It was hard to picture in my mind what our lives would be like without him. I tried to imagine, but I couldn't know. No one knows until it happens. I think your mind won't let you conceive of it because the pain is too great.

The deterioration of Cory's health was escalating. We couldn't remember being warned about what to expect. I'm not criticizing the docs, but it was a tremendous burden to watch my child die an inch at a time. Cory and I talked about it and decided that the doctors couldn't possibly know what to tell us. He was a different case no matter what odds they ever gave us, so we accepted the challenge and dealt with it the best we could. *"Death is beautiful, but dying sucks!"* Another one of Cory's memorable quotes. These words mean so much to me now. It may sound strange, but in fact, it is very true. Cory's trips to the other side told him and me that death was not something to be feared but welcomed. The thing we weren't prepared for was the deterioration of his physical body. That's what he was referring to when he said, "Dying sucks!" We just weren't ready for the blindness, hearing loss, or hypersensitivity and his not being able to carry his own weight.

When we were told he would die soon, we accepted that, but we never gave any real thought to the actual process. Cory's eyes could see, but because the disease affected the nerves that send the impulse to his muscles, he couldn't open his eyelids. Fortunately, both eyes didn't go at the same time. It was a very heavy blow for him when the second eye became useless. He cried and begged me to call Elisabeth to come help him. He just knew she would know what to do to fix his eyes. At one point he wanted me to get toothpicks to prop them open or take him to the hospital to have his eyelids removed. Talk about desperate!

I had to calm him down and explain that Elisabeth was in Europe somewhere and there really wasn't anything anyone could do. Trying to get him to listen and understand this concept was one of the toughest things I had to do for him. He had always been so courageous. Seeing the fear and pain he was experiencing pierced my heart.

Sometimes, I would try to forget he was dying. I was torn between wanting to escape into denial to pretending it was not happening, but my intellect would click in, and I had to reckon with the knowledge that I had to make the most of each precious second of his life. I did not want to deal with regrets later.

I wasn't sure if it was his disease or denial, but once or twice Cory asked me if I thought he would need braces on his teeth in the future.

I responded, "No, honey, your teeth are as straight as mine." I figured it couldn't hurt for him to escape once in a while, but he had the straightest teeth I'd ever seen.

We were sitting up late one evening not too long after he had awakened from the coma. I was watching TV, and Cory was listening to it. His poor little cancer-ravaged body was extremely sensitive, so much so it was hard to hold him. In fact, if anyone bumped his bed even slightly, he would cry out in pain. So I was sitting very still and carefully holding him as he snuggled next to me and said, "All I ever want is for you to remember me loving you."

The beauty of his spirit will sustain me for the rest of my life. No matter how down I get about *anything*—finances, physical pain, fear of failing—it doesn't matter; I think of his swollen little body snuggled up next to me saying those comforting words—him comforting me! And truly, nothing else matters.

"The Courage of Cory"

Elaine Purchase was having a hard time finishing the story about Cory. It was difficult coordinating the camera crew's availability with Cory's physical condition. He was either too sick, or she couldn't get a camera crew. He went into his methadone-induced coma when the piece was nearing completion. To save the project, she changed the focus a little and interviewed people, asking how Cory had affected their lives. It was a good save.

Cory came out of his comatose state in time to see the piece when it aired. It was a wonderfully produced tribute to Cory's courageous outlook on life. He was critical of some of the statements his classmates made, but other than that, I think he appreciated it. He especially liked the scenes shot at his school.

People who saw the story about Cory on television got a sense of who he was—a courageous little boy who was living every moment to the fullest. One of Cory's favorite little ditties that he liked to whisper to me was "LIVE like there's no tomorrow. LOVE with all your heart. LAUGH until your spirit lights up. And BE HAPPY!" He believed those words. In fact, I think he embodied them.

Cards and notes arrived in the mail. They were from strangers who had seen Cory on television or read about him in the newspaper. Cory was very touched by their care and concern. He was a little puzzled by the attention he was receiving because to him the stories were no big deal—he was just being Cory.

As his health slipped away, Cory's spirit retreated. He spent most of his time snoozing. Many of our friends came by to see how we were holding up. They also wanted to say their goodbyes to Cory before it was too late. Donna read Elisabeth's book, *Remember the Secret*, to him. Another friend performed Reiki, an ancient Japanese healing technique, on his aching muscles. Our friends from the Children's Connection came over, and we all sat around Cory's bed, holding hands and silently praying for him. The loving support was wonderful and uplifted all of us.

I have always been fiercely independent which makes it hard to accept help. Learning to accept graciously was a gift I hadn't anticipated. For that I will always be grateful. The experience enriched my life and Brie's as well.

When I look back on my life, I can see how much Cory changed my path, my philosophies, and my sense of who I am at my core. So I guess there is always a silver lining, just as my grandfather had always said. These two shaped my life: Cory's wisdom gave me direction, and my grandfather's words kept me sane.

Dogged Determination

One morning as I was passing the open door to my bedroom, I caught a glimpse of my waterbed. I hadn't slept in it for weeks! I had been sleeping on the floor next to Cory's bed in the living room, mostly, or in the reclining chair. That bed looked so inviting. In a split second, I decided to lie down for just a minute. I was luxuriating in the warmth and, more important, in the fact that it wasn't a hard floor when I heard a sound next to the bed. I rolled over and strained my neck to see over the edge. I peeked over the side rail and to my utter amazement I saw that Cory had crawled all the way to my room, searching for me. I asked him what he was doing, feeling just a twinge of guilt for having left him alone in the living room. Mostly, I was blown away that he was physically able to do such a thing.

He answered me with a half-grin, "Oh, just getting some exercise." I cracked up and rolled off the bed to reach him. His spirit was so strong! It was a struggle, but together we managed to get him back to the living room.

I had a difficult time getting him onto his bed. We were both exhausted afterwards. Cory was especially tired after his trek around the house, but he was so darn proud of his accomplishment. Cory had every right to his pride: He was blind in both eyes and hadn't been out of bed for at least five weeks.

That was his second to the last outing. On his last excursion, I was in the kitchen whipping up some cereal for him. Towards the end, that was all he could eat. As a matter of fact, that's all he wanted. And each day, the amount he was able to consume was considerably less and less. That is such a bizarre experience for a mother, for this mother anyway. A mother is supposed to feed and nurture. And food means mothering, right? It was frightening to have him go almost six and a half weeks hardly eating. And during the coma, he had no nourishment at all. After he came out of the coma, he ate maybe once a day and very little, at the very most, only a few spoonfuls of cereal.

On this particular day, I walked into the dining room to find him trying to climb into a chair at the dining room table. They were wood, ladder-back chairs, but sort of lightweight and not very sturdy. The sight scared the heck out of me! Gasping for air, and trying to remain calm so as not to frighten him, I said, "Cory, what ya doin'?"

He turned his head in my direction and announced that he was sick and tired of being stuck in that bed and he wanted to eat at the dining room table like everyone else. I could see that there was no way to persuade him to do otherwise, so I helped him get up into the chair.

To support his effort, I stepped away. It was only a few feet back, but I watched him carefully because I was unsure of his ability to balance. The sun was streaming into the dining room. It was a glorious spring day, but nothing could compare to the look on his face. His determination had paid off, and he was jubilant. Leaning up against the table's edge, he lasted less than two minutes in the chair. But the short time didn't matter; I think all he really wanted was his dignity.

During this time his pain had been getting worse and worse. I could not understand why he was hanging on to this life that was so filled with terrible bouts of pain. I had come to believe he was a very spiritual soul and that he had more control over his destiny than some of us less enlightened people. It never occurred to me that he wanted to stay for a specific reason.

I kept the house as peaceful as I possibly could. I kept a fire burning in the evenings and candles lit on the mantle. It was important, I felt, to control the number of visitors in the house at one time. My limit was three. Any more than that and people would forget why they were there and make too much noise. Cory's hearing had become unbelievably and excruciatingly hypersensitive.

His normally skinny body was so grossly swollen from the drugs and disease. His skin was stretched so thin. That's why it hurt him so if anyone bumped his bed. In some areas of his poor little body, the skin was actually tearing. I have never seen anything quite like it and hope to Jesus that I never see such a painful thing again.

While he was lying there on his bed in the living room, Cory would eavesdrop on conversations. He loved listening. Most of the time, he appeared to be asleep, but in reality he was merely resting. Every now and then, he would pipe up to correct someone's story. It was so funny one time: His grandfather was reminiscing, and out of the blue this exasperated little voice shouted, "No, Grandpa, that's not the way it happened at all!" And then Cory went on to tell his version of the story. He liked to correct grammar and vocabulary, too. He had always been exceptionally bright, but he was never a "know it all" until then. We were all so happy to hear him speak no one minded that he was being a little snippy sometimes.

One night some friends came by to check on us. Brian and Shirlee and Mark and Brenda brought over Chinese food for dinner. It was a much-needed break from our routine.

We were in the dining room, which flowed right into the living room where Cory was sleeping. We kept fairly quiet, but as I said before, when too many people got together, it was too noisy. We were having fun and had to keep reminding each other to keep it down. Finally, Cory shouted in a very disgusted tone, "Speak up! I can't hear what you guys are saying!" We all broke out laughing. Usually he would complain if the noise around him got to be too much. But for this group, he loved everyone who was there, and I think that made all the difference in how he reacted. Plus he was pretty nosey!

He had always been interested in my stories about growing up. His sense of family was just one of his many strengths. Cory loved to hear my sisters and me talk about the shenanigans we pulled during junior and senior high school. While he was still able to converse, he asked me to retell stories from my teen years. Cory's godmother, Donna, and I were involved in a race riot at our high school. He always wanted to hear the story about us getting the stuffing knocked out of us. The injustice of it always got him fired up. Towards the end, if I even hesitated for a moment, he would finish the story for me.

One day we were home alone chatting. He said, "Mom, I think you should get out of the detective business and go into television. Being a detective is too stressful, and it doesn't serve humanity enough."

I replied, "Sure, kid, easy for you to say. You won't be here, and your sister and I will starve to death. I can't afford to go back to school."

He started laughing. "No, Mom, you need to be in television where you can reach millions of people with what you're supposed to be teaching."

Together we had talked with students about death and dying. I could not imagine what he had in mind, but it didn't sound like something I could just walk into. "We'll see," I said (standard mom response). He went on to tell me I was supposed to help Elisabeth teach people not to be afraid of death. I remember thinking that seemed like his part, not mine. And a very tall order, too.

Cory and Tyler

fter several broken promises to visit Cory, Tyler finally made it over. He had no idea Cory's condition would be so dramatically different from the last time he'd seen him. Again, this guy had never experienced anything even remotely close to the death of a loved one.

Cory gave him a hard time about not showing up the other times and how "un-cool" it is to break promises. I felt badly for Tyler. I could see him fighting back the tears. He finally blurted out the truth. "I love you Cory, and I am having a really hard time with this."

My little boy cared for Tyler, too, but he was never one to mince words. He shot back, "But I'm the one that's dying, and I've needed your friendship. I want you to come see me again. I know how hard it is. Don't you think it's hard for me, too?"

I was hanging out in the kitchen trying not to listen. Tyler came in to talk with me. I tried to comfort him, but guilt and shame consumed him. He was inconsolable. He was obviously struggling with his emotions and his own sense of mortality. He said, "I know that Cory's right, but I'm not sure I can handle coming back. Please forgive me." I thanked him for his honesty, and we said goodbye. He went back to Cory's bedside and kissed him on the cheek. With tears spilling from his eyes, a heavy heart, and a sagging soul, he left. Cory never saw him again.

Cory with Tyler and Brie at Paradise, Mt. Rainier

Christianity, Religiosity —
What's Real?

eligiosity—Religious esp.: excessively, obtrusively, or sentimentally religious. (*Webster's Ninth New Collegiate Dictionary*)

Well-meaning friends and relatives encouraged religious people associated with their faiths to call me. I know they meant well, but it really wasn't helpful to have strangers calling me, constantly trying to sell me their religious beliefs any way that they could. Some people actually went beyond just being intrusive. Guilt was BIG with a number of these helpful folks. A friend of my sister Penny perpetrated one good example of this guilt-inducing behavior. This woman called and chastised me. She accused me of not introducing my dying son to the Jesus she believed in. She was practically hysterical. I couldn't believe my ears. Spouting off at me, in the name of Jesus, this so-called Christian woman really called to unload all of her insecurities on me. She tearfully told me it had to be my fault Cory was dying, because he'd been at the top of HER prayer list, and HER God wouldn't let her down. Therefore, his dying had to be my fault.

Needless to say, I was totally offended. I retorted, "Just because I don't go to your church and share your belief system does not mean your doctrines are right and mine are wrong." She didn't hear me. I didn't want to be rude, but she was ticking me off.

Cory overheard my side of the conversation. He was so weak he could hardly speak. He held his hand up and said, "Let me talk to her, Mom. I *have* met Jesus. I've walked in God's garden. I don't think she can say *that*. I'm closer to God than she is. And she doesn't sound like a very good Christian to be calling here upsetting you when your kid is dying." He was irate and indignant.

I asked her not to call again and hung up on her. I had enough to deal with at that time and certainly didn't need the added stress. Unbelievably, she called back five minutes later. She kept apologizing and begging for forgiveness. I tried to get her off the telephone gently. Within minutes, she was ranting and raving at me again. This time I told her she was harassing me, and I would call the police if she EVER called again. I certainly didn't need her kind of "help." I found it fascinating that people never asked me what my beliefs were. They didn't know that I had been a Christian all my life. My grandfather's faith had been instilled in me as a very young child and had never wavered. I knew that Cory's life and impending death were part of the plan that God had in store for my family and me. I trusted that God would take Cory back to his kingdom and that, even though my heart would break as a result, there was indeed a purpose.

The end was approaching, but I didn't have any sense of how fast. Everything seemed blurred around that time. I think it had a lot to do with physical and emotional exhaustion. Cory's nightly bouts with pain were developing a pattern. And as each one got stronger and lasted longer, my fears mounted.

One evening, Keller came over to sit with Cory and me. Debbie, my friend from work, and her friend, Mike, came by with dinner for all of us. Now they were examples of good Christians—giving, helping, and not pushing their beliefs on anyone. While we were finishing up with dinner, Cory's pains came, and he let out a pitiful cry. I rushed to his bedside and fell to my knees. I began putting the morphine pills under his tongue in an attempt to eradicate the pain. I was never sure if the medication actually worked or if he finally just came out of it on his own. I started to feel panicky inside because this time the intensity of his pain seemed to have doubled since the night before.

Cory started calling out in anguish, "Help! Help! There's a crazy lady trying to poison me!" My friends all looked at each other in amazement. I said, "Cory, that isn't even funny!"

He quietly replied, "Mom, calm down. I'm only dying. It's not the end of the world, so lighten up." That's the kind of kid he was—a practical joker right 'til the end. But at first I thought he was talking about dying right then and there!

The next day, my Aunty Cathy called me from Southern California. She was checking on how things were progressing. I told her Cory was still with us but in pretty tough shape. We chatted about a variety of things. She told me she was going to a class that evening taught by a local psychic.

"Wow, that sounds interesting. Hey listen, will you take the picture I sent you of my kids with Santa Claus and ask this psychic why Cory is still here suffering so?" Don't get me wrong; I wasn't in any hurry to rush him along, but I just could not understand why he had to suffer so much pain.

Elisabeth's stories about dying children usually had a central theme: The kid hangs on because the parents selfishly can't let go. I did not want to be one of those parents who guilt-tripped their kids into suffering longer because I couldn't let go.

Cathy promised to call me the following day with a full report. I could hardly sleep all night. I was so afraid she would tell me it was my entire fault.

The next morning Aunty Cathy called. She was totally freaked out by her experience. Her friend who had invited her to attend the class couldn't make it so she went alone. She couldn't find the picture I had asked her to bring, so she grabbed another one of Cory skiing at Crystal Mountain. His face wasn't even visible because of the hat, goggles, and ski clothes.

Cathy arrived at the class late because her car broke down. She tiptoed into the back of the room and tried to keep a low profile. The subject that evening was psychometrics. It didn't quite fit with her questions so she kept quiet, telling herself she would seek the woman out after class. The people all stormed the front of the room when the class ended, so Cathy told herself, "*Forget it, I'll come back next week.*" As she was heading for the door, Jean Wilson, the psychic, who was in a wheelchair, stopped her and asked, "Did you enjoy the class tonight?" Cathy nodded. "Would you like to come again?"

"Yes, I would."

"Do you feel that your needs were met?"

Cathy had to reply, "Well, no, actually they weren't." Jean told her that she had been picking up that sense from someone in the room all night, and she thought it might be Cathy.

As she dug through her handbag, Cathy told Jean that she had a picture of someone she was worried about. She was apologizing for the picture before she even found it in her bag. When Jean heard her say his face wasn't clear because of the ski clothes, she touched Cathy's arm and asked her to stop. She didn't want to hear another word. Jean called her mother and husband over. She asked them if they recalled the dream she had told them about the day before. Both of them nodded, and her husband said, "You mean the one where the guy dressed in ski clothes burst into your dream?" Well, most folks in Garden Grove don't often dream about skiing, especially Jean, who had been in a wheelchair most of her life.

Then Jean turned to my aunt and described Cory's personality to a tee. Then she said, "Your little nephew is in a great deal of pain, and he will die soon. Your niece wants to know why he's dragging his feet." Cathy was speechless. This woman was repeating word for word the things I had said about Cory. She then talked about my relationship with Cory and repeated whole conversations Cory and I had had in private. She was a stranger, but she was accurate.

When Aunty Cathy called me and recounted her experience, I was amazed. No one could know the things Cory and I had talked about. No one knew he had told me to change careers to television. I hadn't told anyone. Jean Wilson even told Cathy about Cory wanting to come back to me as a new baby named Michael. Then, she instructed Cathy to have me call her.

I didn't get up the nerve until later that day. I had to think about how bizarre things were getting. I wasn't sure I wanted to hear anymore from this stranger who seemed to know so much about us.

I told Cory's nurse, Elaine, about the whole episode. She was fascinated. I was scared. Finally, I dialed the number Aunty Cathy had given me. Jean was very nice and non-threatening, but it was one weird conversation! Throughout our time on the telephone, she kept calling him Michael. Jean knew things no one else could possibly know. She even quoted word for word a conversation Cory and I had had the week before! I asked her how much longer he had to live. "I keep seeing the number three," she said.

"That can't be. He is so sick. Three weeks is so long, but three days is much too soon."

She cut to the chase, "I'm sorry, honey, it is three days."

This was on Friday...

"Tears Heal the Soul..."

*H*ave you ever wondered what happens at the moment that your soul is leaving your body, when your heart stops beating and you've swallowed your last breath? I had not given it much thought until I found out that my little boy was dying. And even then, there was so much going on for me emotionally that I hadn't considered the final moment and what it would be like. I suppose most people would rather not think about it.

Cory's hospice nurse Elaine, put out a call for sublingual morphine. I had no idea it was in such limited supply. I guess that is why they call it a "controlled substance." Prior to that day, I had never considered what that term meant. Pharmacists all over the Puget Sound area were pooling their supplies to fill Cory's prescription so he could make it through the weekend. The prescription was eventually filled. It was for a thousand pills! Just the amount scared me.

In spite of what Jean Wilson, the psychic had told me that morning, I didn't think about it all day. I was so focused on the search for morphine to alleviate Cory's pain.

We made it through Friday. That night, he had his nightly bout of pain. Then he settled down and slept fairly well. I, on the other hand, couldn't sleep a wink. I just sat in the corner of the living room watching him breathe. The psychic's words, "three days," kept running through my mind, and they tore a gigantic hole right through my heart.

The next night I was watching a mindless television movie and talking with Cory off and on. He was very tired and would fade in and out on me. Brie and her cousin Jeffrey were fast asleep up in her room. I was propped up against Cory's bed, sitting on the floor and holding his hand. We were sort of waiting in dread for the pain to come. Cory's periods of intense pain were growing longer, more frequent, and much worse each night.

The pains usually hit around eight o'clock at night. Typically Cory would give out a heartbreaking yelp, and I could just feel the depth of his pain. It reminded me of a wounded animal. I would rush to his side and watch helplessly while he writhed in agony and with such intensity that the pain literally lifted him off the bed.

When I asked Cory to describe the pain to me, he told me with rivulets of tears streaming down his face that it felt as if someone was striking him in the middle of his back with an ax. His answer made me instantly very sorry I'd asked. How does one respond to that description? My stomach burned and I was not able to speak. I could only rub his back and pray that by some miracle his pain would be resolved.

Cory was so burned out from going to the hospital that, when we discussed his wants and needs for his final days, he made me promise that he could die at home without IVs, needle pokes, or doctors. That left us with sublingual morphine as our only means of trying to subdue the pain. To me, it never felt as if we could even "catch up" with the pain much less alleviate it. But I kept placing the tiny pills under his tongue in the hope that it would ease his pain. It was such a horrible feeling to see him suffering so and not have the ability to help him. I was the mommy; I was supposed to make it all better; that was my job. Sometimes I felt helpless, and at other times I just felt like a dismal failure. All I could do was pray for God to give him relief.

Later, my brother Mark stopped by to see how we were doing. I don't know what compelled him to do it, but he decided to stay overnight to give us his support. Within minutes, the waves of pain hit Cory with the most gut-punching force I had witnessed up 'til then.

The sight of Cory levitating off the bed each time pain tore through his body was almost too much to bear. I remember praying to God and begging him to stop Cory's pain. *"Please God, it's not fair. No one should have to endure such pain, especially not my beautiful little boy. Please make it stop!"*

I looked calm on the outside, but inside I was a mass of jangled nerves. I kept faithfully putting the morphine tablets under his tongue. To tell you the truth, I doubt they did anything at all. At the time, I remember thinking; *"All those crazy doctors worrying about his becoming addicted to the pain medication have obviously never dealt with severe pain themselves."* The pain seemed to absorb the drug, and I never felt that we achieved a balance. When the pain would eventually subside, it felt more as if the pain had just run its course and not that my intervention with the tiny bits of morphine had had anything to do with it going away.

Cory's cancer cells had invaded his central nervous system. The multiplying cells filled the ventricles of his brain, which caused the imbalance in his spinal and cranial fluid. The imbalance put pressure on various parts of his brain at different times. This affected the nerve impulses, which resulted in weird muscle reactions throughout his body. At times, we could actually watch a charley horse form in his thigh muscle…the result of a scrambled impulse sent by his confused brain. I assumed the pain in his back was caused the same way.

As the pain took on a life of its own, Mark and I watched helplessly. Just as quickly as Cory's body became racked with the pain, it suddenly stopped.

The room became eerily quiet and filled with a sense of peace. It was as if the air had stopped moving and time stood still. I knew he was gone. Cory had died right there with me holding his little hand. He had not said a word to me. I was sitting on the floor beside his bed. I looked at his still body, and I was afraid to move. I wanted to wail that I had not yet said goodbye. His chest was not moving. Completely frozen by the experience, I sat there motionless—all I could do was stare at him.

A split second that felt like an hour passed, and I heard Cory's voice as if it was far, far away. It is hard to describe, but it didn't sound as if it was even in the room. Over and over, he kept protesting, "No, no, no, I can't go with you. No I don't want to go yet. I want to go home! I want to go home!"

At first, I thought he was talking about going home to God's house, so I leaned over and whispered in his ear that it was okay for him to go home to be with God. It killed me to say it because I thought I had missed my opportunity to tell him how much I loved him and to say a proper goodbye. I wanted the last words he heard to be mine…my telling him how much he meant to me and how much I loved him. I was trying so hard to be benevolent, but Cory ignored me completely. It took me a few seconds before I realized that he couldn't hear me because he wasn't *present*. With each cry his voice got more and more emotional until he was sobbing, "I want to go home to my mommy's house. I want to go home to my mommy's house. I want to go to my mommy." It was heartbreaking to hear the anguish in his voice.

Again, I whispered to him, "Honey, if you're supposed to go, it's okay. It's time, and your body is too sick for you to stay."

Mark, my brother, was sitting behind us completely baffled. He said aloud, "What is he talking about? He *is* at his mommy's house."

I waved back at Mark to quiet him as I continued to eavesdrop on Cory's conversation. The whole time this was going on, Cory's lips were not moving, his chest was not moving, and I felt as if we were in a time vacuum. Truly, nothing else mattered. It was so bizarre because Cory's body seemed like an amplifier of some sort, but his voice did not seem to be coming from him at all. It was in the room surrounding us.

Then we heard Cory's voice still sounding far away and strangling with desperation and defeat say, "This isn't my home. I want to go home." There was a moment of silence. I waited to see what would happen next. I held my breath mainly because I couldn't breathe and I was afraid to move.

Suddenly Cory's voice was present. His lips moved as he spoke to me, "Mommy, are you here?" I was startled at first because I was holding his hand. He apparently couldn't feel it. Then I answered, "Yes, sweetheart, I am right here holding your hand. I'm right here. Mommy's here."

He was physically very weak, but he continued on, saying sadly, "I don't want to go yet, but I don't think I can stay." I told him that he couldn't stay, that his body was too sick, and that if it were time for him to go I would be okay and for him not to argue. I asked if he remembered what Elisabeth tells people about death, "The cocoon can no longer support the butterfly."

He nodded in agreement and said, "Yes, it is time for me to go." I asked what had just happened to him, and he said, "They tried to take me over the bridge, and I didn't want to go yet. And, Mommy? I'll never miss you."

Well, by now my brother was literally draped over my back, crowding me, straining to hear what Cory was saying. He kept asking, "What? What? I can't understand him. What's he saying? Why isn't he going to miss you? I don't get it."

With all of his might Cory pulled himself up on his side. He reached over and grabbed me by the neck so he could pull me closer to him, and with the last reserves of his strength, he whispered in my ear, "Send Uncle Mark to bed." I tried not to laugh because the situation was so intense, but Cory was definitely set on getting rid of my inquisitive brother. Cory had not been able to do anything that physical for weeks!

My brother, bless his heart, was totally freaking out, so he was more than happy to be sent to bed.

After he left Cory said, "Okay, now we can talk. Remember Mama; all the love we've shared will last forevermore. I'll never miss you because I'll always be with you. At the speed of thought, I'll be beside you... whenever you think of me, I'll be there." I thanked him for reminding me. Then with a triumphant quality to his voice, Cory said, "Boy that was close! They wanted me to go across the bridge, but I said no."

I will never forgive myself for not pressing Cory further about who "they" were. He was grinning like the cat that ate the canary. I was stunned to see the smile on his little face because he hadn't been able to use his facial muscles for several months, but it was definitely a big ol' "I got over on someone" type of grin. I asked what he was grinning about, and he replied, "I'm dallying."

I said, "What?" He had *never* in his life used that word before.

Cory said, "You know, as in dilly-dally? Well, I'm dallying. They wanted me to go with 'em, but I said, 'No,' and I won."

Again, I started to feel panicky inside. Feebly I stammered, "What do you mean? They were going to take you? And it was time for you to go? And you said no?"

Cory continued to grin, and he came back with, "It's okay, Mom; they'll be back for me later."

I said something really lame like, "Honey, your body is too sick; you can't stay. How will you know what to do? What if they don't come back?"

To which he replied with a slight bit of annoyance, "Mom, it's OKAY! They said they would be back for me. They weren't too happy, but they said I could stay a little while longer."

My mind was racing. There was so much I wanted to know, and I didn't know where to begin. When I asked what it was like when they tried to take him, he told me it was a secret. He said, "I can't tell you. It's a secret that isn't revealed to you until you die."

Flabbergasted by this information, I pushed a little more, "Come on, Cory. If Elisabeth gets to hear this deathbed stuff all the time, why can't I? Why do I have to wait?"

Cory, always the diplomat, said, "Mom, you are just going to have to find out for yourself."

Remembering Cory's previous statements about reincarnating as a boy named Michael, I thought to myself, *"Okay, maybe he knows who his father will be..." So,* I asked, "Okay buddy, since you know you're going to come back to me as a kid named Michael, do you know what your *last* name will be?"

"No. What???" he asked. I told him I thought he might know. He started laughing at me! I thought I was being pretty sneaky. He finally stopped long enough to say, "You're on your own, Mom."

"C'mon, honey, if you know—please tell me."

"Sorry, Mom. You're on your own." Then it was my turn to laugh.

"Okay, Cory, give me a hint: Is it someone we already know? Or someone I haven't met yet?"

"Mom, I can't help you. You've got do it by yourself."

Then he changed the subject.   He wanted to clarify his funeral arrangements. Cory could be very much like a little old lady with all his details and fretting about every last one of them. Thank goodness he had music changes since his original funeral plans had been made a year and a half earlier. Cory also wanted to be buried in his favorite pair of Knight Rider pajamas. He wanted to look just as if he had gone to sleep.

Over the years, incredibly deep philosophies would just pop out of Cory's mouth. There were many times in his life when the things he said reminded me of Kahlil Gibran. One minute we would be talking about pajamas, and the next he would say, "Tears heal the soul, hugs and kisses heal the heart, but only love can heal mankind." That one prompted a long and involved conversation about life, people, and other heavy topics, such as reincarnation, war, child abuse, and nuclear waste. These heavy topics made Cory pause for a moment and really question his desire to come back to a place with so much pain and sadness. He thoughtfully said to me, "Mommy, I may decide to stay in heaven after I get there. Please don't be too disappointed if I stay."

There were also silly things that I wanted to know, such as what his favorite movie was and who his favorite people were. He again laughed at me good-naturedly and said, "Mom, why are you asking me such dumb questions?" I was just trying to cover some of the things I didn't know. I wanted to make sure I knew everything there was to know about him before they came back for him, and it would be too late to ask.

"By the way, my favorite movie was, *Oh God, Book II*. I asked why that particular movie. He replied, "Because no one believed the character who said he'd met God. I know how he feels."

Cory talked of the love he felt for all of his cousins. Sadly, he articulated how sorry it made him knowing he would not be able to grow up with them. He said, "I wish I could grow up and be just like cousin Markie—he's smart, funny, and nice. And, I'm sad cousin Michael won't have any cousins close to his age to play with anymore."

There were messages for specific people, too. "Tell Christina I said to *Remember the Secret*." It was obvious to me that Cory had a list of messages in his head as he went on. "Give my love to all my relatives, especially Grandma, Grandpa, and Brie-Brie. Let them know, especially Brie, that I will always watch over them...and tell Brie she better be good! Tell Tyler I forgive him for not coming back. And tell Keller thanks for being my friend and teaching me to love soccer. Tell David [Hasselhoff] thanks for being so nice and being my friend. And when you talk to Elisabeth, tell her I couldn't wait for her call any longer, but when she thinks of me, I'll be beside her."

We finally fell asleep around 4:00 a.m., only after he told me to go to sleep because he needed to rest. He said, "Dying is hard work. I need to get my rest so I can manage it." I told him I was afraid to fall asleep because he might leave without my being able to say goodbye. He promised that he wouldn't do that to me. We made the solemn agreement. I fell asleep sitting up with my head resting on my arm on the edge of his bed.

As One with God

"The Sun Is Down"

The morning dawned with the sun shining magnificently and the sky a beautiful blue, as can only be seen in Seattle on a spring day.

There was an early knock at the door. I was asleep on the floor next to Cory's bed, and although I heard the door, my first thought was to check to see if Cory was still breathing. I sat up and saw that his coloring had changed drastically and had taken on a sort of mottled, blotchy look. His little chest was still rising and falling. It was very erratic though; a sure sign death was imminent. I had heard that somewhere... I'm not sure where, but I knew it meant the end was near.

Leaning over his body, I asked, "What are you doing still here?"

Cory whispered, "They haven't come back for me yet. But they will." He then told me that he would be resting most of the day in preparation for dying He reminded that "dying is hard work, ya know."

In the meantime, my brother had answered the door and let Beverly Barnard in. She had come to say goodbye as she was heading out of town. She quietly came into the living room and knelt beside Cory's bed. She told me that she was leaving for a conference and wanted to be sure to say "*Aloha*." She kissed his little face and said, "Bye, buddy; see you around next time." Then we heard the eagle in the back yard.

An honest to goodness eagle had been hanging around my back yard for weeks. Cory's grandfather had seen it in the tree and so had Beverly. Beverly had worked with Native American Indians at one time. She told us how they believed the eagle was a mystical bird that transported spirits to the other side. "*How appropriate,*" I thought. Cory had been telling me about his friend the eagle. I know it sounds really dumb, but I hadn't really paid that much attention to his eagle story. But when I realized it really was out in our yard, hanging around, presumably waiting for him, I got chicken skin (also known as goose bumps). Well, wouldn't you? I lived in the city. I hadn't even seen an eagle when I'd gone up to the San Juan Islands much less sitting in a tree in my own back yard! (Things kept getting weirder and weirder.)

Beverly didn't stay long. She bid Cory adieu, gave me a hug, and slipped out the door.

My brother fixed us breakfast. I went in to my bedroom to telephone Cory's hospice nurse, Elaine, to tell her he was definitely getting ready to die. I was shocked to find out she had left for New York that morning. One of her grandparents had passed away unexpectedly, and she had gone to be with her family. "Okay," I said to myself. "I'll just call his hospital clinic nurse, Mo, to find out what I can expect." I dialed the telephone, and there was no answer. I was lying on my bed and for a brief moment, I closed my eyes and imagined her hiking on Mt. Rainier. (I found out later that that is precisely where she was.) I thought to myself, "*Why am I not surprised we are going to be doing this by ourselves?*" I went back to Cory's bedside and told him we were on our own. He nodded sleepily and said, "We don't need anybody else, Mommy; we've done it all alone this far. Don't worry." I mumbled something about it being easy for him to say...

Cory's dad came to visit, and I described Cory's condition to him. I encouraged him to finish up his business with Cory before it was too late. Then I left them alone.

The day dragged on. I spent most of the time in my bedroom so Cory and his father could have their last visit together. By evening, I could see it was time for me to take over the vigil.

While I was cooped up in my bedroom, I had telephoned our friend, Shirlee Kimball, to give her an update on Cory's condition. When she found out I wasn't able to reach either of our nurses, she offered to come keep us company during Cory's last hours. She was a nurse but hadn't practiced in a few years. In fact, Shirlee had never worked with terminal patients, so I really appreciated the courage of her offer. I said yes, knowing that her presence would be a comfort to both Cory and me.

Cory had insisted that he be allowed to die at home without medication or anything else that might remind him of the hospital. I supported his choice, but it was very scary. Of course, when I had agreed to his requests, I had no understanding of how much pain his dying would generate for both of us, how we would have to endure his blindness, acute hearing sensitivity, some confusion, and many bouts of excruciating pain.

Cory's death was not peaceful. It was not quiet and dignified, as I had envisioned. Nor was it horrible as I had foreseen during one of those weak moments filled with anxiety and dread. Cory's death for me was our final adventure. The whole process when we got right down to it was fascinating and rather mysterious. Of course, it was sad and awful for me as his mother to watch him die, but as strange as it may sound, it was truly an adventure, almost as incredible as his birth. And, like his coming, we did his parting together.

The night he left felt long, but when it was over, for me, it was much too short. Shirlee and I had been sitting with Cory for several hours. The wracking pain turned into something totally unexpected for me. His nervous system went haywire. He was struggling to keep his limbs from spasming. He was working very hard at it by doing relaxation breathing. Watching him suffer and my feeling so helpless gave me a whole new understanding of what he had said, that it would be a lot of work.

It was so much more than that. I thought to myself, "So THIS is what he rested up for." Cory would puff-puff a few breaths and then say, "I love you, Mom" or "Auntie Shirlee" and then pucker up his lips to kiss us. Then he would continue with his breathing. He was such a brave little soldier. It still brings tears to my eyes to remember how courageously he confronted his death.

At one point, I was nearly hysterical because obviously the morphine wasn't working. He finally said, "Mom, forget it...it doesn't matter; I'm okay." I tried so hard to believe him, but the contortions his body was making were very hard to witness.

Close to midnight, exhausted, I became quite desperate. Then I remembered Cory had been prescribed Valium for his leg cramps, so I ran to the medicine cupboard to search for it. Unfortunately, the medications were labeled with generic pharmaceutical names, so I couldn't distinguish between them. I ran to the telephone and dialed the hospital to ask for help in deciphering the labels. Cory called me back to the bed and said, "Forget it, Mommy. The drugs won't help anyway." Numbly, I hung up the receiver and took my place beside his bed again to wait for the end.

"The sun is down."

Shirlee and I both heard it—a very deep masculine voice. A very deep disembodied male voice. We looked at each other in astonishment. Then we silently shrugged our shoulders. We were alone with Cory. It was just after midnight, and we were hearing a man's voice! What I wanted to know was WHO in the heck was talking and to WHOM was he speaking? I have experienced some pretty weird things in my time, but this had to be the weirdest. Not only that, but our sun had gone down hours before! I decided it had to be God's voice telling Cory and his escorts that it was time for the journey to begin.

After the initial statement, we heard nothing more. We kept waiting for something to happen. It was painfully clear that my son would be leaving me at any moment. Talk about living in the moment...there was nothing else to do but wait.

What I couldn't figure out was why he was suffering so. All the stories I had heard about our other little friends' deaths sounded peaceful and otherworldly. Here was this very special, wise-beyond-his-years, God-loving little soul being forced to go through this tremendous amount of pain and suffering. It just didn't seem quite right. Where was the loving God waiting with outstretched arms that Cory had described after one of his trips to Summerland? I couldn't help but wonder if he was being punished because of his "dilly-dallying" the night before.

If he had died when he was supposed to, it would have been very peaceful. So why was he going through this intense, bone-wracking pain and out-of-control flailing? I begrudgingly gave fleeting attention to those thoughts, but his labored breathing brought me back to reality and the task at hand. I couldn't hold him because his body was so sensitive to touch, and besides, his flailing would have made it impossible to do. I was worried that if we hindered his flailing, it would have hurt him in some way. So, we sat helplessly by and told him how much we loved him and how much we would miss him.

Cory was having a harder and harder time with each breath. His body thrashing did not seem to be dissipating at all. He said, "I love you, Mommy." Then Shirlee went to the bathroom to get a wet washcloth to wipe his face. I was sitting next to his bed holding his hands when he suddenly stopped moving. No more than an instant later, I heard his voice, which sounded distant again. He asked someone I couldn't see, "Where's Quackzser?" He sounded puzzled, apparently because his precious dog wasn't there to greet him. He said something else, but I couldn't make out what it was because he seemed to be moving farther away. I pictured the Rainbow Bridge in my mind.

I knew then that Cory was leaving me and nearing the bridge. I could actually hear him leaving! I imagined him walking over the bridge, looking for his beloved dog, wondering where Quackszer was.

I quickly leaned over and kissed my baby boy's cheek. I whispered, "Goodbye, buddy, I love you...and I promise I'll never forget you." His chest was still rising and falling shallowly, but I could feel that his presence was gone.

Shirlee came back to Cory's bedside, and I told her that he was gone. She immediately dropped to her knees beside me. She looked at his chest and insisted, "But he's still breathing." I said, "Yeah, but he's gone. Can't you feel it?" Then, I reached over and pulled him toward me so I could give him a last hug. As I drew him to my chest, and held him in my arms, everything stopped. I felt a sense of relief for him, because I knew his suffering had just ended. As for me, my heart shattered into a million pieces, and my lungs went numb. It was difficult to breathe, or maybe it was more that my brain didn't instruct my lungs to function normally.

I gently laid him back down on the pillows. Shirlee and I took turns wiping his little face with the cloth. We both kissed his face, and I brushed back his hair. I sat there looking at his swollen face and body. I thought, *"No, this is not my little boy. This is a sick, worn-out macaroni box. My little boy is gone. He just crossed over the Rainbow Bridge to enter the kingdom of Heaven...and I know 'cuz I heard him!"*

Eventually, I went to the telephone and with great resignation called Children's Hospital to report that Cory's pain and suffering was over. I'm not sure why I called them first; I guess I was just following instructions. It could also be that I needed to tell it to a neutral party before I could relay the tragic news to the people who loved him. I had to rehearse hearing the words come out of my mouth.

Then I called my parents and Cory's other grandfather to tell them he was gone. My last call was to the mortuary. Have you ever imagined how it would feel to call a mortuary in the middle of the night to come take your child's body away forever? No? Neither had I. It was a moment in time that I wish I could forget. Anyway, they said they would send someone right over. I felt as if I had been punched in the stomach hard when I heard those words. It sounds kind of crazy, but I felt glad that he died in the middle of the night so that the whole neighborhood wouldn't be out there watching as his body was packed off like used luggage. I have always had a weird thing about prying neighbors...something left over from my childhood.

When the men from the mortuary came, they were very nice. I cannot remember anything they said or if I even talked to them. I'm sure I must have. I do remember that I couldn't be in the living room with them. I was afraid they would put him in a body bag; you know the kind we've all seen in the movies? I knew I couldn't watch as they zipped him up and took him away. I have to admit, at the time, I was not as attached to his body as some parents I've met. But it definitely was not the way I wanted to remember him. So I purposely stayed in the kitchen. Now, all these years later, I regret that I didn't spend more time with him before they took his body away. Twenty-twenty hindsight—isn't it great?

My parents came over. They didn't say much. Really, what could they have said? I appreciated their presence, their quiet support. They didn't stay long. They left after telling Shirlee and me that we should try to get some sleep. I was exhausted, or if there is a word that describes being beyond exhausted mentally, physically, and in every other way, I was it. I felt completely drained...empty...hollow.

Shirlee and I did fall asleep for a while. But it must have only been a few hours. By morning, the house was bustling with people. I felt as if everyone else was in a much higher gear than I. Lynn came over, stripped Cory's bed, and started cleaning my house. My sister Penny took my telephone book to her house to inform my friends and our relatives.

Barbara Clark stopped by. She was on her way to the airport because she was going on vacation. I had intentionally not called her the day or night before because I didn't want to ruin her trip. She knew Cory was dying, and there was nothing she or anyone else could do. She started to cry, and I gave her a hug. She looked over my shoulder at his empty bed and said, "Where is he?!" Dumbfounded, I blurted out that he had been taken away at four in the morning. When the realization sank in, she really started crying. I thought she knew he had died and that's the reason she had stopped by. But she had just come by to see us, believing he would go while she was on her trip. Instead, the poor thing had to rush off to catch her plane, carrying the sad news with her. I felt so sorry for her starting her European vacation in that emotional state, but there was absolutely nothing I could do for her.

"I'll Be Beside You..."

Cory told me right before he died that, when he went out of his body to Summerland and saw people that he had known before, they appeared to him as regular people like you and I, "only better because they aren't sick or in pain." He also said that when you die, your "being" is manifested in sparks of light energy that look like the sparks on his drawing of Summerland. He said when others get there they have a special "knowing" about their loved ones, that they immediately recognize each other. But if someone is newly passed over, he might be frightened by the whole experience, so his loved ones appear like regular people. After passing, the one really "cool" thing about appearing in body is that you get to choose the age you want to be. For example, he wanted to be remembered at the age he felt the strongest and looked the healthiest, so he told me in private that he would appear as seven-year-old Cory. He told me that Grandpa Nick wanted to appear as a healthy thirty-year-old. I have no idea how he knew that since he died before Nick.

Several people who came to me with stories about seeing Cory or having dreams where he appeared to them all describe him as around age seven. I hadn't told anyone what he had said either! I always smile and nod.

The very first report of an appearance by Cory was the morning he died. His Uncle Adam (my friend Mairie's husband) was driving home from work early that Monday around 3:00 a.m. or so. Adam and Mairie lived in a rural area, on the way to Steven's Pass. Adam had been working way too much overtime at his job, and he had already pulled over on the highway two times because he was falling asleep at the wheel. He was so exhausted; the third time he felt his body and mind drifting off towards sleep; he didn't care.

All of a sudden Cory was beside him on the seat of his car, whacking him on the arm with one hand and holding the steering wheel steady with the other. "Wake up, Uncle Adam! Wake up. You have to get home safely. Wake up. The boys and Aunty Mairie need you." Startled awake, Adam looked over at Cory. Cory chastised Adam about taking better care of himself on behalf of his wife and children all the rest of the way home.

They chatted. When Adam arrived in his driveway, he parked his car. As he turned to hop out, he looked back towards Cory's side of the seat, and it was empty. He shook his head and walked away acknowledging that Cory was absolutely right, that he had been working too hard and not taking care of himself. Adam went into his house and went straight to bed.

That morning, I telephoned Mairie around 7:30 a.m. to tell her Cory had died. We talked for a while, but I had several other calls to make.

Later, this is what Mairie described to me. When Adam was beginning to awaken later that day, he told her about his drive home. He told her about falling asleep while driving and his dream that Cory helped him get home safely. Mairie said, "Adam, you weren't dreaming. Cory died this morning about an hour before you saw him. I don't think it was a dream. I think he really helped you."

When I asked her how Adam described Cory's appearance, she said, "He looked healthy and thin like when he was around seven."

Cory's death occurred on Monday, May 13th around 2:00 a.m. On Wednesday, two days later, I was soaking in the bathtub when I heard the telephone ring. Then I heard Brie answering someone's questions. I realized by what was being said that it was Elisabeth Kubler-Ross. I leapt out of the tub and ran to the living room. Brie was having quite a chat. I had to wrestle the telephone away from her, worried that she would conclude her conversation and hang it up. Elisabeth was calling from Austria. Amazingly, our connection was fairly good, which always helped with Elisabeth. Even with a clear line, because of her accent, it was sometimes difficult to understand her.

The very first thing she asked was, "He's gone, isn't he?" I responded in the affirmative. Elisabeth then said, "Was it Monday?"

"Yes," I said, wondering where she was going with her questions.

"Was it closer to Sunday?" Curiously it was. So when I confirmed it, Elisabeth said, "I knew it. I was bragging on Cory and showing the people at my workshop his drawing of the crystal castle, and I could feel his presence so strongly beside me that I knew he was there with me." Together we calculated the time difference and determined that she had felt his presence right about the time he had died in Seattle.

With a laugh I told her that one of the last instructions he had given me was a message to her: "Tell Elisabeth I couldn't wait for her phone call any longer. Tell her I love her and that when she thinks of me, I'll be there."

Cory appeared to Brie quite soon after he died. She dreamt that the two of them were floating down a beautiful river in the bright sunshine. There were exquisite, fragrant, colorful flowers growing along the riverbanks. Cory told his sister he would always watch over her; he would be her own private guardian angel. Then the board drifted over to the riverbank. Cory stepped off, steadied the boat, and held out his hand to Brie. She followed him onto the land. Together they began to climb up the steep riverbank. Cory walked ahead of his little sister and pulled her up the hill. He told her over and over again that, even if she couldn't see him, he would always be beside her whenever she needed him, just like he was right then. He also said she would recognize him when she got to heaven.

So, for you parents whose child has died, according to Cory, you will know your loved ones, and they will know you. It's a given...instant recognition. Besides, his descriptions always made it sound as if your loved ones guide you to the other side. You never transition alone.

I felt bad that Brie wasn't able to say goodbye to her brother. The body contortions were so disturbing that I thought they would definitely frighten her. It didn't seem like the kind of thing a six-year-old could put behind easily, so I made the decision as a mother not to subject her to them. (I hope and pray that she understands that someday.)

When she got up in the morning and discovered that Cory was gone, I sat her down and explained what had happened. I promised to take her to the mortuary later in the day so she could see his body. That seemed to satisfy her.

When my mom, Brie, and I went to the mortuary that afternoon, we were trying to keep it light for Brie's sake. We wandered in to the room where his casket was and found it half-closed. Brie's eyes got huge with fear. She began to cry, insisting that they open the bottom half of the casket for her to see him, because she needed to know that he was whole. So to accommodate her, the lovely man who owned the mortuary came and opened it all the way. Well, to our dismay and disgust, Cory's best friend, "Wubie," formerly known as "Blanky," was wrapped around him, tucked completely out of sight. He had loved that raggedy ol' blanket since day one. Even though it was worn thin and full of holes, I had envisioned him holding it just the way he slept with it all nine years of his life—close to his heart. So we made the nice man rearrange the nasty old Blanky.

After Brie recovered from the half-opened casket scare, she took one look at him and said, "Oooh, he's wearing lipstick." Then she paused, looked around the room and stated, "He's not in there." My mother and I looked at each other with curiosity. Brie again stated emphatically, "He's not in there. His body looks like a big sleeping dolly, but Cory's not there."

We said, "How do you know?"

She calmly looked from him to us and said, "Can't you feel it? He's not in there." Then she again remarked about his face having make-up on it. She wanted to touch him. We held her up so she could kiss him goodbye. We stayed as long as Brie needed.

Then she wanted to see where his service would be held. As we entered the chapel, Brie told us she could feel Cory's presence there flying around the room. My mother and I nodded to acknowledge her declaration. Then we walked completely around the chapel so she could inspect it. Apparently, it met with her approval because she turned to us and said with a toss of her head, "Okay, we can go now."

The next few days were a blur of activity. We had relatives arrive from out of state. I had people staying at my house wanting to keep me busy, talking until the wee hours of the night. I drank more tea and smoked more cigarettes than I ever want to remember. This overdose of tobacco smoke prompted me to quit.

Cory had instructed me to stop the night before his death. He told me he was worried about my health. I was only a part-time, on-social-occasions type of smoker (really dumb). When he told me to quit, I said, "But I'm stressed out. You're dying, and I can't quit right now. Give me a couple of weeks." He said, "Okay, but then you need to take better care of your health." Well, it only took about three days of late night smoking and gabbing to do it. I haven't smoked since. And, as everybody who has ever smoked and quit knows, I hate being around smoke, tobacco, or anyone who smells like cigarettes. There's nothing worse than a reformed smoker.

The day before Cory's funeral, five of my friends were over visiting with me. There was a knock at the front door. I looked out to see a woman I recognized as a neighbor, but I didn't really know her. Believing she was probably stopping by to offer her condolences, I opened the front door. The woman inquired, "Are you Cory's mother?"

I replied, "Yes." She proceeded to prattle on—telling me that the same night Cory died her boyfriend's mother died, too. They apparently lived with the boyfriend's mother up the block a few houses. Well, big surprise to me, this woman stopped by to tell me she was upset because Cory had told all of the kids in the neighborhood not to be afraid of death. So her seven-year-old daughter was not crying and carrying on like everyone else in her house!

"What did you say?" I stammered incredulously. "You are upset with my son because your kid isn't as fearful and frightened as the rest of your family?"

Not only that, she said, "Yeah, and my daughter walked up to my grandma the other day and said, "Just think, Grandma, next time, it could be your lucky day!"

I wanted to laugh out loud on that one, but I decided I had had enough. I had to get rid of this woman. My patience had evaporated, so I said, "Look, I'm sorry you have a problem with your child not responding the way you think she should. Maybe you should be glad she's not freaking out. Everyone grieves in his or her own way and time. You need to respect that. And, right now I have a house full of guests because we are burying my little boy tomorrow. So, I'm closing the door now."

As I turned around, I could see that everyone in the living room was stunned. In fact, they were speechless. No one could believe the conversation they had just witnessed. In total exhaustion, I sank onto the couch and shrugged my shoulders. I said, "Just think how lucky that silly woman is to have children with healthy ideas about death, and she doesn't even appreciate it."

Celebrating Life

The next morning was incredibly chaotic. We had several relatives sleeping over with us. Brie and I got up to get ready for the funeral. My stomach was already in knots when I got a frantic call from the man who owned the mortuary. It seems my ex-husband and some of his family had called that morning demanding impossible, last minute changes. The poor man was frazzled, and he wanted my help. That was all I needed. I would have lost it if Keller and my nephew, Mark, hadn't been there. They helped calm me down and I was able to focus again.

I telephoned Cory's grandfather, (his dad's dad) and begged him to intervene. He assured me he would. As a precaution, I then called several of my brothers and a dear friend of ours who was a local policeman and asked them to arrive at the chapel early.

Other than their late arrival, my ex-husband and his family behaved themselves. The service went beautifully. We really couldn't have blown it since Cory had pre-arranged everything himself. We just had to stick to his instructions. Brie had dictated a beautiful prayer for her brother. Since she wasn't able to write, our friend, Steve Geller, had taken her dictation a few days before Cory died. During the service, Steve stood up at the front of the chapel with Brie. They held hands as Steve read for her:

God bless everybody - and Cory, I love you Cory.

You were a good brother to play with. You were a good brother to me.

I am glad you are going to be able to do anything you want, flying and playing around, and playing with other friends and old people, and playing with angels.

You will never turn older. I'm glad you don't need oxygen.

When you were sick, I wished you felt better and didn't have leukemia. I know now it will be funner for you up there than it is down here.

To the people here - you love Cory, too. As soon as he got up there, I'm sure he was playing with Quackszer and Aaron.

Dear Cory - I love you.

Amen

Brie shyly curtsied at the end and said, "Amen." As you might imagine, that nearly brought the house down. There wasn't a dry eye in the place. She quickly scrambled to the floor back to her previous spot with Cory's best friend, Christina. I could tell she was proud of the warm response her tribute to Cory elicited from everyone present.

Cory had asked his stress management doctor, Bill Womack, to give the eulogy. Bill was instructed to keep it "light and funny." Cory asked that no one wear black—only bright, happy colors. Cory chose the music, too—the theme song from E.T., Tim Noah's "Friends and I Can Do Anything," Raffi's "Baby Beluga," Peter Alsop's "No One Knows for Sure," and a beautiful folk song entitled, "Thanksgiving Eve." He was very eclectic. I was just relieved that he had changed his mind about Michael Jackson's Thriller tape. I honestly didn't push it; he chose to eliminate Michael Jackson all by himself.

The chapel was filled with colorful helium balloons, several hundred of them. We passed them out at the door. Christina, brought a bouquet of balloons just for her. She had written messages on each of them with a magic marker. I guess she figured if they went up in the sky, they'd make it to heaven.

The service was a mixture of tears, laughter, hope, and memories. It was just as beautiful as Cory had wanted. Bill Womack did a fantastic job of capturing Cory's essence and actually got through his tribute without breaking down.

Wayne, one of Cory's teachers, showed up dressed in a dark suit. When I approached him to say hello, he started babbling about how it was the only decent thing he had to wear. He thought so much of Cory's instructions about the attire that the poor guy was consumed with guilt for dressing up in dark clothes! I just smiled at him and told him not to worry; I didn't think Cory would haunt him or anything.

The school bus brought about thirty or forty of Cory's schoolmates from AS#1. Some had never attended a funeral before Cory's. I could tell it was a good experience for them. It wasn't scary or maudlin; it was a true celebration of Cory's life. The students at Cory's school had made a huge colorful poster in his honor. We propped it up against the podium so everyone could see what the students had written.

Brie wanted to sit with her friends on the floor of the chapel, just in front of the podium. I wondered what was going through her mind. She gave no indication, except when I tried to pull her up onto my lap or seat her next to me she pulled away. Brie made it clear she wanted to sit with the other children.

"May We All Fly Like Eagles..."

May we all fly like eagles, fly so high, circling the universe on the wings of pure light...

This was a song we learned at the Children's Connection, the support group we had helped start for terminally ill children and their families. When Cory designated who would do what at his funeral, he put Ilene and Christine, our friends from the group, in charge of the graveside part of his celebration. They thought it only appropriate that we sing the eagle song that day. It was such a beautiful spring day, and the collection of voices sounded like a beautiful choir. It's sung in a round, which really makes it special.

As we finished singing the song, Christine instructed everyone to join her in saying a brief prayer. Then she asked everyone to think wonderful thoughts of Cory and let go of the balloons. Up, up, and away they went.

There were so many people, and I was so tired. I felt like a spectator. Friends started to approach me after the brief graveside service, which brought me back to reality. It was amazing; people I had not seen in years came to offer their thoughts and prayers. It was so sweet and thoughtful of all of them. The outpouring of love and support was overwhelming.

I was marveling at the presence of a woman I had known from the parents' support group. Her little boy was one Cory had seen in Summerland. Then Cherri, one of my oldest and dearest friends, ran up to me and grabbed me by the arm. She said, "Oh my God, Shirl, look up there..."

I looked up at the balloons floating away and said, "Uh huh, they're pretty, aren't they?"

Cherri said, "No Shirl, not the balloons, look over there." I followed her finger pointing to an eagle flying in a circle right over the cemetery. My mouth dropped open, and I looked at Cherri. Now, I was even more convinced that the eagle in our backyard had indeed been waiting for Cory.

In unison we said, "Woo woo," and then we just stood there and shivered. The rest of the time spent at the graveside I was overwhelmed by our friends and acquaintances offering their condolences and giving Brie and me hugs. Cory's classmates and soccer buddies were so attentive. And, of course, there were people I didn't know or maybe just didn't recognize.

I watched Brie flit from friend to friend, seemingly oblivious. But I knew she wasn't unaffected by the events of the day. She had always been a very private child. This concerned me because Brie had a tendency to internalize whatever was bothering her.

My sister Penny invited most of the people there to stop by her house for lunch. My friend Keller, my mother, and I had the limousine take us back to my house. I wanted to change into more comfortable clothes. Then Keller drove mom and me over to Penny's house for the wake.

The food was plentiful and so were the people. I stretched out in a lawn chair and watched the activity. After Keller left, I didn't feel too much like interacting. It was just nice to feel all the love and support from so many people. It also felt good to see that so many people loved my little boy.

When it was time finally to go home, Lynn suggested we go to her parents' house to soak in the hot tub. My Aunt Cathy thought it sounded like a good idea, too. We went home and grabbed our bathing suits and some towels.

While we were there, Brie got very angry for no "apparent" reason. I took her into the bathroom and tried to hold her on my lap, but she kept wiggling away. I finally had to block the door to prevent her from leaving. I needed to know what she was angry about and what was going through her six-year-old mind.

Finally, Brie let go of her anger and began to cry. She blurted out how it didn't make sense to her that Cory hadn't been made well by the doctors at the hospital. Her six-year-old understanding was that everyone who goes to the hospital gets well. From her ramblings, I deciphered that she was angry with me for not putting him in the hospital.

We cried together on that bathroom floor, as I tried to explain why some people live and others die. (Like I'm supposed to know everything?) I tried desperately to help her understand that Cory knew he was going to die and that it was his request that he stay at home and not be put into the hospital. I told her how he hated the hospital and that, even if he had gone there, he would have died anyway because it was time for him to go back to heaven to be with God.

What was the other thing that was on Brie's mind? She wanted to know who was going to take care of her when I went with Cory. I kept reassuring her that I wasn't going anywhere and that she would always be taken care of. Brie did not believe me. And I finally figured out what the real question was. When I told her that if anything ever happened to me, she was to go straight to my parents' house and they would take care of her FOREVER, she quieted down. That whole exhausting episode was really a lesson in how to listen to underlying questions, not just what the child sounds like she is asking. (I haven't mastered it yet, but my kids keep me actively trying.)

A few weeks after Cory died, I went back to work. It was so hard to concentrate and get back in the groove. But being a single mom, I didn't have a choice.

My desk was piled high with five weeks worth of work. I was knee-deep in report writing when my telephone rang. It was Beverly Barnard, the principal of AS#1. She asked how I was and commented on how well Brie seemed to be coping at school. Beverly told me that Cory's favorite teacher, Karen, was there with her and that she had a story to tell me. Beverly handed the telephone to Karen who said, "Just last night, I woke up in the middle of the night to find Cory sitting on the edge of my bed. I was surprised to see him, but he was very casual. I told him his funeral was great. He said, "Yeah, I know;

I was there." Then, I asked him about the eagle everyone saw flying over the cemetery, "Cory, did you have anything to do with the eagle we saw?" He said, "Yeah, I was flying on his back." Then Cory said, "Don't you remember my telling you about my friend, the eagle, a long time ago?" Karen said, "Vaguely." Cory went on to say that he had drawn a picture of the eagle for Karen. "It's hanging on your bulletin board behind your desk, but somebody stapled a bunch of papers over it. Check it out." Karen asked, "Where is it?" Cory told her, "If you sit down at your desk and look over your right shoulder, lift up the papers stapled there, and it's on the bulletin board."

Karen then went on to say that she had gone to school and followed Cory's instructions. The eagle drawing was precisely where Cory had indicated it would be. She ran down the hall to Beverly's office, and then they called me.

That same evening, I went to a Children's Connection board meeting. While I was sharing Karen's story about the visit from Cory and the eagle, Steve Geller jumped up from where he'd been sitting, and he had a funny look on his face.

He came back with his journal and read it aloud. Steve and Cory had agreed to trade artwork. The day he painted the picture for Cory, he had driven north to a place called Deception Pass. While there he did a watercolor of two eagles flying near the bridge. Then he fell asleep.

During his nap he dreamt about two huge eagles swooping down to give Cory and him a ride. They flew to Summerland, and Cory's eagle let him off at the door to the crystal castle. As Cory was being taken into the castle, his eagle flew up and perched above the door. Then Steve's eagle flew him back to where their journey had begun. He wrote in his journal that he felt sad to leave Cory behind.

When Steve awoke from his nap, he added two figures to the backs of the eagles.

After he read us the story we all got "chicken skin," as my grandfather would say. It was a wonderful story, which prompted us all to talk about the eagle that had been flying above the graveside ceremony. I hadn't realized that everyone had seen it circling the cemetery.

Eagle drawn by Cory

Mother's Day

As I explained earlier, when Cory came out of his coma, the first thing he asked me was if he had missed Mother's Day. I was so happy to see him awake and to hear his voice I did not even try to understand the significance of his question. Silly me. Actually, I didn't figure out why for a number of days. The biggest clue I had was something that happened to me three weeks after Cory died.

I was in the alpha-state of sleep, and I heard Cory calling me. It was real. It sounded as if he was calling me from his bed in the living room. He kept calling, "Mama, mama..."

I'm not sure how long it took me to hear him, but as I was rolling over, I began to answer him. Then my brain clicked, and I told myself that Cory couldn't be calling me because he was no longer in the living room, and in fact, he was dead.

Then I woke up all the way and began to cry. I cried because he was gone. I cried because I wanted to hold him again. I cried because I knew I had blown it. In fact, for three days I was distraught and angry with myself for waking up. I believed Cory wanted to tell me something significant, presumably something he had forgotten to say before he died. I kept berating myself... *"If only this, if only that."* Then it grew to, *"If only I had just answered him and stayed in the alpha state..."*

I pouted until I couldn't stand myself any longer.

On the fourth day, it happened again. Cory's voice was calling, "Mama...Mama...Mama." I stayed calm and concentrated on remaining in the alpha state. I answered him, "What Cory? What is it?"

Very clearly, Cory called back to me, "Mama, what are you going to do with my money?"

I started to question him about this money, "What money are you talking about, honey?"

Cory said, "You know, Mommy, the money in my savings account." I had totally forgotten he even had a savings account.

Again, I questioned him about the account. He was beginning to sound completely distraught with my lack of understanding, as he responded with, "Mom, you know, the money in my savings account!"

I finally realized I was asking all the wrong questions. I thought to myself, *"He obviously wants me to do something with the money."* Then my next thought was, if he had money in his account, it couldn't be much or I would have remembered.

So I asked, "Is there something you want me to do with your money?"

Cory's voice sounded slightly relieved that I wasn't being so dense, as he replied, "I want you to go see Gordon." One of my best friends is a diamond broker. Cory loved to go visit Gordon because his office was filled with interesting rocks, and one time Gordon gave him a pretty polished agate out of the safe. But, I figured no way does Cory have enough money in his account for me to make a visit to a diamond wholesaler, even if the guy is one of my best friends.

"Honey," I said, "I don't know how much money you have in your account, but I'm sure it's not enough for me to go see Gordon."

Never one to hang back, Cory shot back, "Mom, just go see him. When you see 'it,' you'll know. You'll think of Elisabeth and me." Then he was gone.

While still lying in bed, I woke up all the way and thought about what had just happened. Telling myself I was losing my mind, I jumped out of bed and threw on some grubby clothes.

Cory's room was pretty much the way he had left it, minus the things that he had instructed me to give away. It felt rather strange going in there to look for his bankbook. To honor Cory's requests, I had cleaned out most of the things he wanted given away the week after he died. And since I had not run across his bankbook, I assumed Cory had hidden it.

Several searches of his room did not turn up the missing bankbook. After a few days, I put the whole thing out of my mind.

A few days later, I woke up with a pounding, throbbing, pulsating ache in one of my molars. I kept ignoring it because I had missed five weeks of work while Cory was dying, and I knew my boss would be upset if I took the time to get my tooth checked.

It got worse over the next few days, and I began to feel nauseated from the pain. I was sure the tooth had abscessed. Finally, my friend Debbie said she was calling the dentist to get me an emergency appointment.

The dentist was nice enough to make an early morning appointment for me. (Debbie was pretty persuasive.)

I went in. After a thorough exam, Dr. Scharman pronounced my mouth healthy. He said there was absolutely no sign of any problems with any of my teeth. I insisted he look again. We went back and forth, and finally he agreed to send me to an oral surgeon for another opinion. Shaking his head, Dr. Scharman walked to his office. I know he thought I was a nut.

When he came back into the room, Dr. Scharman handed me a scrap of paper with the address of the oral surgeon he wanted me to see. I froze for a second because the doctor's office was in Seattle across the street from my friend Gordon's but in the same building as the showroom Gordon's brother, Jerry, and his partner operated.

I asked why he wasn't sending me to the man who had done my root canals. Dr. Scharman said, "Would you just get outta here?" So, I left with that eerie spine tingling feeling.

When I arrived downtown, I parked my car and headed into the 4th and Pike Building. On the ride up in the elevator, I told myself that after my dental appointment I would just pop into the showroom and ask Jerry what Gordon was up to.

The oral surgeon did a complete examination, including checking the nerves of each tooth and hitting each one with a little hammer. He finally put down his instruments and said, "There is nothing wrong with your teeth."

I said, "C'mon doctor, I have been in terrible pain, and the tooth has been giving every sign of abscess. I am not crazy."

The doctor then looked at me very seriously and said, "Yes, you are. There is absolutely nothing wrong with your mouth."

So in a mild state of confusion, I got up from the chair to leave mumbling, "Okay, I must be crazy." Adding to my confusion was the fact that my tooth hadn't throbbed or anything all morning, even when the surgeon was probing the nerves or hitting my teeth with the tiny hammer.

I got on the elevator and hit the button for the floor where the jewelry showroom was located. Peering through the glass door, I rang the buzzer and was admitted in. Inside I saw Gordon's brother, Jerry, his partner, Norman, and a couple of female assistants. I wandered over to where Jerry was standing. As I was talking with him about Gordon's whereabouts, I found out he was rafting on a river in Oregon somewhere.

I thought to myself, *"Well, Cory, why did you want me to go see Gordon if he wasn't in town?"* Then as I leaned on the top of a showcase, I glanced down and saw a beautiful necklace displayed on a large piece of petrified wood. It was a gold butterfly with a diamond for its head hanging on a very delicate chain. I immediately remembered Cory's words...then I actually heard Cory's voice whisper in my ear, "See, I told you you'd think of Elisabeth and me." Elisabeth Kubler-Ross' logo is a hand releasing a butterfly, and Cory's artwork prominently featured those beautiful creatures. Ironically, Elisabeth found thousands of butterflies carved into the walls of the Polish prison camps she visited after World War II.

While I was staring at the necklace and hearing Cory's voice chiding me, I felt as if I was sucked out of reality and flung headlong into the foggy alpha-state. In the middle of the day and wide awake!

I snapped out of it long enough to ask how much the necklace cost. One of the sales assistants took the necklace out of the display case, and I saw her turn the price tag over. It was over three hundred and eighty dollars. I felt pretty sure it was out of my league, even with

Butterfly necklace

Cory's money. Norman said, "Let me look at it. You know, Shirley, we'll give you a deal."

"You better, 'cuz I could buy a car for that amount," I said to him. Norman laughed. Little did he know that I wasn't kidding.

While I was standing there waiting for him to check it out, my knees were feeling rubbery and non-supportive. I could hear my own blood rushing inside my ears and the pounding of my heartbeat. I watched as Norman weighed the gold and examined the diamond. He seemed to take a long time, but I'm sure it was only seconds.

Finally, Norman looked up at me and said, "How does two hundred dollars sound?"

Nodding slowly, I told him I would take it, but that I had left my checkbook at work. We made arrangements for me to stop by after work to pick it up.

Now, looking back, a really weird part of the whole occurrence is I have absolutely no recollection of leaving the showroom, finding my car, or driving to my office. I just wandered off into the fog.

When I reached my office, I spoke to our receptionist and asked not to be disturbed for a while. I closed my office door behind me. Mechanically, I got out the telephone book and looked up the number for the bank where Cory's account was located. I dialed the number listed in the book. When a woman with a pleasant-sounding voice answered, I started babbling to her that my son had recently died and that he had an account with her bank. I went on to explain that I was unable to find the bankbook. I wanted to know how much was in the account and what the procedure would be to retrieve the money without the bankbook. I could tell the woman was crying after hearing my sad story. She put me on hold while she looked up his account information.

When she returned to the phone line, I heard her say, "How does two hundred dollars and forty-seven cents sound?" Without thinking or even uttering another sound, I hung up the receiver. I know that sounds rude, but I was in a total state of shock.

Somehow I made it through the rest of the day. I was afraid to tell anyone my story because it was so bizarre. Most of my friends have always thought of me as a little "out there" anyway, but this time it was a whopper.

I picked up the necklace on my way home. All the way there I kept telling myself that I was a nut, that I could not afford to buy myself a necklace when I had missed so much work and had to accept monetary help from my family to pay my bills. My family had been wonderful about helping me, but I felt embarrassed to be in need. And so here I was with this necklace, feeling quite guilty. I began to question my whole experience, starting with Cory's instructions about seeing Gordon, the bank account, my dental mystery, etc. My biggest concern at that moment was my sanity.

Brie was at my parents' house, and the house was quiet. So, I walked into my bedroom and sat on the edge of the bed. I flipped open the jewelry box and stared at the beautiful butterfly necklace inside. Next thing I knew, I felt an elbow jab at my upper arm, and at the same time I heard Cory's voice say to me, "Put the damn thing on. It wasn't your money, anyway!" I looked over, and he was sitting next to me with a funny look on his face. It was a look of irritation, with perhaps a healthy dose of amusement, at my silly behavior.

Cory looked like he did when he was seven years old. Just the way he told me he wanted to be remembered. Now I was embarrassed. As usual, Cory was right. After all, it was not my money. It was his. I took the necklace out of the box. As I closed the clasp, I heard my son say, "Happy Mother's Day, Mama." I turned to show him how beautiful it looked, but he was already gone. I was sad and happy at the same time. Then I understood why he had suffered for so long...he wanted to be with me for Mother's Day.

The cherished necklace has remained on my neck ever since.

Epilogue

Dos and Don'ts

Within several months of Cory's death, he appeared to me in my sleep. The first few times it was like a dream. In one, he was sitting in the waiting area of the lobby at my office. I looked up to see him peeking at me through the doorway. When we made eye contact, he waved and smiled.

The saddest dream-visit was the last. I was sitting with him at my dining room table and he was crying. He looked swollen and achy the way he did near the time of his death. The last thing he said to me was, "I can't come anymore, Mommy. They told me I can't keep coming to see you—I have work to do. Remember, Mommy, I'll always be your best friend." I can still see the tears rolling down his chubby little cheeks.

Every now and then I can feel his presence. Sometimes I feel a butterfly kiss on my cheek or a little touch of my hair. But, I haven't had the full-blown visits as in the beginning. I pray at night sometimes to be able to see him and hold him. It works once in a great while.

I sincerely hope Cory's story will help bereaved parents because, although his experiences were quite incredible and unique, at the same time they were very spiritual. Again, my intention in the telling of these stories is not to convert anyone or change religious beliefs. I personally became a Lutheran after trying out many churches over my lifetime. I believe Cory had these "woo woo" experiences happen to him so that I could share them with others and they could derive comfort from his simple explanations. He was a very wise old soul.

It has taken me a bit longer than I had anticipated to get these stories down on paper, but I am compelled to do so now because several people who don't know Cory's real story have stolen bits and pieces of it for their own gain.

Unfortunately, they don't know the real story because they didn't even know him, which is why they could not tell it accurately. Maybe the false accounts kept coming out to force me to finish my book.

One of the worst rip-offs of Cory's story was when it showed up in a national tabloid. My mother received a number of telephone calls from upset friends and relatives. This happened because another man who didn't know Cory at all wrote about him in "his" book, but he couldn't tell the story accurately, so he made up stuff. My mother was traumatized, I was judged unfairly, and my daughter was teased on the playground at school because the author accused me of letting my son die unnecessarily by allowing him to go off his life-saving chemotherapy because of his "visions." In fact, he accused me of child abuse. That's okay, because I believe that what goes around comes around and he will get his due some day for profiting off of my family's grief.

Part of the reason I have hesitated to finish this project is because the reliving has been excruciatingly painful for me. I miss him terribly, and I have accepted that I always will. I am convinced that the pain of a child leaving you *never* goes away...it just changes with time. But, people who have not experienced such a loss in their lives cannot fathom the depth of pain a parent is left with when her child dies. It doesn't matter how he dies. Whether your child dies from a long and horrible illness, an accident, or suicide... pain is pain, loss is loss, and gone is gone.

For those people out there who, for whatever reason, feel the desire or need to measure your pain, I am truly sorry for you. I honestly do feel your pain. I have been approached at seminars and speeches after giving a talk and asked the most inconceivable questions such as, "Do you think your pain is greater than mine?" This comment was from a parent whose baby died from SIDS. From another whose child apparently died in an accident, I was told, "At least you got to say goodbye." And the mother of a teen who committed suicide said, "There's nothing worse than having a child commit suicide. It is far worse than what you have experienced."

After much thought and careful consideration, I finally decided to tell people the following: "I will not compare my child's death and the pain left in its wake to your experience, but I can tell you this: Watching my child die a centimeter at a time was not easier, nor was it harder than anyone else's experience. Dead is dead and pain is pain."

The other side of such insensitivity comes from "well meaning" people who don't have a clue about your pain. Three months after Cory's death, I was stopped on the street by an acquaintance. He politely asked, "How are you?" When I told him that I was feeling sad and missing my son, he snapped, "Are you still grieving? It's been three months! Shouldn't you be over it by now?" This came from a father of four! (All healthy, of course.)

I mustered up a half-smile and looked him straight in the eye and shot back, "I will NEVER be *over it*." Maybe not so coincidentally, I never spoke to the man again. Sheesh, can ya blame me?

Grieving parents are forced to endure such incredible insensitivity. I am truly amazed by how people who consider themselves "nice" can be so stupid.

There's another group of well-meaning people, the unsolicited advice givers. These people offer wonderful tidbits, such as, "You can always have another child." For some reason, they think of children as possessions that once worn out or lost can easily be replaced! Or how about, "Get over it. Bad things happen to everyone." This type of helpful person has usually never experienced anything worse than her child having strep throat or drainage tubes put in his ears.

When I started to reckon with the truth, that my little boy was about to be gone from me for the rest of my life, that I would never hold him in my arms or see his sweet face again, I couldn't get enough air in my lungs to breathe. My heart wanted to stop beating in my chest while my brain screamed out for mercy. Those easily given thoughts and feelings pale in comparison to reality. It is far worse, and the pain hopelessly indescribable. The sun is never again as bright, nor the sky as blue. Mountains aren't as majestic or music as beautiful.

It's very difficult to find happiness, and you begin to forget what the word "joy" means.

Some days, it takes all your energy just to get out of bed. Imagine the heartbreak from your very first thought in the morning being the painful recognition that your child is gone and you won't get to see him that day, or any other day for that matter, or especially to touch him. Yeah, it's hard to get out of the bed. Often it is hard to sleep. In my experience I would finally fall asleep just before I had to get up.

Being emotionally exhausted makes it really hard to go to work. It's hard to sit through meetings and pay attention to what is being discussed in the room. The ol' memory is filled with blanks...kind of like Swiss cheese. I was a single parent; I *had* to work. I had to go on with my life for the sake of Cory's sister, Brie. It was hard though. Grief and loss cause such powerful emotions.

If you work with someone who is grieving, please don't expect him or her to "get over it" right away. There are even grief counselors out there in the community who think they can predict the stages of grief and outline how long it should take. Everyone is different. There is no such thing as a proper time to stop grieving or a proper way to behave.

It is a given that grieving people have memory difficulties. You are not firing on all pistons. Believe me, it is difficult to stay on task or to concentrate. Please be supportive and do not give your co-worker a hard time. I am sure that he or she is doing the best under the circumstances. If this goes on too long though, say more than four or five months, do encourage counseling, especially if you find that he or she is not sleeping or eating regularly.

No, being a bereaved parent is the pits. No one around you truly understands how you are feeling. With that lack of understanding comes the judgment and the well-meaning but totally useless advice.

Whenever people ask me how to approach a bereaved friend, I strongly suggest they write a note stating how sorry they are and include an offer to listen anytime the person needs an ear. The key is to *really* listen. Don't offer any advice unless the grieving person asks for it, and even then don't be surprised if they blow you off. If you don't have an answer, don't manufacture it; admit you don't know and refer your friend to someone who does, such as a good grief counselor. And make sure the counselor is "REAL," a highly educated, well-trained therapist who graduated from a reputable program. In Washington, anyone can hang out a shingle and call him- or herself a "Registered Mental Health Counselor" just by taking a four-hour AIDS class and paying forty dollars. So, you really need to be careful.

And, whatever you do, PLEASE don't judge *anything* your friend says or does while in the throes of grief.

There is no "right" thing to say, but there are a lot of wrong things. The absolute all-time worst thing to say to anyone who is grieving: "I understand how you feel." You could get punched in the nose for that one. The second worst: "Can't you just concentrate on the good things? At least you had your child for a little while."

Please respect the grieving person's space, sadness, and memories. Don't avoid mentioning the child. Believe it or not, the parents and siblings will be comforted knowing you miss him/her, too. They DO want you to talk about their child or sibling. You may worry that it will make them sad, but guess what? They are already sad, and hearing you talk about their child may cheer them up. It is a comfort to know their loved one is still in your thoughts.

Just remember: One person's depth of pain is a shallow mud puddle, while another's is a bottomless ocean. Having a child die puts you near the bottom of that ocean. Unfortunately I know, and I'm a lousy swimmer.

Life Without Cory

A week after Cory's death, I found the instructions he'd given me for distribution of his possessions. It was essentially his last will. I had already sorted his things, and as people came by to visit, I gave them away according to Cory's wishes. My niece April was to receive Cory's blacklight painting of Jimi Hendrix, which was taped to the backside of Cory's bedroom door. I peeled the tape off carefully so I wouldn't ruin the edges of the painting. Much to my surprise and pleasure, I found little scraps of paper with notes on them taped to the door. Some were cartoon drawings of Garfield, the cat. All of the drawings had names on them. I assumed that meant I was supposed to pass it on to that person. Some were little notes that said, "I love my mommy" or "I love you, Mama."

I found more notes when I took his waterbed apart. Cory had stashed them between the wall and the base of his bed. Little love notes fell out of books on my headboard. I even found one hidden in the bottom of my travel makeup bag. (That was almost a year later.)

On Cory's drawing pad that he left at my parents' house, he had written on the inside cover a whole list of love notes. "I love my grandma...I love my grandpa...I love my mommy...I love my dad...I love Brie-Brie...I love my uncles, aunties, cousins (each one by name), I love Elisabeth..." I think you get the idea.

In an old drawing pad, I found a series of pictures of muscular looking action-type characters wielding swords. Cory labeled them with the names of his first-grade classmates, so I deduced they were drawn at that time. The second to the last drawing depicted a bleeding "Cory," suffering from a chest wound. The last one showed his friends Alex and Coleman standing over his lifeless body. It was pretty bizarre for me to think he'd drawn it two whole years before his death.

I took Cory's advice and went into television production. Actually, not long after Cory died, Elaine Purchase, the producer/reporter who had done the two stories about Cory, convinced me to change professions so I could come to work with her. I started out as the Associate Producer of the KOMO-TV documentary unit. Under Elaine's mentorship, I blossomed. Together we won numerous broadcast industry awards. I learned a lot from her. Elaine's piece, "The Courage of Cory," won a special Emmy Award the year after he died.

I also followed Cory's instructions about helping Elisabeth with her work. I was part of a group that assisted Elisabeth's foundation with the planning, organization, and execution of grief workshops for children and teens. Kids came from Canada and across the United States to attend. They were awesome. We witnessed and helped facilitate the amazing healing transformation of broken, sad, self-destructive children and teenagers. The process was so empowering. The kids we still hear from have grown up to be happy healthy adults.

Another life changing event happened for me the year that Cory died. I fell in love. Remember Steve Geller? He was the human jungle gym, our wonderful friend from the Children's Connection. Steve and I worked on the inception of the Kubler-Ross workshops together. We were just friends at first, but things just magically evolved. Steve offered his kindness and gentle care and support to Brie and me during our darkest days leading up to and following Cory's death. Brie and I enjoyed our time with Steve so much. She told me one night, "Mommy, we should marry Steve." See, Cory opened yet another door in my life.

Because of his friendship with Cory, Steve decided to go back to school and become a child psychologist. (He loves it.) Cory's death touched Steve deeply, too, and that makes it so much easier for me to share my feelings and my sorrow.

After we got married, we moved to North Carolina because Steve chose UNC Chapel Hill for graduate school. Being a Tarheel came easy for him since his mother grew up in Charlotte and he has so many ties to the state.

Brie loved it there, too. She especially liked the fact that the sun shines most days in that part of the country.

I went to work for the CBS affiliate in Raleigh. I loved the friends that I met, and I learned so much more about the television business. I also learned more than I cared to about the Civil War. Ooh-weee! Some folks in the Carolinas are still whining about the damn Yankees! I asked somebody if I was a Yankee since the depth of their pain confused me for something that had occurred eons before they were born. Well, the response I got knocked my socks off. "No, you're a westerner, and that ain't much better." Oh yeah, baby, welcome to the south!

One year after our wedding, while in North Carolina, Steve and I had a beautiful little girl that we named Keili Elisabeth (after EKR). I guess Cory decided to stay in Summerland and wait for us there since he said he'd never come back as a "dumb ol' girl"—no offense to Keili or Brie, I'm sure.

My first assignment after getting back from maternity leave was a report about babysitters abusing babies. A couple suspecting that their sitter was hurting their baby set up their camcorder and caught the woman on videotape in living color slapping the infant around. It freaked me out to know that anyone could do that to a helpless baby. It also set the stage for the next change in my life.

When Keili was six months old, I decided to move back to Seattle. This left Steve to commute for several years. I had a terrific job offer back at my old station, and I just couldn't handle leaving Keili with babysitters that I didn't know. My best friend Mama Lynn offered to watch her for free if I came home.

Steve was very understanding. He finished up his education and several internships in North Carolina and in Washington. He worked for a community mental health agency for a number of years before finally deciding a few years ago to hang out his shingle. He is happily working with children, teens, and their families. Of course, he is an extremely gifted therapist and doing wonderful work. He loves to work with adolescents. When he first started his private practice, it immediately filled up with angry teenaged boys. What does that say about our society? Steve also works with couples. I love it. He comes home sometimes and thanks me for being so normal, and if he's had a very unhappy or angry couple, he comes home and worships me. Works for me!

Although Brie misses her brother tremendously, she is doing well. I've noticed it has been especially hard for her in what would have been his milestone years. I think the worst was the year he would've graduated high school and gone on to college. Like me, Brie feels a deep sense of loss, and I am sure that she always will. As I said earlier, "The pain never goes away—it just changes over time." We learn to cope and compartmentalize our feelings. That little trick is good some days and bad others. I hope that someday Brie will write her own book about her experience as a bereaved sibling. She went through several angry, awful years. A few well-timed visits from Cory gave her something to think about and gave us some relief. I would love to share them with you, but they are not my stories to tell; they are Brie's. Suffice to say, they were pretty incredible, extremely woo woo, and Cory got his point across in very creative ways.

Keili feels a strange sense of loss, too, even though she never knew her brother. It can only be described as Keili feeling as if something very important is missing in her life. Have you ever heard about a surviving twin experiencing a deep sense of sadness and loss even when he didn't know 'til years later that he'd lost his twin at birth? I think it's like that.

I did years of volunteer work for the American Cancer Society and helped to start several support groups for parents experiencing diagnosis and then, later, a group for dealing with after-death emotions.

I still facilitate a bereaved parents group for Candlelighters, which is an organization that offers support to families dealing with childhood cancer issues. The pain a parent goes through when his or her child dies is debilitating. Some Sundays I have to choke back my tears as I listen to the parents whose children have died recently. They see me as a role model, someone who survived the horror and came out okay enough to help others. That makes me feel good, but I would still rather be watching my son become a man.

Through the hospital, I made friends with several little boys who were far away from home for treatment. Their families were split up with dad usually back home working and trying to cope with the needs of the siblings while mom and the little patient were living at the Ronald McDonald House with no breaks from dealing with the hospital and all that entails.

My little friend Samuel, a six-year-old from Alaska, called me his "second mommy." He had the most beautiful green eyes and the most expressive little face. We used to sing together in the car while I drove him to his favorite seafood restaurant for clam chowder. He craved it so much that I started calling it Sam chowder. That tickled him so. One night he lovingly told me, "You have the sweet voice of an angel—just like mine!" I cried. Actually, I still cry whenever I think of him saying that. You see, I got kicked out of the eighth grade choir at my junior high school and never really thought much of my singing because of it. Sammy had an old soul feeling about him similar to Cory's. I never once heard him complain about his situation. He went blind, too, and was eventually in a wheelchair. I took him to my brother's place to feel the horses, and he got to go for a ride with my sister-in law. We also took him camping. We had a blast.

Unfortunately, my little buddy Sammy didn't survive his disease, either. I still keep in touch with his family, as they became a loving part of mine.

In 1987, I was awarded a Jefferson Award for Outstanding Public Service for helping terminally ill children and their families through the support groups, the one-on-one time I spent with the families, and the Elisabeth Kubler-Ross grief workshops for children and teens.

After Sammy died, Brie asked me, "Mommy, can we please make friends with kids who aren't dying? It is too sad for me to have to say goodbye all the time." I hugged her and told her that of course we could and that I was sorry if it had been too rough on her. She assured me that she loved Sammy and the others but that she just needed to have friends who were going to live. After that I told the social worker at the hospital that we couldn't offer support to others, that we—especially Brie—needed a break.

After we moved back to Seattle from North Carolina, Steve and I helped start some grief workshops with children and teens for a local hospice and homecare agency. At times it is hard to feel their pain, but working with them is so extremely rewarding. Steve bailed on the workshops after a few years, but I stuck with it, and we are now moving into our tenth year of these powerfully healing workshops.

In his short life, Cory touched thousands of people. Keller helped me create a poster from Cory's drawing of Summerland. We sold it to fund scholarships for the Elisabeth Kubler-Ross kids' and teens' grief workshops. The posters had been sold worldwide through Elisabeth's newsletter and at her lectures. I've met people from as far away as Sydney, Australia, who have heard of Cory and even own his poster! I've also walked into several mental health agencies where almost every private office had a framed Cory poster hanging on the wall. Several doctors and therapists told me that the poster is a great icebreaker with new clients. Pretty wild, eh? He's still helping people after all these years!

In 1993, I produced a children's television special entitled, "Cancer through the Eyes of Kids," which won an Emmy award. We taped the program on Cory's birthday, and it was dedicated to him and other children who have been teased because of what chemotherapy has done to their little bodies, survived incredible losses, and shown strength of spirit, something that regularly escapes most adults.

I realized a few years ago that Cory's dying process could have been less stressful if I had only known how healing music could be. This is my biggest regret about how I handled Cory's death. I wish with all my heart that I had played more music for him. I advise anyone going through the same process to think about playing soothing peaceful music for your loved one. Even though I sense his presence around me all the time and once in a while I feel those butterfly kisses, Cory hasn't visited me in body for a few years, but that's okay. The last time was a dream-visit on Halloween (his favorite holiday), and we talked for what seemed like hours. He was lying across my lap while I rubbed his back. At one point I bent down and smelled the back of his neck—just like old times. It was wonderful. Cory's body started looking frayed around the edges, and he sighed deeply. I asked what was wrong. He just smiled and said, "It takes so much energy to manifest a body. I know I am starting to look weird, and I better get back now."

I told him that I wasn't at all afraid of what he looked like and that I was just glad that he had come to see me. Then he left and I woke up. I was sitting up in bed leaning against the wall. I could still feel the warmth of his body and smell his scent. It was lovely. Steve woke up and asked me why I was sitting there. It took me a moment to reply because I just wanted to luxuriate in what remained of Cory's essence.

Brie is now a mommy. She had a boy, and they named him Cory Keawe. It was very difficult for all of us to call him Cory for the first year or so because he looked just like his uncle. Their baby photos are indistinguishable. Even his dad couldn't tell them apart. Cory's friends burst into tears when they saw Brie's baby. I felt really bad when Christina Moloney saw him the first time. She almost went into shock. Now, he is taking on more features from his daddy, and the resemblance isn't as striking. They called him "Baby" for the first year. I told them, "You cannot call a child who is half Samoan 'Baby.' It will just cause him to get into fights when he gets older! So either call him Cory, or call him Keawe, but stop calling him 'Baby.'"

Baby Cory does interesting things at our house. One day, he found his uncle's favorite teddy bear, Danger, in my bedroom and immediately snatched him up and walked around the house hugging it and babbling in baby talk. I could never tell if he was speaking Samoan or baby gibberish. This time I think it was baby gibberish. Ever since he was a little toot, he'd point to Cory's photograph in my bedroom and say, "The boy. I want to see the boy." Gosh, who knows what connections they have shared?

So, you see, life does go on after a tragedy such as the death of a child. People often ask me, "How did you do it?" and they are seemingly amazed. My usual answer is very simple, "You gotta do what you gotta do and move on." Grief is so different from other emotions that no one really knows how to deal with it. You just have to feel it no matter how much it hurts. If you try to ignore the pain or deny all the other confusing emotions, it waits for you. When you least expect it, it will rise up and bite you in the *okole* (butt, behind, tush, tookas, backside). Believe me, grief can take on a life of its own. I've seen it happen, and it's not pretty. So get a good therapist, or find a support group and get on with it.

Our remaining children don't want us to shrivel up and die, too. They want us to continue on with our lives. As my wise and very brave little boy said, "I'm going with God to the land of the sun; my lessons on earth are all done." He knew that my lessons are many and that I had to go on to help others.

I would like to leave you with this beautiful poem (author unknown). Lynn gave it to me in a nice wooden frame. I am grateful to whoever wrote it. It says it all...

Though distance
May come between
A mother
And her child,
The bond
That holds them close
Will never weaken.
The love they share
Will never be more
Than a memory apart.

With the help of my family and friends, I have been able to keep my promise to Cory...he will *never* be forgotten.

2001 Odyssey

Okay, so I didn't finish this book in a timely manner. My friends who have read the manuscript have been after me to get it published. I made a few feeble attempts to get some interest generated, but in reality I was not satisfied with the ending. It didn't feel complete, so up until now I just waited to see what might happen. I continued to let people who wanted read the manuscript. I relished the feedback that I received from each and everyone who took the time to go through it. There were only a few folks who could not handle the material, and one person thought it was too "woo woo." But hey, we can't please everybody all the time, now can we? At times I became a bit bummed out because nothing seemed to be happening, and then, I started wondering if maybe I needed to change something. As I had not been too happy with the ending anyway, I decided to add a little more here and there. But still I kept wondering. Then, finally the real reason for the delay revealed itself, and now here I am sitting at my computer again, writing with tears in my eyes and a mixture of love and sadness in my heart.

I have already told you a little bit about Cory Keawe, Brie's little guy. Well, he is three years old now and quite the handful. He has been hanging out with me during the day for the past few weeks. He is very much a little boy and totally "into" super heroes such as Spider-Man, Batman, and Superman.

A few weeks ago as we were climbing the stairs to my office, Cory stopped at the picture frame on the wall, pointed to a photograph of my son, and said, "Oh, there I am in my Spider-Man costume."

I immediately replied, "No, honey, that's your Uncle Cory."

"I know," he said quite emphatically. "I AM Uncle Cory. That's ME."

Startled, I blinked at first and looked down at his little smiling face. Then I said, "Oh?" He continued to point to other photos in the frame. Then, he said very matter of factly, "There I am with Goofy at Disneyland…and that's my mommy when she was my little sister."

Well, some might brush this off as a small child's imagination, but I know enough about child development that no three-year-old can even conceive of his or her parents being small children. And where would the idea of his mother being his sister come from? It is too complicated for one so young. I confirmed my theory with child psychiatrist Bill Womack, who agreed with me that it was too much of a concept for someone so young.

At any rate, I was not blown away by this bit of news but extremely intrigued. Part of me was excited to think that my Cory had come back almost as promised. But there is a part of me that then mourns the idea that when I die, Cory won't be there to greet me. Sounds pretty selfish, I know, but what's a mother to do?

Okay, so the next day, I was at my desk when Cory arrived. He bounded up the stairs to see me. He leapt on to my lap to give me a hug and to chat a while. After a few minutes the screensaver on my computer monitor popped up, and Cory pointed at the picture of the crystal castle and said, "I made that. I made that picture."

I casually asked, "Oh? Really?"

He replied, "Yes, I made that picture for you."

"What is it?" I asked.

"That's the castle where God lives, and that's the Rainbow Bridge." He pointed at each image as he spoke.

Now, it is pretty hard to ruffle me, but this was too much information. I had been mulling over the first day's events, and I didn't want to ask him questions that might taint his answers so I just nodded my head and waited for him to tell me more.

"How did my picture get in the 'puter?" he asked with a puzzled look on his face. I could not find the words to explain this process to a three-year-old. But he really didn't care that much for an answer because in the next instant he hopped down to run after the dog.

Over the next few days Cory talked to both Steve and me about the photos on the wall. Consistently he described himself by saying, "That's 'me-Uncle Cory.'" He runs the names together as if they are one word.

Brie called one morning that same week and asked if I had been showing Cory old photographs. I said, "No, but he's been showing me a few. Why?"

Her voice was quivering when she told me that he had run to her in the morning and said, "Mom, guess who I just saw? I saw Trista. I haven't seen her for such a long time. She looks good." Well, Brie was shaken because her cousin Trista, who is alive by the way, lives a distance away, and the last time Brie saw her was at her baby shower *before* Cory was born. So, Cory had never seen her.

I told her that the only photo that I have out with Trista in it was taken when she was an infant and no one in my household knew the names of the kids in the picture except me. So there was no way that he heard about Trista from anyone else, and I knew that he hadn't heard about her from me. I then told Brie what Cory had been telling us about being "me-Uncle Cory." I asked her if she had been talking to Cory about her brother. She said that no, she hadn't and that I have all of the photographs of when they were small. She was very puzzled because she had not spoken to him about her brother, the crystal castle, or their relatives.

The very next day Cory was having breakfast at my dining room table, and he looked up at me and said, "I used to be a girl once."

I was amused and asked, "Really? How was that?"

He shrugged his shoulders and said very casually, "Ah, it was all right." Then he started talking about the cartoons on the cereal box. This behavior was very much like that of my son at the same age. He would drop little "bombs" and then immediately go on to another subject, leaving me with my mouth gaping open and my head spinning.

A week or so later as I was working at my computer, Cory came upstairs to play. He was walking past my file cabinet and spotted the snapshot that shows my son Cory feeding a bottle to Trista the infant cousin, her brother Travis sitting next to them, and then Brie who was about a year old sitting on the end. Cory stopped, rose up on his tiptoes so that he could see the photograph, and murmured to himself, "Hmmm, who is that in that picture?" After a very thoughtful moment he replied to his own question, "Oh yeah, that's us and our cousins." I almost fell out of my chair.

I turned and said, "Who is that in the picture?"

Cory looked at me with a look that showed a cloudy memory might be surfacing and becoming more clear and answered, "Oh that's me and my mommy with our cousins Travis and Trista." Then, he started playing with his toys again, and the conversation ended.

Shortly after all these amazing insights started happening with Cory, my father became quite ill. Within six weeks my father died—on Christmas Eve. That is really such a sad time to lose a loved one.

While Brie and I were sorting through my mother's old photographs so that I could make a collage for my dad's memorial service, she found some studio photos of herself and her brother. As Brie was showing the photos to her son's father Cory Keawe pointed and said, "That's me-Uncle Cory and my mommy." His dad isn't too open to the idea and argued that it was his Uncle Cory not him. Cory Keawe got very defiant and indignant and said, "I AM Uncle Cory. That's ME." Then, he stomped out of the room. He came scowling into my mother's bedroom where I was sitting and he jumped up on my lap and growled, "Puna, my dad is bugging me! And I don't like it! You need to spank him. He doesn't believe me." My mom and I exchanged looks, and I just patted his back to calm him down.

I finished the collage. The service was sad but very nice. People gathered at my brother's house for the wake to celebrate my dad's life. Folks were crowded around the collage looking at the collection of photographs for hours and hours. Finally, Cory pushed his way to the front and stood staring at them.

"Hey, there's me-Uncle Cory," Cory said pointing to a picture of my son on a carousel horse. Then, he pointed to a current photograph of himself and said, "And there's me when I am not Uncle Cory. I am me, and I am with cousin James." My daughter Keili yelled over her shoulder, "Mom, he's doing it again!"

So, there you have it. Some would call it proof of reincarnation while others might say an incredibly active imagination or worse—the work of the devil. Although I have always wondered why those folks who are so willing to believe that Satan is everywhere think that he would want me to feel comforted and happy about my son's whereabouts whether it's Heaven or back here on Earth.

My son Cory will always be indelibly etched on my heart and in the fabric of my soul. I will always remember his smile, his laughter, his courage, and his ability to reach out to others. He taught me about life not death. He taught me to love and to forgive. I feel his presence with me whenever I think of him…just as he had promised. And I believe that God is enjoying his company, and that gives me the strength and comfort to know that death is another aspect of life. "It is what it is."

2007

Cory Keawe still talks once in a while about being Uncle Cory. When he was eight years old he, was having dinner with his mom. Brie thought he sounded just like her brother and burst out laughing. Cory Keawe asked her what was so funny? When she replied, "Sometimes you just remind me so much of your Uncle Cory." Cory Keawe sighed and with great exasperation said, "Brie! When are you going to get it? Why don't you listen? It's me Brie. I have been telling you since I was little. I am Uncle Cory. I came into his body. It's me!" Brie was still having a hard time with the whole "I gave birth to my brother thing" so she called me to report what they had talked about over dinner.

A few days later while I was driving with him I said, "So Cory I heard that you and your mom had an interesting conversation the other night." Cory Keawe asked innocently, "Really?" I said, "Uh huh." Without a flicker of an eye he answered, "Oh, you mean about the fact that I am reincarnated?" To which I chuckled and said, "Yeah, that would be it." I looked in my rearview mirror and he smiled back at me and then switched subjects.

Now, my grandson's insistence that he is Uncle Cory "reincarnated" has me wondering how that all works. Can he be in two places at one time? Or did he leave the comfort and wonder of Summerland to come back here one more time? So, as long as Cory Keawe is determined to talk about his experiences and his identity, I will always be listening carefully, taking notes, and looking for that familiar glint in his eyes.

About the Author

S hirley Enebrad is a certified grief specialist and has been an award-winning television/video producer and writer since 1985.

As a result of Cory's illness and subsequent death, Shirley started a number of support groups and workshops for terminally ill children and for grieving children and their families through the Elisabeth Kubler-Ross Foundation, the American Cancer Society, and Candlelighters Childhood Cancer Foundation of Western Washington. Shirley is the current president of Candlelighters of Western Washington. For her tireless volunteer work for ill and dying children, she was honored in 1987 with the Jefferson Award for Outstanding Public Service, and in 2004 she received the Angel of Hospice Award for her work with grieving children and teens.

Shirley grew up in Seattle and, now with her husband, Steve, still calls the Puget Sound home. Her two daughters and grandson live in Hawaii. For relaxation she loves to travel and hike with her husband, play with her dogs, and spend time with her many friends.